AT JOURNEY'S END

THE COMPLETE GUIDE TO FUNERALS AND FUNERAL PLANNING

ABDULLAH FATTEH, M.D., PH.D., LL.B.
WITH NAAZ FATTEH, M.D.

HEALTH INFORMATION PRESS
Los Angeles, California 90010

Library of Congress Cataloging-in-Publication Data

Fatteh, Abdullah
    At journey's end : a complete guide to funerals and funeral planning /
    Abdullah Fatteh, Naaz Fatteh.
        p. cm.
    Includes bibliographical references and index.
    ISBN 1-885987-19-6
    1. Funeral rites and ceremonies--United States--Planning.
    I. Fatteh, Naaz. II. Title
GT3203.F38 1999   99-32680
393'.0973--dc21   CIP

Disclaimer:
The information presented in this book is based on the experience and interpretation of the author. Although the information has been carefully researched and checked for accuracy, currency and completeness, neither the author nor the publisher accept any responsibility or liability with regard to errors, omissions, misuse or misinterpretation.

ISBN: 1-885987-19-6

Printed in the United States of America

Health Information Press
4727 Wilshire Blvd., Suite 300
Los Angeles, CA 90010
1-800-MED-SHOP
Internet: HIPBOOKS.COM

Dedicated to my grandchildren:

Naseef

Nabeel

Saher

Imtiaz

and the ones to follow.

ACKNOWLEDGEMENTS

The interviews, comments and counsel of numerous funeral profession-als, medical examiners, pathologists and consumers are the principal basis of this book. I am grateful to many colleagues and friends, especially Julian Almeida, Theodore F. Brill, Esq., Don Boyd, Cy Case, Steve Cheyney, Lee Drake, Michael Evans, David Hoodiman, Page Hudson, M.D., Fred Hunter, Douglas Jennings, Joseph Jodrey, Edward Kalis, Richard Kurtz, Thomas K. Marshall, M.D., Roshan Moraes, M.D., Ronald Morrison, Mark Panciera, Joshua Perper, M.D., Dan Perrine, Jose Portela, Thomas and Patricia Ralph, Lawrence Schuval, Larry Sherman, Cyril Wecht, M.D., David Wiecking, M.D., and Bradford Zahn.

I received great help from the National Funeral Directors Association, the Cremation Association of North America, and the American Association of Retired Persons. They responded to my requests generously and promptly, and I sincerely extend my thanks to the staff members of these organizations. I am especially indebted to Chris Raymond, Editor of The Director, and to Robert Harden, Executive Director of the National Funeral Directors Association.

With love and affection, I open my heart of gratefulness to my younger daughter and co-author of this book, Naaz Fatteh. She is board certified in Internal Medicine and Infectious Diseases and a legitimate poet. She was my constant companion, a mind reader, a morale booster, and an astute researcher at all times. She was an invaluable asset in writing and editing this work and made the task of writing this book easy. My older daughter and a partner in my medical practice, Sabiha Khan, was always considerate and generous in letting me get out of the office to research and write this book. She also supported me in various ways by providing advice, encouragement and ideas. My son, Faiz, an Internist, a medical software developer and a computer visionary helped put together "The Future" of the funeral industry. My daughter-in-law Shahnaz Fatteh, an Allergist and Immunologist and my son-in-law, Mohammed Nasir Khan, a Family Physician, contributed immensely with their youthful wisdom, knowledge and constructive criticism. My wife, Mahlaqua, was a silent but major contributor in her own ways. I thank them all.

I sincerely appreciate the arduous efforts of Sareh Beladi, who painstakingly edited and typed the manuscript as well as contributed to the research and writing of the sections on the Taj Mahal and the Muslim Funeral.

I wish to extend my sincere thanks to the managing editor of Health Information Press, Kathryn Swanson, who was always courteous, polite and prompt. She made the production of this book a real pleasure.

Abdullah Fatteh, M.D., Ph.D., LL.B.
Spring, 1999

TABLE OF CONTENTS

Acknowledgements i

Preface v

Foreword *by David R. Pearson* ix

Introduction: The Future of "Death Care" xi

Section I: Planning Your Own Funeral

Chapter 1: Preneed Planning 3

Chapter 2: A Personal Example: My Own Funeral Arrangements . . . 11

Chapter 3: Protect Your Estate:
       Don't Leave the Door Open for Uncle Sam 19

Chapter 4: Living Wills 25

Chapter 5: Charitable Dead 27

Section II: Planning the Funeral of Your Loved One

Chapter 6: At Need Funeral Planning 39

Chapter 7: Funerals and the Grieving Process 45

Section III: What Happens to the Body?

Chapter 8: Embalming 57

Chapter 9: Burial 65

Chapter 10: Cremation 73

Chapter 11: Autopsy 85

Chapter 12: Don't Pick Up a Living One! 91

Section IV: The Price of Death

Chapter 13: Economics of Funerals and How to Cut Costs 97

Chapter 14: Memorial Societies 115

Chapter 15: Funeral Fraud & the Funeral Rule 119

Chapter 16: Paying for a Funeral: Federal Help 127

Chapter 17: Death Overseas 141

Chapter 18: Death . . . Here Come the Lawyers 147

Section V: Regulation of the Funeral Industry
Chapter 19: All Funeral Directors are Not Crooks! 159
Chapter 20: Laws Governing Funerals 163
Chapter 21: The Funeral Industry and OSHA 175

Section VI: Death Rites & Customs Around the World
Chapter 22: A Brief History of Funerals 185
Chapter 23: The Chinese Funeral 193
Chapter 24: The Jewish Funeral 201
Chapter 25: The Christian Funeral 209
Chapter 26: The Muslim Funeral 215
Chapter 27: The Hindu Funeral 221
Chapter 28: Funerals in Japan 229
Chapter 29: Other Funeral Traditions (Humanist, Amish,
    African-American, Mormon, Hmong, Vietnamese, Mexican) . . 237

Section VII: Final Remarks
Chapter 30: All of the Questions You Ever Had But Were
    Afraid to Ask 253
Chapter 31: The Ultimate Checklist: 100 Things to Do for
    Peace of Mind 261

Section VIII: Appendices
Appendix A: Famous Funerals 269
Appendix B: Famous Burial Monuments 279
Appendix C: Words of Comfort 287
Appendix D: Disposition Instructions and Other Forms 301
Appendix E: Funeral and Memorial Societies 309
Appendix F: Organizations 321
Glossary 329

Index 339
About the Authors 349

PREFACE

*D*eath is inevitable, and hence a funeral has to be a part of life. The lack of one comprehensive source on funerals created a compelling reason to write this book.

I have been associated with funeral professionals for nearly forty years and have understood their concerns and questions when faced with variables in laws or traditions. Directly or indirectly I have been involved in the investigation of over 32,000 deaths. This has created a disturbing picture in my mind of the dilemmas the survivors of a death go through. *At Journey's End: A Complete Guide to Funerals and Funeral Planning* is an attempt to provide comprehensive information that would help the surviving consumer. A book that provides information on the funerals of many different ethnic groups, on the changing laws, modified funeral customs, increasing litigation, altered economic patterns and an array of alternative funeral options, is long overdue.

The United States is a country of immigrants. This is a land where cultures and religions adopt altered status. Lifestyles change, and death styles too must change. The ceremonial acceptance of death, the rituals surrounding the dead and the disposition of the deceased take different forms. Funeral customs vary from country to country and from religion to religion. The immigrants from different parts of the world bring their traditions and try to follow them but, they may have to modify their traditions to fit circumstances in the United States. The original traditions, altered versions and the differences with respect to each ethnic group create a multitude of diverse funeral ceremonies. This indeed creates a challenge for the funeral director. Most ethnic groups do not have specialized funeral homes that can provide help specifically fitting their needs. Therefore, a general funeral director has to research and be ready to handle funerals for every conceivable ethnic group. One of the missions of this book therefore is to present a broad view of the funerals of different ethnicities. The general population of immigrants most often is not fully knowledgeable about their own traditional funeral customs and they become even more confused when their funeral arrangements do not fit the procedures and the laws of their adopted land. The discussion of the funerals of most of the religions and ethnic groups presented in this book should ease the survivor's pain at a very critical time of the death of a loved one.

Another significant fact is that most people do not like to discuss death and do not think of making preneed funeral arrangements. This results in confusion and unnecessary expenses. The chapters on preneed funeral arrangements, the "Ultimate Checklist" and even my own funeral arrangements are intended to prepare the consumer to think and act in advance.

The lack of advanced preparedness combined with sudden death usually lands the survivor in a situation demanding that quick decisions be made. Under these circumstances, things can and do go wrong, resulting in increased grief.

Since death creates one of the major expenses in life, the subject of the economics of funerals is presented in several chapters. A significant segment of *At Journey's End* is dedicated to help the consumer save on funeral expenses. The methods of reducing the cost of funerals through prearrangements, body donations, use of memorial societies, third-party shopping for goods, and choices for less expensive methods of disposition are detailed to help the consumer. Prepaying for a funeral and receiving federal financial help are also discussed.

The state and federal laws governing the funeral profession that protect the consumer and the employees in the funeral business are also addressed. The all-important FTC Funeral Rule and important parts of the updated laws of some states are included in the book to clarify the consumer's rights. The importance of wills as well as living wills is stressed.

In this book, there are reflections on the funeral industry with an honest quashing of indictments served by some on the funeral directors. At the same time, the consumer is warned to watch out for fraud —a byproduct of human nature in every profession.

In essence, this is a total guide for the consumer to fall back on at the time of the most crucial event in life —death.

The ultimate goal of *At Journey's End* is to provide peace at the time of death and a complete closure after death.

FOREWORD

*W*hen I was in mortuary school, I read books on funeral history, funeral customs, the technical aspects of funeral service, and consumer practices when faced with arranging funerals. At that time, I spent hundreds of dollars to have all of these books in my library. Had Dr. Fatteh's book been around then, I could not only have saved money but considerable shelf space as well.

As I read Dr. Fatteh's book, I found many topics of interest to both consumers and funeral service professionals. The book examines the fastest-growing section of the funeral service market —preneed or funeral planning in advance of death— and offers consumers many good ideas as well as things to watch out for. It also discusses the legal and economic aspects of funeral service. From the laws governing funeral service practices to a discussion of estate taxes, Dr. Fatteh covers the legal and financial aspects facing consumers and funeral directors before, at and after a death.

Dr. Fatteh also reviews the history of embalming from ancient Egypt to the present, explaining why embalming is performed and describing the process itself. He discusses cremation, burial, autopsy and other procedures related to death care. America is a melting pot of cultures and, in that spirit, Dr. Fatteh discusses the funeral customs and traditions of a number of these cultures. He also describes how these varying traditions adapted and evolved because of cultural assimilation within the United States.

Since our society has become one of lists, Dr. Fatteh provides the ultimate checklist of 100 things to do before, during and after a death. The book closes with answers to frequently asked questions, and a number of appendices. One of these appendices highlights two of the most memorable funerals of my lifetime: President Kennedy and Princess Diana.

Dr. Fatteh does a great service to consumers by shedding light on a mysterious business while reinforcing the sentiment of the American people that the funeral service is an honorable profession. Dr. Fatteh has succeeded in writing a book that everyone should read.

David R. Pearson, President
National Funeral Directors Association
Spring, 1999

Introduction

THE FUTURE OF "DEATH CARE"

There are more people alive today than have died in the history of mankind. Does this sound impossible? Consider the simple concept of exponential growth and you may become convinced—as well as frightened. In August 1998, the U.S. Bureau of Census estimated the U.S. population to be 270 million and the world population to be 6 billion. In the United States, the elderly will comprise an ever-increasing proportion of the total population due to the aging of the baby boomers. Combine this fact with the escalating costs of funeral services, and it becomes easy to understand why "death care" is a multi-billion dollar business.

This book helps readers to negotiate, emotionally and financially, through life's final rite of passage. After a house and a car, a funeral is often the third most expensive purchase we make. According to recent surveys, the average cost of a funeral today is over $4,500. As discerning as today's consumers are and as competitive as the market is becoming, they still need all of the help they can get regarding funerals, for the decisions that must be made are significant and usually come at a time when they are emotionally distraught. *At Journey's End* guides you through planning your own funeral before death has occurred—one of the most loving things you can do for your family—and it also assists you in making good decisions when a loved one has just died. There's no way to take away the pain of a loss, but there are ways to minimize it, and both preparation and knowledge are keys to this. This book describes the many choices available concerning funerals, wills, and other preparations for death. It shows how you can save money and avoid anxiety and frustrations. It explains the important role of the funeral director, and it describes consumer and health laws which are in place to protect you. It also provides a glimpse of the ways different cultures, past and present, honor the dead and assist survivors to recover from their loss.

Two of the most significant anticipated influences on funerals are the use of the Internet and the development of funeral "supermarkets." The funeral industry has already begun to feel the effects of these and other changes. What follows in this introduction is a glimpse of what's to come. The remainder of this book helps readers to understand how to work with what already is available.

COMPUTERS, THE INTERNET, AND THE FUNERAL INDUSTRY

The Internet has brought and will continue to bring revolutionary changes to almost all aspects of our lives. The funeral industry is no exception. Already there are hundreds of Internet sites dedicated to the marketing and sales of funeral services and products, such as caskets, urns, urn vaults, cremation, stone monuments, stone memorials, cemeteries and more. The Internet may prove to be a comfortable medium through which individuals can learn more about topics like funerals which they normally might not discuss. Thus, as a repository of useful information on funerals, the Internet is both abundant and accessible, and will only get better.

Today the Internet already offers access to information on services, merchandise and preneed and at need funeral planning. For instance, FuneralNet (*http://www.funeralnet.com/*) lists over 20,000 funeral homes in the U.S. and over 1100 in Canada, with addresses and phone numbers. It also carries helpful information on funerals, cremations and cemeteries.[1] In the coming years, perhaps information about most of the funeral homes, cemeteries, crematoriums, mausoleums, memorial societies, funeral product manufacturers and mortuary schools will be available on your computer screen.

If they haven't already, funeral homes will put their price lists, photographs of the facilities, qualifications of their staff and even laudatory letters of recommendation on the Internet. There are even now a few "virtual" funeral homes who do business on the Internet. There will be advances in this field with the offerings of down-to-earth funerals and "designer" funerals (e.g., for people willing to spend $200,000 for a "state-of-the-art" funeral).

We are also already seeing Internet visitation of relatives and friends of the deceased in "virtual" cemeteries. The Internet Cremation Society (*http://www.cremation.org*) allows consumers to view and print out online brochures from each participating cremation society. These activities will be expanded in the future.

Memorials on the Internet

Internet memorials sometimes appear only as epitaphs, but other times are more detailed written and pictorial tributes to the deceased. As might be expected, there are companies that provide services so that you can create an Internet memorial for yourself or a loved one that can be seen by anyone for many years. For a fee, you can purchase "perpetual care" for such a web site as well.

The computers and the Internet will be used more often for death notices and obituaries, printing of prayer cards, eulogies, replicas of state and federal forms, as well as death certificates. They will be increasingly used for record-keeping, creating a database for families and presenting choices of goods and merchandise to the families through video-conferencing and scanning of pictures. They will also be involved in automated purchasing, billing and electronic fund transferring in business transactions.[2]

In 1995, Michael S. Wilson presented a summary of his predictions for the year 2010. He stated his belief that by that date, computers will file all legal work electronically, will handle cash allowances, e-mail obituaries, select caskets, make flower arrangements, design cemetery markers, transmit purchase orders and write checks, file credit card charges and verify insurance.[3] Computers will help with a funeral by "putting together a puzzle with tons of pieces."[4] So far, his predictions appear to be on-target.

Electronic Death Registration

Electronic communication and commerce will also begin to play a role in the funeral industry as transfer of electronic forms by government agencies becomes standardized. State governments are required to register deaths in a timely fashion. It is expected that the process of electronic death registration will soon become commonplace and mandatory in a matter of years.[5] Some states, such as Ohio and Alaska, already have Internet sites where the death certificates of any person who died in that state can be found. The departments of vital statistics for states can become extremely important when survivors try to locate the assets of a deceased relative. Likewise, the easy collection and dissemination of that information allows states to minimize expenses.

ONE-STOP FUNERAL SHOP

A second major change affecting the way consumers interact with the funeral industry is that the funeral business is going supermarket style. This idea began when a company called Roc Eclerc opened a funeral supermarket store in Paris in 1991.[6] The store is no different from any other supermarket outlet in setup or appearance. However, it houses only funeral products and services. It contains the following departments:

- Casket and showroom
- Monument department
- Memorial placard and accessories area
- Flowers and plants
- Funeral arrangement office.

Roc Eclerc has prominent signs on the exterior, and large glass windows so that passersby can easily see the products inside. The casket showroom contains many wooden caskets of different qualities and prices. The extras for the caskets, such as interior finish and hardware of different types, are also displayed. The garden-like flower area exudes fragrances of flowers in small and large arrangements with artificial counterparts. There are many decorative grave covers and marble and granite edifices in the monument room. The accessories in the store include memorial pieces made of glass, marble, granite and Lucite, which can be ordered plain or may be etched to provide information about the deceased or even to show his or her face. There are also private offices, filled with brochures, which are used to discuss funeral arrangements with clients. Funeral price packages are openly displayed on the glass partitions.

The prices in this store are said to be 20 to 30 percent less than elsewhere. This business idea was so successful that two years after opening the first store, the company added three more stores and opened 48 additional stores for franchisees with about 300 affiliated outlets throughout France. All of these stores are doing good business. In fact, the first store's revenues are about six million dollars a year. Roc Eclerc claims that the outlets handle over 100,000 funerals a year, which is 18 percent of all deaths in France.

Another death-care supermarket in London called Regale acts as a one-stop shop for funeral needs. Customers can purchase tombstones that may be used as bookends and coffins that can serve as bookcases or wine-racks until they are needed for their ultimate purpose.[7]

There are many advantages to funeral supermarkets. They encourage consumers to think about preplanning. When a consumer enters the store, he does not get the eerie feeling he would get in a funeral home. He knows that there are no dead bodies in the funeral store, there is no embalming fluid smell, and he can shop around without being interrupted by a funeral service or funeral attendees, which may happen in a regular funeral home. Finally, the prices one finds at these stores are much better.

Is America ready for this kind of a change? The idea is inescapable. In fact, the thought-barrier has already been broken, and a one-stop funeral shop is now a reality in Hollywood, Florida.[8]

What is touted as the first funeral shop in the United States was opened by local entrepreneurial funeral director, Mark Panciera, in April, 1998. The interior of "Alternative Funeral and Cremation Care" looks like a wedding store. It has a soothing atmosphere, pleasing fragrance and chamber music. In one corner, there is a memory garden, serene and relaxing with fichus trees, flowers and the sound of a fountain. As in the French funeral stores, in different sections of the store one finds caskets, urns, treasure boxes, wind chimes and garden stones displayed, each with a price tag. An adjoining, interconnected store offers a large variety of head stones.

Panciera plans to place a computerized kiosk for placing orders in the store, and to construct an Internet web page where customers can design a preneed funeral for themselves or for their loved ones.

The fact is, it's time for this kind of store. Baby boomers, the most likely target for this kind of store, look for convenience, choice and value. Although many can afford the expensive funeral, they will prefer to get the best for less. These consumers are educated and knowledgeable, but they have less time and are perhaps less spiritual or religious than their ancestors.

What is the future for these one-stop funeral shops? The sales figures at the Hollywood store and at the stores in France indicate that so far this is an attractive venture. Increasing numbers of people are preplanning their funerals. These preplanners are finding better value at such stores. These factors, together with comfort, convenience and wider selection of choices, are likely to attract more investment in this business. There will not only be more stores, but a properly managed franchise company may usher the country into a new era of funeral shops in every major town in the United States.

SOME UNUSUAL PREDICTIONS

Some of the "current trends" in the funeral industry may not appeal to as large an audience. For example, a bookbinder and printer in Kentucky called Timothy Howley Books offers a line of "bibliocadavers." These are handsomely bound volumes with blank or printed pages created from the ashes of a deceased loved one.[7]

Another company, Relict Memorials in Mill Valley, California, specializes in creating granite-like slabs from cremated remains. Finally, it's possible to purchase DNA kits for swabbing samples from the deceased and preserving them for future DNA studies such as for identification of the deceased, establishment of paternity, etc.

THE TREND TOWARD CONGLOMERATION

Less obvious to consumers are the behind-the-scene changes taking place in the funeral industry. Until 1970, nearly 100 percent of funeral homes were independently owned. At the present time, corporate conglomerates are swallowing these independent businesses at a rapid rate. The latest figures, as of September 30, 1998, show that the largest corporation, Service Corporation International (SCI), owns 3370 funeral service locations, 430 cemeteries and 180 crematoriums in 18 countries on five continents.[9] The Loewen Group and Stewart Enterprises are two other large funeral companies. Altogether, five large conglomerates together own over 20 percent of the funeral industry, and further acquisitions are expected. The empire-builders and the dreamers on Wall Street are probably already working on mega-mergers. These mergers will first involve intra-industry acquisitions. But more significantly, the death-care industry will eventually be a small part of a massive conglomerate, consisting of other related giants such as the health insurance industry, hospitals, health maintenance organizations and hospice. Ultimately, a global union of similar industries in other countries will probably follow. At this point, there will be no bargaining room for the consumer.

As competition increases in coming years, consumers will find they have more options and more information available. They can expect even more radical changes in the death-care industry.

THE ULTIMATE QUESTION

You are with a grieving family in an era of a state-of-the-art funeral system with computer, videos and the Internet. Are you going to allow all these advances to replace a box of tissues, kind words and firm hugs? Regardless of what may come down the pike, a warm, caring, compassionate human touch will always be needed.

REFERENCES

1. "FuneralNet." Online. Available: *http://www.funeralnet.com/ search.html*, 1997.
2. Horvath S: "Funeral Service Automation, Past and Future." *The American Funeral Director*, June 1995:27.
3. Wilson MS: "Any Funeral Firm USA on a Day in 2010: A Look Ahead to How Technology May Transform Funeral Service." *American Funeral Director*, June 1995: 29, 60-1.

4. Schafer S: *Mourning Becomes Electric Inc.* Tech 1997;3:66-71.

5. Horvath S: "Total Computerization and the Information Revolution." *The Director*, February 1996: 26.

6. Doody AF: *Reinventing Funeral Service.* New Orleans, LA: Center for Advanced Funeral Practice Management, 1995.

7. Murphy C: "The Time Has Come." *The Atlantic Monthly*, September 1998: 24-6.

8. Walker E: "Hollywood's One Stop Funeral Shop." *Miami Herald*, Jan 9, 1998.

9. *SCI News*: "SCI Earnings." Oct. 22, 1998.

Section I:
Planning Your
Own Funeral

Chapter 1

PRENEED FUNERAL
PLANNING

It is time for action. . . now.
Everything that has to be done
before death, must be done before death.

*E*very *death presents a challenge. Meet these challenges ahead of time:* preplan. Increasing numbers of people are doing so, and about 98 percent of the funeral homes in America offer a funeral preplanning option. Those who do preplan secure peace of mind for themselves and their loved ones.

Preplanning a funeral serves three important purposes. First, it allows you to determine what type of funeral service and disposition you want. You have time to think about the details and to discuss them with your loved ones. This prepares them in advance for handling your funeral. You will have time to purchase a cemetery plot at a location of your choice, as well as to gather funds and pay for the services, plot, and other goods and merchandise. Preplanning eliminates uncertainties and surprises. The French poet Jean De LaFontaine (1621-1695) wrote,

"Death never takes the wise man by surprise,
He is always ready to go."

Secondly, preplanning a funeral spares your survivors the burden of making last minute decisions. Death brings with it grief, confusion, uncertainty, emotional upheaval and, at times, irrationality. Under these circumstances, it becomes extremely difficult for survivors to make the best decisions. This may result in delays, much worry and unnecessary expenses. If you preplan and prepay, you will be giving your family some financial security and relieving them of any future financial burden. Preplanning eliminates unnecessary difficulties in a time of stress and sorrow. It creates comfort and peace for the survivors and gives them the feeling of satisfaction in carrying out your wishes. We must not forget the words of Herman Hesse (1877-1962):

"The call of death is a call of love.
Death can be sweet if we answer it
in the affirmative, if we accept it as one of
the great eternal forms of life and transformation."

Finally, the pre-selection of a funeral home eliminates efforts to search for one at the last minute. The funeral home will know what to do at the time of your death, and your family will know who to deal with and what to expect.

STEPS TO TAKE NOW

If you are interested in preplanning a funeral, you should do the following:

- Research the subject. Call a few local funeral homes for general information. Follow up with visits to some of these with your close relatives to "feel out" the places. Obtain brochures and compare the funeral homes with respect to services, goods and costs.

- Request brochures from your local association of funeral directors, the National Funeral Directors Association (NFDA) and the American Association of Retired Persons (AARP). These brochures contain excellent information on various aspects of preplanning.

- Study the Federal Trade Commission's (FTC's) Funeral Rule (see Chapter 15) and obtain FTC brochures on the topics of funerals, caskets and vaults. You should also study the Consumer Preneed Bill of Rights, which you can find later in this chapter.

- Visit the cemetery of your choice to select the specific location of your grave. If you purchase a lot in the cemetery, the funeral director will prepare a contract.

When preplanning a funeral, your funeral director is going to be the most helpful source of information. Get to know him. Ask him questions.

He has the answers you need to make decisions. He will discuss the options, services and costs, as well as help you to personalize your funeral. He will show you the facilities, the merchandise, and the cemetery. He will set the stage for completing all the arrangements.

Now in the absence of any emotional pressure is the best time to make decisions. It is the time to investigate, shop around, compare and even bargain on prices. This is the time to complete a preplanning agreement with no loopholes. The American Association of Retired Persons recommends that everyone preplan and prepay. They indicate that preneed plans are especially attractive to the elderly. In 1991, the average age of a preneed plan purchaser was over 70 years. Forethought Life Insurance company estimated that one million adults preplanned and prepaid for their funerals in 1990.

A traditional funeral, including the ceremony, transportation of the remains, a casket, and the services provided by the funeral director, usually costs about $3,500. This average amount does not include a cemetery lot, head stone, mausoleum space, or the costs of opening and closing a grave. It may or may not include the cost of a vault, limousines, flowers, obituary notices or an honorarium for the clergy. For an in-ground burial, add one to two thousand dollars to this price. When you are making arrangements with a funeral director, insist on clarifying in writing what is and what is not included in the package.

The Federal Trade Commission is the ultimate watch dog. The FTC's Funeral Rule operates to protect the consumer. It requires that a funeral director provide consumers with itemized price lists, which can then be used to compare costs. This general price list must be in writing, and must contain the cost of each individual funeral item and service offered. Once you have selected the items you want, the funeral director must give you a statement of goods and services selected along with the individual prices of each item.

Based on the FTC's Funeral Rule, the National Funeral Directors Association has created a Consumer Preneed Bill of Rights.[1] This self-explanatory document is reproduced here with the permission of the NFDA.

CONSUMER PRENEED BILL OF RIGHTS

Prior to purchasing any funeral goods or services or signing any preneed funeral contract, you are urged to ask any and all questions you may have regarding your preneed purchases.

To ensure that you, as our client family, have a full understanding of the preneed funeral transaction, we guarantee the following rights and protections.

We, as the funeral providers, will:

- Provide you with detailed price lists of services and merchandise before you select services and merchandise.
- Provide you with, at the conclusion of the funeral arrangement conference, a written statement listing all of the services and merchandise you have purchased and the price.
- Give you a written preneed funeral contract explaining, in plain language, your rights and obligations.
- Guarantee in the written preneed contract that if any of the merchandise or services you have selected are not available at the time of need, merchandise or services of equal or greater value will be substituted by the National Funeral Directors Association at no extra cost to you.
- Explain in the written preneed contract the geographical boundaries of our service area and under what circumstances you can transfer the preneed contract to another funeral home if you were to relocate or if death were to occur outside of our service area.
- State in the written preneed contract where and how much of the funds you pay to us will be deposited until the funeral is provided.
- Explain in the written preneed contract who will be responsible for paying taxes on any income or interest generated by the preneed funds that are invested.
- Inform you in the written contract whether and to what extent we are guaranteeing the prices of merchandise and services you are purchasing. If the prices are not guaranteed, we will explain to you in the written preneed contract who will be responsible for paying any additional amounts that may be due at the time of the funeral.

CONSUMER PRENEED BILL OF RIGHTS *(continued)*

- Explain in the written preneed contract who will receive any excess funds that may result if the income or interest generated by the invested preneed funds exceeds future price increases in the funeral merchandise and services you have selected.
- Explain in the written preneed contract whether and under what circumstances you may cancel your preneed contract and how much of the funds you paid to us will be refunded to you.

ADDITIONAL STEPS TO TAKE

Purchasing a Plot

Now and then cemetery lots are advertised to be "on sale," like any other consumer product. Keep an eye out for such ads as you may end up paying less. Once you decide to buy a cemetery lot and a purchase contract is being prepared, make sure you look it over carefully before you sign. Make sure the care and maintenance of the grave site are provided. The contract should have a description of interment rights, merchandise, and should itemize charges and details of a payment plan, including trusting, refunds and possible cancellation.

Pre-Paying for the Funeral

Before you pre-pay for funeral goods and services, consider the following issues:

- Be sure you know what you are paying for. Are you buying only merchandise, such as a casket and vault, or are you purchasing funeral services as well?
- What happens to the money you have pre-paid? Some states have different requirements concerning the handling of funds paid for pre-arranged funeral services. Check with the NFDA or your local funeral directors association to get clarification of these requirements.
- What happens to the interest income on money that is pre-paid and put into a trust account?

- Are you protected if the firm with which you are doing business should go out of business?
- Can you cancel the contract and get back any money you have prepaid if you should change your mind about the preplanned funeral?
- What if you should move to a different area or if death occurs away from home? Some pre-paid funeral plans can be transferred, but often there is an added cost in doing so.

Keep copies of the pre-payment documents and inform your family about the whereabouts of these documents.

Three of the most commonly used methods are payment from personal accounts, payment through a trust and payment from a life insurance benefit.

Payment from a Personal Account

This is the easiest method. No lawyers are needed. Simply open a savings account in a federally insured bank containing the amount needed to cover the cost of the funeral. This account should be designated as "payable upon death" to the funeral home. Alternatively, you may open a joint account with your next of kin who has the right of survivorship. Upon your death, this survivor will pay for your funeral.

Payment from a Trust

This method requires prepayment of the funeral costs to the funeral home. The funeral director puts this payment into a trust account. The beneficiary of this trust will be the funeral director and he will receive the funds upon your death. Most funeral homes offer this funding option. If you choose this method, make sure the trust is regulated by your state.

Payment through a Life Insurance Policy

This method requires purchasing a life insurance benefit equal to the cost of the funeral. The benefits are either assigned to the funeral home or the funeral home is named as the beneficiary. When you die, the funeral home collects the benefits of the insurance policy.

The AARP Product Report entitled "Pre-Paying Your Funeral"[2] is an excellent source for additional information on this subject.

Information on Social Security benefits, veterans' benefits, federal government retiree benefits and the military's funeral policy is provided in detail in Chapter 16.

Prepare an Information Brochure on Yourself

This is one of the most important aspects of preneed funeral planning. Between the finalization of the preneed agreement and your death, a considerable length of time may pass. Many of the details of the arrangement may be forgotten. At the time of your death, your family will be at a loss to understand what was done. Therefore, it is vital that you create a composite document containing all the pertinent information.

This important brochure should include the following:

- Personal information: your name, date and place of birth, current address and Social Security number.
- Names, addresses, telephone numbers of your spouse, previous spouses, children, parents, brothers, sisters, and other relatives.
- Names, addresses and telephone numbers of friends, employers, attorneys, executor of your estate, funeral director and clergy person.
- Information on your education, organizations you belong to, religion, obituary notices and organ donation.
- Details about your veteran status.
- Your wishes regarding disposition of body, funeral home, cemetery, casket, vault, music, flowers, visitation, and donations in your memory.
- Location of your passport, drivers license, real estate papers, insurance policies, checkbooks, passbooks, credit cards, safe deposit box and key and preneed funeral contract.

Tie Up the Loose Ends

After you have researched the preneed funeral plan, made the decisions, signed the preneed contract and prepared the information brochure, it is time to put it all together. Place all the papers in a safe place and tell your next of kin where they are. This is when you will experience personal satisfaction and contentment, knowing that you are giving your family peace of mind.

REFERENCES

1. National Funeral Directors Association: "Consumer Preneed Bill of Rights." NFDA, 1998.
2. American Association of Retired Persons: "Pre-Paying Your Funeral. FTC Funeral Rule Statement." *AARP Product Report*, 2:2, 1992.

Chapter 2

A PERSONAL EXAMPLE

My Own Funeral Arrangements

For a man who has done his natural duty,
Death is as natural and welcome as sleep.

—George Santayana (1863-1952)

*C*harles Lindbergh planned the details of his own funeral just a few days before he died of cancer on August 26, 1974. He arranged to be flown from New York to his home in Hawaii. He ordered a coffin to be constructed out of eucalyptus wood. He composed a prayer to be read at the grave site. He asked to be dressed in simple clothes and requested the pallbearers to wear ordinary work clothes.

Besides Charles Lindbergh, millions of people in the past have prearranged their funerals, be they "ordinary" members of the public or kings. Many preplanned their funeral years before their death. The Egyptian pyramids are the classic example of preplanning by pharaohs.

Most people don't want to think about death. They find it even harder to think about preplanning their own funeral. I believe preplanning one's own funeral is the most unselfish act of life. Besides, since we know that death is inevitable, why not prepare for it?

There are many reasons why I have preplanned my funeral. However, my ultimate goal was to leave my loved ones with comfort at death and peace in mourning. I wanted to write the last chapter in the book of life before I go to bed for a "long sleep." Death brings turmoil for survivors, creates chaos, unfolds uncertainty and sinks them in sorrow. I want to spare my survivors of these agonies.

As a pathologist and medical examiner for 39 years, I have been involved in the investigation of over 32,000 deaths. I have been a partner in pain with those grieving, shared in the agony of the dying process and counseled survivors on death and on life after death. During this period, I have dealt with every facet of life and death. I have attended numerous funerals of my patients, relatives and friends. All of them have left the poignant message for me that I should preplan for my own passing.

My father, a farmer, businessman, Islamic priest and novelist, died at the age of 62. My oldest brother died at 60 from stroke, and another brother of mine died at age 51 from a heart attack. Each time, the lack of planning took a toll on my family. In all these experiences, I was most touched by situations created by sudden and unexpected death. The survivors were left completely helpless and had no concept or knowledge of what to do or who to turn to. Some succumbed to shock and could not even communicate with anyone. Some sank into an emotional "coma" from which they could not be roused for a long time. Many were left with no financial resources to pay for the handling of the remains of the deceased. Indeed, I was immensely moved each time I dealt with these survivors. Reflecting on all these fragile episodes, it became ever clearer to me that I must preplan.

I am 66 years old now and in perfect health. I am not afraid of death, but I want to be prepared. Death is not only inevitable, but many times it is also unpredictable. While it could be too late to prepare for it, it is never too early to prepare. I know this will help my family. Beyond that, I feel deeply that I must publish my preneed arrangements of my funeral. I know this will help many others.

PRELIMINARIES

I started by putting the important matters of my house in order. I began with matters that I knew would consume a considerable amount of time. I made a list and started working on it:

- Family discussions
- Preparation of will (estate planning)

- Preparation of living will
- Search for cemetery plot
- Selection of a place for services; and
- Selection of goods and merchandise.

FAMILY DISCUSSIONS

I live in Fort Lauderdale, Florida. All of my children practice medicine in this town. One day I called them for a family conference to discuss my funeral preneed arrangements. Being totally unprepared for such a discussion, they were initially startled. Nevertheless, I proceeded to explain why I thought this was important. In particular, I brought up my family history. They saw my point, and I solicited input from each of them. I discussed my choices and expressed my wishes and together we developed a consensus.

Family discussions are extremely important in advance planning of a funeral. Your loved ones will know what your wishes are and they will get tremendous satisfaction in fulfilling those wishes when you die. They will also get satisfaction from participating in these preparations. These discussions should not be limited to the idea of prearranging your funeral, but they should also include other important aspects of your will and living will.

PREPARATION OF WILL

Preplanning for my funeral disclosed an important lapse in our lives. My will was in a closet untouched for nine years despite a few letters from an estate planner. Laws change, and an outdated will may not be what you want to leave behind. So, if you don't have a will or if you have one that is outdated, make an appointment with your estate planner as soon as possible. There may be serious consequences if you do not do so. My will is updated and current now.

PREPARATION OF YOUR LIVING WILL OR ADVANCE DIRECTIVE

A living will, also known as an advance directive, is another important document. The following story exemplifies this.

Once I took over the care of a hospitalized patient who had been treated by another physician for several months. The patient was a young man in a coma resulting from injuries sustained in an automobile accident. His life was sustained by all imaginable modern therapeutic measures because his wife insisted on such measures. After two-and-one-half years, he died. He did not have a living will. His medical bills by this time were over one million dollars.

Seeing this man every day for over 800 days, I felt his exhaustion and the futility of my efforts. He convinced me that everyone should have a living will. My living will is in order and my family and my doctor know where to find it. This book addresses what a living will is, how to prepare it and what to do with it.

My religious faith requires that after my death, my body be undisturbed, except for bathing. Therefore, no procedures will be performed to remove my corneas, tissues or organs. My faith also requires immediate burial, and hence embalming of the body and the donation of the body will be precluded. Thus, I have prepared no papers describing embalming, organ/tissue or body donation. However, if you wish to donate your body to science or to donate tissues or organs for transplantation then your preneed funeral arrangements should include preparation of the appropriate papers. You will find details about this in Chapter 5.

CEMETERY PLOT

Only unforeseen circumstances will prevent me from being buried in plot number 515 of Forest Lawn Cemetery in Ft. Lauderdale, Florida. After researching the area, I bought this plot on April 8, 1998. I also bought plot 516 for my wife. Several factors played a part in this purchase. The plots, which are normally priced at $1,500 each, were advertised for sale at $445 each, and I took advantage of it. The cemetery is well landscaped and maintained, and my contract provides for perpetual care and upkeep. One important religious factor in the selection was the positioning of the graves. They will be opened in such a way that the head-end of our bodies will be towards Kaba, Mecca. The cemetery is only one mile from my home and it is located by the side of Interstate Highway 595, with easy access.

I bought these lots for my reasons; your reasons might be different. To find the right plot for you, visit a few cemeteries, factor in location, quality, convenience and cost and then make a decision. Pay for it as discussed in Chapters 1 and 13, and you will relieve your loved ones from the worry of a last minute search and high prices.

SELECTION OF A PLACE FOR SERVICES

The facility where I intend to have my funeral service is about 100 yards from the cemetery plots. Therefore, no hearse, flower car, or limousines will be needed. The building is a large pyramid-shaped structure, unlike any other in the area. It is visible from several miles away, is easy to find and can accommodate over a thousand people for a service. It was selected to cut down on the travelling time and to assure a rapid burial.

SERVICES, GOODS AND MERCHANDISE

The above preliminaries took several weeks to complete. The next thing I did was to identify the services and goods. In my case I picked the following essential items:

- Transportation of body from home to the funeral service facility
- Casket for viewing and services
- Use of the facility for three hours of services
- Opening of grave
- Vault
- Closing of grave, and
- Grave marker with epitaph.

I sat down with the funeral director and negotiated the prices and the contract.

MISCELLANEOUS ITEMS

After completing the preliminaries, I turned to other items, such as the preparation of a detailed information brochure on myself. This contains all the information in the brochure discussed in the previous chapter and a copy of it will be given to my family and to the funeral director.

Finally, I gathered my wife and children and presented to them a package containing all of the family's important documents, including birth certificate, passport, driver's license, will, living will, real estate papers, marriage certificate, cemetery contract, funeral director's contract, stock and bond certificates, and the information brochure. I told them where exactly they can find these papers.

My job is done, and I feel good.

FUNERAL PROTOCOL

The conduct of my funeral will be based on our religious beliefs, which are described in Chapter 26, the Muslim Funeral. The emphasis will be on simplicity, dignity and expediency.

When my own death occurs, immediate family and close friends will be called. Their telephone numbers are in my information brochure. The *Haaji* (Muslim priest) will be called to perform the ritual bathing, and the funeral director will be alerted.

When the Haaji arrives, the ritual of bathing will be carried out by men as is described later in this book. Light make-up will be applied to the face. As is typical, women and men will recite from the Koran while awaiting for the arrival of the funeral director. In the meantime, the exact hours for the viewing will be determined and all to be invited will be called by chain-calling system.

The body will be taken from my home in the casket and placed in the funeral service facility for viewing. There will be no music. Only one rose will be placed on my chest. The guests will be requested to donate to the charity of their choice, in lieu of flowers.

Eulogies will by read by a few close relatives and friends. The following poem will be read by a family member on my behalf:

I'm Free

Don't grieve for me, for now I'm free!
I'm following the path God laid for me.
I took His hand when I heard Him call,
I turned my back and left it all.
I could not stay another day.

To laugh, to love, to work or play.
Tasks left undone, must stay that way.
I found peace at the close of day.
If my parting has left a void,
then fill it with remembered joy!
A love shared, a laugh, a kiss
ah yes! These things I, too, will miss.
Be not burdened with times of sorrow,
I wish you the sunshine of tomorrow.
My life's been full, I've savored much,
good friends, good times, a loved one's touch.
Perhaps my time seemed all too brief,
don't lengthen it now with undue grief.
Lift up your heart and share with me,
*God wanted me now, **He set me free**.*

After the viewing period ends, the casket with the body will be taken to the grave site with only relatives and friends serving as pallbearers. No hearse will be used; there will likewise be no limousines. At the grave site, the casket will be placed in the vault. After grave site prayers are completed, the grave will be closed.

My grave marker will carry the following epitaph:

I am dead,
but I shall not die.

Chapter 3

PROTECT YOUR ESTATE

Don't Leave the Door Open
for Uncle Sam

Death is the most convenient time to tax people.

—David Lloyd George (1863-1945)

*A*s *a conscientious, tax-paying citizen, you know the importance that* Uncle Sam plays in your life. Therefore, it should come as no surprise that Uncle Sam will also play an important role after you die. Depending on your situation, the government may take as much as 50 percent of what you leave behind in the form of federal estate tax or "death tax." If you are leaving money behind for your loved ones, then you must care about their future. Thus, you should care to take the time to consider estate tax laws so that you leave behind more to your legacy and less to the Internal Revenue Service (IRS).

Remember Joe Robbie, the former owner of the Miami Dolphins, who died as a billionaire? He did not do estate planning. The U.S. Government took 60 percent of all he had left behind.[1] In this chapter, general information on estate planning and taxes is presented, so that you may take appropriate steps to safeguard the fruits of your life's labor.

PREPLAN AND BEAT THE IRS

When a spouse dies, the surviving husband or wife must provide a list of all assets if the total value of the such assets exceeds $625,000. This includes cash, stock, bonds, funds, accounts shared with children and property. When the remaining spouse dies, if total assets are greater than $625,000, the survivors must file an estate tax return. It is important to note that the total of $625,000, known as the lifetime exemption, excludes any money given as gifts, not exceeding $10,000 per year, to heirs at any time during their lives. In order to minimize the amount that your survivors will have to pay in estate taxes, you must consider acting on the following points:

1. Give to your children before you die

The government allows you and your spouse to gift anyone $10,000 per year tax-free. Thus, if you give your child $10,000 per year for five years, your estate will be reduced by $50,000 and when you die your child will not have to pay estate taxes on this amount. Also, the $10,000 gift will appreciate for your child. Although the amount that is not gifted would also appreciate, it would be subject to estate taxes.

2. Spend while you are alive

The more you spend while you are alive, the less you will leave behind for Uncle Sam when you die. What, after all, are your hard earned dollars for but to enjoy?

3. Create a house trust

Your home may appreciate during your lifetime, resulting in a large percentage of your total assets. If you transfer your home to what is called a "house trust" before you die, then the amount the house appreciates between the time you create the trust and at the time of death will not be subject to estate taxes.

4. Create a family real estate partnership

If you own property that amounts to a large dollar value, you can avoid having to pay enormous taxes on it upon death by creating a family real estate partnership which constitutes the total value of all of your properties. Your children and other relatives can be included as members of the partnership. You can assign shares of the partnership to your loved ones at the rate of $10,000 per year. As long as you retain more than 50 percent interest in the partnership, you can determine the fate of the property and prevent anyone from selling their share of the property. By the time you die, you will have already transferred a substantial proportion of the value of the property to your survivors and the amount transferred before you die will not be subject to estate taxes.

5. *Transfer the business, keep the income*

Tax laws permit you to transfer the net value of a business or income property to a relative while maintaining the income for yourself. This way, when you die the total value of the business will avoid estate taxation. For instance, just as with real estate, if a business is worth $500,000 and is transferred to an heir before your death, the value of the business will not be subject to estate taxes after you die.

6. *Have your child take out a life insurance policy on you*

If you are an individual with high net worth and you expect that your estate taxes will be high, then you should consider a life insurance policy for yourself that is paid for by your children. For example, you can gift the amount of money needed to pay the premiums for a one million dollar life insurance policy to your children. Then when you die, your children will be awarded the one million dollars tax-free, which would enable them to pay the estate taxes on the rest of your assets.

7. *Good news on the horizon*

Thanks to recent changes in legislature, the lifetime exemption, which is the exemption on your principal residence when it is sold, will be raised gradually over the next decade. Lifetime exemption is scheduled to increase as follows: $625,000 in 1999, $675,000 in 2000 and 2001, $700,000 in 2002 and 2003, $850,000 in 2004, $950,000 in 2005 and $1 million in 2006. Furthermore, your heirs will be exempt from paying capital gains taxes on the first $250,000 (single) or $500,000 (married couple) of profit from the sale of property used as the principal residence for two of the past five years.

STATE TAX LAWS

Although the federal estate tax laws are discussed above, it must be mentioned that estate laws for states vary significantly. There are some general concepts that deserve mention. For example, if you own property in different states, your heirs will have to go through probate in each state, whereas if the properties are in a trust all of the matters can be settled locally. Most states do not charge a separate estate tax. Rather, any money that is collected by the state can be used as a credit against federal estate taxes that are due. States with a large population of retirees may charge taxes in excess of federal estate taxes. If you have further questions, consult with an attorney in your state who specializes in estate planning.

AVOID DEATH (PROBATE) COURT

Transferring your assets to your children when you die is a legal process that involves a significant amount of paper work, legal fees, probate court and a judge. Probate court is where the judge legally transfers ownership of your assets to your children. Even if you have a will, your children must go through this process, which can take years and may cost them thousands of dollars. The good news is that you can avoid probate court and its expenses by creating a living trust. The living trust is a document that allows your children to act as agents in transferring the ownership of your assets. They act in place of the probate judge. Thus, they will be able to avoid probate court and the associated legal fees and delays.

PREVENT FAMILY FEUDING AFTER YOUR DEATH

You have seen your children grow, succeed and fail while maintaining beautiful relationships with their siblings. You may think that they will be able to get along after you die, and will be able to decide together on how to distribute your assets. Think again. All rules of conduct may go out the window when money is on the line. Their spouses may act as selfish agents who create tension and lawsuits. It is for this reason that thoughtful planning is necessary. You should consider the following points when developing an estate plan to minimize family tension.[2]

1. *Treat all of your children equally*

While the incomes of your children may be different, you may create tension between your children if you give more to one child than to another. If a child feels shortchanged (or the spouse of your child feels shortchanged) there may be arguments, and lawsuits may even result.

2. *How your child can lose his inheritance*

Like winning the lottery, an inheritance represents a windfall of assets that can change your child's life. Your child can get divorced, thereby losing the money to alimony; he can get sued, he can irresponsibly spend it all, or he can be cheated by others. If you are concerned that your inheritance will be lost to alimony rather than going to your grandchildren, you can create a trust for all of your assets and name only your child, and not the spouse, as the owner of the trust. This way, if there is a divorce, your estate will stay in the family. As with divorce, a child who becomes bankrupt puts his inheritance at risk to his creditors. If you create a trust, the creditors cannot lay claim to your assets. It must be noted that such a trust should be irrevocable, meaning it cannot be changed. Your attorney will help you prepare this. If your child can revoke the trust, his creditors can get the assets. In the case of a young child, you can appoint a trustee, such as a banker, to oversee your assets and transfer ownership of the assets from the trust to your child at a certain age. Or, you could appoint a relative whom you trust to act as a caring party that will make decisions on your behalf.

3. *Deciding on what to do with your home after you die merits an open discussion with your children*

Your home may be your most significant asset. If your children agree ahead of time to sell the home and divide the proceeds, then you can avoid future problems. If one child is wealthy, then you may want to give the house to the more needy child. This may seem unfair to the wealthy child. You can consider writing a clause to let your more needy child live in the house for several years and then be required to buy out the sibling's share or sell the house and divide the proceeds equally. This way the more needy child gets help sooner after your death and the wealthy child is not punished for being successful.

Alternatively, you can give the house to one child and buy a life insurance policy for another child in an amount equal to the value of the house.

4. *If you don't leave anything to your children, at least leave something for your grandchildren*

If you leave all of your assets to your children then your grandchildren will not benefit from your estate until your children die. Also, the amount of your inheritance will be subject to estate taxes once you die and again when your child dies. Gifting to a grandchild also has the advantage of allowing more time for the assets to grow.

SUMMARY

The points mentioned in this chapter highlight important generalities about estate planning.

- You must take an active role in estate planning.
- You can take measures to minimize the amount that the government collects when you die.
- Leaving your assets in a trust can save on taxes and protect your assets from the tax collectors and others who will appear when you die. Trusts can also help minimize family tension and keep lawyers out of the picture.
- While estate planning can be a touchy subject, it is vitally important that you discuss it openly and honestly with your family.

The information in this chapter is meant to provide general guidance on estate planning. For individual situations, expert legal assistance must be sought. Like William Shakespeare said,

"He that dies pays all debts"

—unless he has properly planned his estate, that is!

REFERENCES

1. Blum J: "Your Heirs and the IRS: A Partnership from Hell." *The Director*, 1993:18.
2. Condon GM and Condon JL: *Beyond the Grave: The Right Way and the Wrong Way of Leaving Money to Your Children (And Others)*. New York: Harper Business, 1996.

Chapter 4

LIVING WILLS

By medicine life may be prolonged,
yet death will seize the doctor too.

—William Shakespeare (1564-1616)

*I*mpending death creates a lot of questions. One of the important ques- tions concerns the continuation or withdrawal of medical treatment. Every individual has a constitutional right to request the withdrawal or withholding of medical treatment. In our society, a person's right to refuse medical treatment is the most widely practiced and accepted right-to-die policy. All fifty states and the District of Columbia have laws authorizing the use of some type of advance directive such as a living will or medical power of attorney.[1] These documents help individuals make a valid direc- tive to their physicians stating their wishes in the event they should suffer from a terminal illness.

Generally, the living will directs doctors to withhold or withdraw treatments when you suffer from an illness or injury from which you are not expected to recover. It allows you to make your preferences known regarding life-sustaining treatment to prolong your life.

The Society for the Right to Die recommends that in addition to signing a living will, you should also complete a document called Durable Power of Attorney for Health Care or Health Care Proxy. With this document, you appoint someone you trust as your agent or proxy to make decisions for you when you cannot make these decisions yourself. This is because living will statutes do not always cover every possible contingency you may face in a situation of health care crisis. The standard living will forms are limited in what they can accomplish and what conditions they cover. Living will instructions will always be subject to interpretation at the time of a terminal illness. The health care proxy or agent, on the other hand, can respond to actual circumstances and variables known at the time decisions have to be made.

If there is no one close to you, a living will is safer than leaving matters in the hands of an agent. If you sign an advance directive you do not lose your authority or choice. As long as you remain able to make decisions, your consent will be obtained for medical treatment.

Every state recognizes living will and health care proxy types of advance directives. Many states even accept and honor out-of-state advance directives if they meet the legal requirements of the state where they were made or the state where treatment decisions have to be made.

You can obtain the living will and health care proxy form for your state and other forms from many places, including the American Bar Association, 740 Fifteenth Street, NW, Washington, D.C. 20005-1022. You can also call or fax them at (202) 662-8690 or (202) 662-8698 respectively. Alternatively, you get forms from Choice in Dying, 1035 30th Street NW, Washington, D.C. 20007, telephone (800) 989-9455.

These forms can be personalized to include your wishes. Consult an attorney if you have any questions or need help. After you have selected and prepared the forms, it is important that you discuss their contents with your physician, as well as your close relatives and the person you appoint as proxy. Also, once the forms are completed, sign and date them and have two disinterested persons sign as witnesses. Give copies of the signed forms to a close relative, to your physician and the appointed proxy.

REFERENCE

1. Choice in Dying. Online. Available: *http://www.choices.org/ issues.htm*, September 23, 1998.

Chapter 5

CHARITABLE DEAD

My name is Death;
The last, Best Friend am I.

—Robert Southey (1774-1843)

*M*ost of us are generous at heart. However, while we are alive we believe "generosity begins at home." By this we mean we do things for ourselves and the ones closest to us. When death becomes imminent we become less selfish. We start to think of giving what we believe we cannot take with us in death. We become less selfish, more generous. We see value in sharing and giving. Some of us consider sharing our bodies for research or to give life to others. We decide to be charitable dead, believing, in the words of poet Emily Dickinson (1830-1886):

> *If I can stop one heart from breaking,*
> *I shall not live in vain,*
> *If I can ease one life the aching,*
> *Or cool one pain,*
> *Or help one fainting robin*
> *Unto his nest again,*
> *I shall not live in vain.*

The charitable donation of human bodies or individual parts for medical purposes was facilitated by the Uniform Anatomical Gift Act and endorsed by the American Bar Association in 1968. This act, developed by the National Conference of Commissioners on Uniform State Laws, was designed to serve as a basis for laws in all of the states. The American Medical Association has summarized the essential elements of this act,[1] which is based on the belief that an individual should be able to control the disposition of his own body after death and that his wishes should not be frustrated by his next-of-kin. To encourage donations and to help meet the increasing need for organs and tissue, unnecessary and cumbersome formalities should be eliminated and only those safeguards required to protect the other varied interests involved should be included. The rights of the appropriate next-of-kin should be clearly provided, physicians working in this area should be protected, and the public interests in a dead body, as represented by the medical examiner, should be maintained.

Since the inception of the Uniform Anatomical Gift Act, the District of Columbia and all states have enacted their own laws dealing with the donation of parts of the human body or the whole body after death. These laws are presented later in this chapter.

CONSUMERS AND ANATOMICAL GIFTS

In life you can give gifts, and in death you can give life, the most precious gift of all. In death, you can give a part or all of your body. A stranger may be able to see with your eyes, breath with your lungs. This is the ultimate gift and it will give you comfort knowing that you have made a difference in someone else's life, even as your own has ended.

If you are planning to donate all or part of your body for research or to help others, the following discussion will help you understand various aspects of anatomical gifts and answer your questions.

General Guidelines

If you wish to donate your entire body for teaching and research, or parts of your body for transplantation, the following guidelines will help you.

- Plan ahead and let your next-of-kin and your physician know about it.
- Familiarize yourself with the details of the Uniform Anatomical Gift Act, pertinent parts of which are presented in this chapter.
- Make a will or document and that includes the details of your wishes.
- Carry a signed and witnessed Uniform Donor Card, indicating your desires about anatomical gifts. See Appendix D for this card.

- Complete the form "Anatomical Gift by a Living Donor" (see Appendix D) indicating your desires.

- Give copies of above documents to your next-of-kin and to your physician and hospital. Ask your next-of-kin to sign the documents to make things easier.

- Inform the donee and your funeral director about your pre-arrangements.

- Most major religious denominations encourage donation of organs or body.

- Any individual age 18 or over can make an anatomical gift.

- The whole body or the organs such as heart, kidneys, liver, lungs, pancreas, skin, bone, veins and connective tissue can be donated.

DONATION OF BODY

There is always a shortage of cadavers for medical education; thousands are needed each year for research and education of medical students. The shortage is even greater in foreign countries than in the United States. For instance, in Argentina, 200 medical students may share one cadaver for dissection and learning.[2]

If you plan to donate your body to medical research after death, it is always advisable to make prior arrangements. The body may not be acceptable to a medical school if they are oversupplied. They may not accept the body if there has been prior surgery or autopsy, if a limb or major organ is missing, or if a body has been mutilated because of a violent death. Some diseases and obesity may make the body unacceptable. Contact the National Anatomical Service, a nonprofit organization, at (800) 727-0700 if you wish to donate the body. They help in prearranging and transporting cadavers to various medical schools.

The donation of the body to a medical school is not only a generous and thoughtful gesture but it also is an economical choice. This saves the family the cost of the funeral. While the medical schools do not pay for bodies, they may reimburse the family for the cost of transporting the body.

Generally, the body is cremated after it has been dissected in a medical school. If viewing or services are desired, they can be arranged prior to the body's transfer to the medical institution. The surviving family and the funeral director should contact the medical school to find out how that body needs to be prepared before transportation. The family may also ask the school to return the ashes for disposition as they wish. The cremains may be returned within one or two years after the donation.

DONATION OF ORGANS

With recent advances in transplantation medicine, the organs for transplant are also in short supply. Many thousands of people have been spared of blindness because of corneal transplants, and thousands have been kept alive without dialysis machines due to kidney transplants. Many have earned new lives because of heart, liver, lung and pancreas transplants. Burn victims have been helped by way of skin transplants.

Whereas donated bodies can be preserved and used later, the organs for transplants have to be used fairly quickly after the donor's death. Some organs can be "banked" for a day or two. The donor has to express his desire to donate the organs on his driver's license or through a will, document or Uniform donor card. In the absence of this, a family member can give permission. The order of priority for giving such a permission is spouse, adult son or daughter, parent, adult sibling or guardian.

The donation of the organs does not necessarily result in much delay for the funeral. The surgical retrieval of major organs usually takes less than six hours. The family should feel reassured that the surgical procedures to obtain organs from the dead body will not result in disfigurement of the body. The retrieval of corneas is a simple process and will not cause a delay in funeral.

CONSUMERS, FUNERAL DIRECTORS AND
ANATOMICAL GIFTS

The Anatomical Gift Act is very important for consumers. It faciliates the donation of organs. For proper execution of this Act, the funeral director can help in several ways. He becomes a crucial link between the donor and the donee. Therefore, it is important for him to understand his role. The following are special points to note:

- The Anatomical Gift Act contains several applicable laws which affect the funeral director and therefore, he must be fully familiar with its contents.

- The funeral director must be aware of the changes made by his state that affect his functions.

- The funeral director/embalmer must complete a course in eye enucleation (complete removal of the eye without damage to it) and be licensed in his state to enucleate eyes for a gift.

- If the body is donated for research and medical education, the funeral director should help the family by calling the medical school, preparing the body as required by that school and arranging for funeral ceremonies prior to transporting the body to the medical institution.

- The funeral director should help by getting the death certificate, making sure the appropriate forms are signed for anatomical gifts, and by obtaining authorization for embalming the body and restorative work.

DONATION LAWS

The following are portions of Part I: Uniform Anatomical Gift Act–1968 and Part II: Uniform Anatomical Gift Act–1987 that are pertinent to the funeral directors, embalmers, donees, donors and others making anatomical gifts. They are reproduced here with the kind permission of the National Funeral Directors Association. For full details, check the Act in its entirety and check your state laws or consult your attorney.

PART I: UNIFORM ANATOMICAL GIFT ACT–1968[3]

Section 1 – Definitions

Section 2 – Persons who may execute an anatomical gift.

- Any individual of sound mind who is 18 years or older may give all or any part of his body for any purpose specified in Section 3, the gift to take effect upon death.

- Any of the following persons, in order of priority stated when persons with higher priority are not available at the time of death, and in the absence of actual notice of contrary indications by the decedent or actual notice of opposition by a member of the same or a prior class with higher priority, may give all or any part of the decedent's body for any purpose specified in Section 3:

- Spouse
- Adult son or daughter
- Either parent
- Adult brother or sister
- Guardian of the decedent at the time of death
- Any other person authorized or under obligation to dispose of the body

• If the donee has actual notice of contrary indications by the decedent or that a person with the same or higher priority opposes a gift, the donee shall not accept the gift. The persons authorized to make the gift may do so after or immediately before death.

• A gift of all or part of a body authorizes any examination necessary to assure medical acceptability of the gift for the purposes intended.

• The right of the donee created by the gift are paramount to the rights of others, except as regard to state laws regarding autopsies.

Section 3 – Persons who may become donees and purposes for which anatomical gifts may be made.

• The following persons may become donees of gifts or bodies or parts thereof for the purposes stated:

- Any hospital, surgeon or physician, for medical or dental education, research, advancement of medical or dental science, therapy or transplantation.

- Any accredited medical school, dental school, college or university for education, research advancement of medical or dental science or therapy.

- Any bank or storage facility for medical education, dental education, research, advancement of medical science, advancement of dental science, therapy or transplantation.

- Any specified individual for therapy of transplantation needed by the individual.

Section 4 – Manner of executing anatomical gifts.

• A gift of all or part of the body must be made by will.

• A gift of all or part of the body may also be made by document other than a will, such as a donor card.

Section 5 – Delivery of document of gift.

• If the gift is made by the donor to a specified donee, the will, card or other document or executed copy may be delivered to the donee to expedite the appropriate procedures immediately after death.

Section 6 – Amendment or revocation of the gift.

• If the will, card, other document or executed copy has been delivered to a specific donee, the donor may amend or revoke the gift by:

- The execution and delivery to the donee of a signed statement.
- An oral statement made in the presence of two persons and communicated to the donee.
- A statement during a terminal illness or injury addressed to an attending physician and communicated to the donee.
- A signed card or document found on his person or in his effects.
- By destruction, cancellation or mutilation of the document and all existing copies.
- Amendment or revocation of wills.

Section 7 – Rights and duties at death.

• The donee may accept or reject the gift. If the donee accepts a gift of the entire body, he or she may, subject to the terms of the gift, authorize embalming and the use of the body in funeral services. If the gift is of a part of the body, the donee, upon the death of the donor and prior to embalming, shall cause the part to be removed without unnecessary mutilation. After removal of the part, custody of the remainder of the body rests in the surviving spouse, next-of-kin or other persons under obligation to dispose of the body.

Part II: Uniform Anatomical Gift Act–1987[4]

Section 1 – Explains the differences of the two acts with emphasis in the areas that affect funeral directors/embalmers.

Section 2 – Making, amending, revoking and refusing to make anatomical gifts by individual.

- An individual who is at least 18 years of age may make an anatomical gift for any of the allowed purposes, may limit an anatomical gift to one or more of those purposes or refuse to make an anatomical gift.
- A donor may amend or revoke an anatomical gift only by:
  - A signed statement.
  - An oral statement made in the presence of two individuals.
  - Any form of communication during a terminal illness or injury addressed to a physician or surgeon.
  - The delivery of a signed statement to a specified donee to whom a document of gift had been delivered.
- The manner provided for amendment or revocation of wills.
- An anatomical gift that is not revoked by the donor before death is irrevocable and does not require the consent or concurrence of any person after the donor's death.

Section 3 – Making, revoking and objecting to anatomical gifts by others.

- Any member of the following classes of persons, in the order of priority listed, may make an anatomical gift of all or part of the decedent's body for an authorized purpose, unless the decedent, at the time of death, has made an unrevoked refusal to make that anatomical gift.
  - The spouse of the decedent.
  - An adult son or daughter of the decedent.
  - Either parent of the decedent.

- An adult brother or sister of the decedent.
- A grandparent of the decedent.
- A guardian of the person of the decedent at the time of death.

Section 4 – Authorized by coroner, medical examiner or local public health official.

- It authorizes the removal of any part of the body for transplant or therapy. Section 4 specifically permits enucleators to remove eyes.

Section 8 – Rights and duties of death.

- If there has been an anatomical gift, a technician may remove any donated parts and an enucleator may remove any donated eyes or parts of eyes, after determination of death by a physician or surgeon.

Section 11 – Examination, autopsy and liability.

- The new act is more specific in that it individually names the people who are not liable for civil and criminal actions if they act or attempt to act in good faith. Funeral directors/embalmers would be covered as enucleators or technicians.

Part III: Applicable Laws Providing for Funeral Directors/Embalmers to Perform Tissue Removal[5]

Many other states have enacted legislation permitting funeral directors/embalmers to enucleate eyes or parts thereof. For details the reader is advised to refer to Appendix B of Part III of the Uniform Anatomical Gift Act.

MODEL FORMS

The forms "Uniform Donor Card" "Anatomical Gift by a Living Donor," "Anatomical Gift by a Relative or the Guardian of the Person of the Decedent," and "Authorization for Permission to Use Eyes" can be found in Appendix D.

REFERENCES

1. National Conference of Commissioners on Uniform State Laws: "The Uniform Anatomical Gift Act." JAMA 1968; 206(11):2501.
2. Funeral and Memorial Societies of America: "Body Donation, A Gift to Science." FAMSA, 1998.
3. Part I: *Uniform Anatomical Gift Act*, 1968.
4. Part II: *Uniform Anatomical Gift Act*, 1987.
5. Part III: Applicable Laws Provided for Funeral Directors/Embalmers to Perform Tissue Removal. *Uniform Anatomical Gift Act of 1987.*

Section II:
Planning the Funeral of
Your Loved One

Chapter 6

AT NEED FUNERAL PLANNING

Dying is the most embarrassing thing that can ever happen to you, because someone's got to take care of all your details.

—Andy Warhol (1927?-1987)

*T*here are many differences between preneed planning and at need planning. Preneed planning allows you to attend to funeral details while you are at peace, with no grief or emotional handicaps. It allows you the opportunity to express what you want done and allows your family members to participate in the decision-making process. Also, you can take care of any financial arrangements ahead of time.

However, in the case of a death of a loved one who has not made pre-arranged funeral plans, you have a totally different set of circumstances. Since death is usually unexpected, it immediately creates a crisis situation. You may not know what to do, who to turn to or how to handle the unexpected financial burden. Death can leave you totally unprepared in the midst of your shock, panic and grief. The objective of this chapter is to guide you through this difficult time. A step-by-step plan is presented to eliminate confusion, uncertainty and helplessness.

WHEN A LOVED ONE DIES

It is important to reach out to people who can help you at this time. This is no time to act alone. Call the following people as soon as possible:

- Immediate family members
- Close family friends

- Your family doctor
- Funeral director
- Clergy person

Calling these people will help you to feel supported and secure. Immediate family members will share in your sorrow, help to comfort you and take steps to solve immediate problems. These family members and friends can advise you, make phone calls to other relatives and friends, run errands and help with the funeral arrangements.

The family physician may have to pronounce the person dead. He may also help by providing immediate care to family members. If the death is unnatural, such as the result of a suicide, accident or homicide, the local police and the medical examiner or coroner will also need to be called.

One of the most important people to call is your funeral director. He will help in many ways: he will provide immediate care to the deceased and help you and your family through the entire funeral process. At the time of death, if you do not know which funeral home to call, consult with family members or friends to find one.

The clergy person also plays an important role in advising the family, both on religious aspects of the funeral and in attending to the details in cooperation with the funeral director and the family members.

IMPORTANT DECISIONS

In the process of arranging a funeral, one is faced with a task of making several decisions. Some of the important decisions pertain to:

- Selection of a funeral home
- Immediate burial
- Direct cremation
- Burial, in-ground or above
- Embalming
- Casket
- Autopsy
- Organ/body donation

- Size of funeral
- Cost and payment plan

FUNERAL HOME

Under this heading let us consider the following:

- Selection criteria
- Initial call and services
- Follow up conferences
- Discussion of choices
- Contract and arrangement for payment
- After care services

The selection of the right funeral home is important. Many criteria should be considered in making your selection. During your first conversation with the funeral director, you should feel comfortable. He should sound compassionate and caring, not rushed and indifferent. The funeral home should be able to handle the type and size of the funeral you want. If death has occurred out of town or overseas, the funeral home should be able to make appropriate arrangements. Of course, you should choose the funeral home that specializes in or has experience dealing with your religious beliefs.

Once you select a funeral director, don't hesitate to call him, no matter what time of day or night it is. During this initial call, ask any questions you might have. Let the family-member who is in the best state of mind talk to the funeral director. During this call, the funeral director will need to get the following information to help him start funeral arrangements:

- Your name, address and telephone number
- Name, address and telephone number of the next of kin or person in charge of making arrangements
- Name of the deceased and location of the body
- Name of the person who pronounced death
- Name and telephone number of a doctor who can sign the death certificate

41

- Brief description of the type of arrangements you desire
- Appointment for follow-up conference.

With this information, the funeral director is prepared to help you. Although he cannot make decisions for you, he will make decision-making easy for you. He will make arrangements to move the body from the place of death and take care of it. He will make sure to keep the remains in a refrigerated space to prevent deterioration.

It is advisable to schedule the follow-up conference at the funeral home. That way you can personally inspect the facility, and the funeral director has the opportunity to show you the merchandise available. Take one or more of your close relatives with you to provide both emotional support and to help you to make decisions.

The type and size of funeral service, the location of the service, the method of disposition (burial or cremation) and the budget are some of the major topics you should be thinking about. Try to make these decisions before you see the funeral director, so that he can handle further arrangements.

At the funeral home, the funeral director will go into all of the details regarding the funeral. First, he will advise you on the options you have and present you with the information required to be given according to the FTC's Funeral Rule. He will show you the facilities. He will discuss various aspects of the funeral service, and show you the merchandise, including the caskets so that you can make a selection. Your selection should be based on your budget. Do not hesitate to ask for less expensive items. Find out what the minimum requirements are and buy only what you need. If time permits, shop around. If there is a funeral merchandise show room in your town, you may want to purchase what you need from there and have the items shipped to the funeral home.

After you have selected what you need, the funeral director will discuss the contract. He will specify services and costs and will itemize the prices of the merchandise you have selected. This contract should be clear and all-inclusive. There should be no hidden expenses or contingencies. The contract must include statements by the funeral home showing compliance with the FTC Funeral Rule, your authorization statement and the terms of payment. If a promissory note is prepared it should be part of the contract. Finally, do not sign unless you are completely satisfied with the contract.

The funeral director will ask you to provide several documents for securing payment for the funeral, processing the life insurance, probating the estate and preparing an obituary and other notices.

Some funeral homes offer after-care services to survivors. These are usually counseling sessions to help you deal with your grief. If these services are included in the contract, make sure that the terms are explicit.

IMMEDIATE BURIAL

Burial is the most common method of disposition. If you choose this method, you will have to let the funeral director know that you want immediate burial. The funeral director will arrange with the cemetery owner the time of burial. The cemetery will open the grave site you selected and have the vault ready to receive the body. After the ceremonies at the grave site or elsewhere, the body will be placed in the grave and it will be closed. See Chapter 9 for more information about burials.

DIRECT CREMATION

Without services, this is probably the most inexpensive method of disposition. Once you tell the funeral director that you want direct cremation he will make arrangements for cremation, either in his own funeral home or in a crematorium. If viewing is desired, he will embalm the body. Embalming is, however, not required for cremation. The funeral director must obtain the death certificate and the cremation certificate to carry out the cremation. No casket is required; a cardboard container is sufficient to carry the body. Many states require a lapse of 48 hours after death before executing cremation. Chapter 10 provides more information on cremation.

BURIAL, IN-GROUND OR ABOVE GROUND, WITH SERVICES

The decision to bury the remains involves the selection of a grave site or mausoleum. The funeral director will advise you on the burial site, casket and details of funeral service based on the size of the funeral and any special requests.

AUTOPSY, EMBALMING, ORGAN/BODY DONATION

These are other areas where you will need to communicate your wishes to the funeral director. If you wish to have a private autopsy performed the funeral director will find you a pathologist. It will not be covered by insurance. If the death is unnatural, unexplained or from violent causes, the medical examiner or coroner may order an autopsy and you will not be charged. If the body needs to be embalmed for viewing or for other reasons, the funeral director will ask for your authorization. If the deceased's organs or the body are to be donated, it is critical that you inform the funeral director as soon as possible after death, so that he can take appropriate steps for the best results. Chapters 5, 8 and 11 respectively discuss donation, embalming and autopsy in greater detail.

COST OF FUNERAL

Death brings many expenses. Decide ahead of time how much you want to spend and how you are going to pay. This is an important decision for you and for the funeral director. Cost determines many things —the type of disposition, quality of goods, the size of the funeral, etc. To get a clearer picture of the costs, refer to Chapter 13, which addresses the economics of funerals.

LEAN ON OTHERS

The time of a loved one's death is not the best time to have to make decisions. Emotions, grief and confusion can hamper your decision-making. Yet, you have to act, for death has created a time schedule for you. You will need to move within the framework of that schedule. Receiving help from others will contribute to your strength and endurance and help you make it through the sad times.

Chapter 7

FUNERALS AND THE GRIEVING PROCESS

Death is the season
We all must pass through
And just like the flowers,
God awakens us too
So why should we grieve
When our loved ones die,
For we'll meet them again
In a cloudless sky.

—Helen Steiner Rice (1900-1981)

*D*eath thrusts grief upon you, whether you are prepared for it or not. When you are submerged in immense grief following the death of a loved one, there are certain fundamental philosophical approaches you may take for your own emotional health. You should know that it is perfectly all right to ask family members and friends to be involved. It is acceptable and appropriate to cry, to show your emotions and to acknowledge the pain you are experiencing. It is all right to use rituals to reflect your spirituality.[1] In fact, one the most important functions of funerals and other death rituals is to help survivors to express their grief and pain. By allowing yourself to grieve and to be supported by others, you will proceed through the healing process faster.

In the middle of taking care of the necessary funeral arrangements, it is important for you to think of God (if you believe in a divinity), your loss and yourself. Funerals are a way of getting relatives, friends and the community together to help and support you in your time of absolute need.

Funeral rituals not only affirm death but allow us to accept the finality of death. They help us remember the deceased by exploring the memories of the meaningful life that was lived and to acknowledge the importance of that life. Finally, funerals give us strength in bidding "farewell" to our loved ones. They can be personalized by mourners to remember a loved one in a special and unique way. Thus, all the elements of a funeral combine to ease our grief.

GRIEVING

The grief that arrives with the death of a loved one is inevitable. You may be confronted with the death of a relative or friend in many different ways. Death may be natural but it may be sudden and unexpected. An infant may be found dead in a crib. A high school athlete may collapse and die during a basketball practice. A young man of 30 years may die of a heart attack, and a 60-year-old may succumb to a stroke. Accidents can occur at any time, any place and to anyone. Deaths occur as a result of automobile accidents, plane crashes, motorcycle mishaps, skiing or swimming misfortunes, earthquakes, tornadoes and hurricanes. A disturbed person may kill himself with drugs, guns or other means. Lastly, a criminal may take the life of your loved one. Even if not sudden, death may be lingering but still unexpected and premature, a result of a condition like AIDS, cancer, heart problems or a stroke.

The Intensity of Grief

Regardless of how death occurs, there are three factors that affect the degree of grief a survivor experiences. The first is the timing of death. If the death is untimely and sudden, the grief is usually intense. On the other hand, if a person succumbs to a prolonged illness and the death has been anticipated, the survivors might already be mentally prepared and thus have a shorter grieving period, because they have had the chance to develop an understanding and acceptance of death.

A second factor that affects the intensity of grief is dependent upon the relationship one had with the deceased, while a third factor is the survivor's ability to cope with death. He or she may have had a prior experience with death within his or her own family or may have helped others go through the process. Thus, grief is highly individualized, and rarely will two people respond to it in the same way.

No matter how you are confronted with death, no matter what ethnic or religious group you belong to, you must be prepared for a funeral and grief management. You must look at the deceased:

> *When you look at the dead body,*
> *it will make you realize the beauty of life,*
> *and the finality of death.*

This will help you with the grieving process.

Loss of a Parent

While the death of a parent is inevitable, we are never really ready to say good-bye. Since parents provide nurturing, advice and guidance throughout our lives, at the time of their death, we have a multitude of feelings. The sadness, pain and fear that accompany the loss of a role model and advisor make the grieving course long and difficult. Oftentimes people in their twenties or thirties seek parental advice on making a first house purchase or raising children, and they want to finally make a parent proud by showing the parent their accomplishments. The parent's home is often a gathering place for reunions, and the loss of this adds to the feelings of loneliness and sadness. In addition, a grandchild may have been close to their grandparent, and he or she will need to be helped through the grieving process. The combination of all these factors creates intense grief.

Loss of a Spouse

"Widow shock" is the term used for reactions to the demise of a spouse. For the surviving spouse, in addition to the numbness and anger, there may be guilt over arguments and feelings of secondary losses. These may include loss of help in child rearing, financial support and changes in relationships with other "couple" friends. Most importantly, there is the loss of the most significant companion and partner. All of these things parlay into a very intense grieving process.

Loss of a Child

With the loss of a child, there is always the feeling that this is not what nature intended. It is felt that a child is supposed to outlive a parent. Because of this, it is very difficult to accept. Although one will still proceed through the stages of grief, one does so to a greater degree and with more intensity. There may be a particularly strong need to blame someone for the death in order to make it seem more justifiable. A parent may feel guilty simply for being alive. Replaying the events of the death is common. The parents keep wishing they had been there a little earlier to prevent the tragedy. Often, both parents do not mourn in the same fashion, and this could put a strain on their marriage. Generally, the sorrow felt should be equal because of the loss of the same child, but this does not always hold true. This can lead to difficulty in communication between the parents of the deceased child. In spite of this, it is important for a parent to explain the death to the other surviving children, to avoid blame, ease guilt and assuage any fears that the same illness or fate may await them.

Infant death often leads to self-blame by the mother who may feel as if she did something during her pregnancy to harm the baby. Parents perceive that they should have received medical attention sooner or somehow been able to protect the baby. Such guilt feelings are very common in cases of Sudden Infant Death Syndrome (SIDS), which is the leading cause of death for infants one week to one year old. An autopsy does not provide any answers, so parents often censure themselves for the death. In addition, a medical investigation is required by law, and this furthers the onus of guilt.

Pregnancy is a time for parents to adjust and prepare for the birth of a baby. There are many expectations. Baby clothing and furniture are bought, all of which remain unused if the baby is stillborn. Many times the cause of stillbirth is not known, and parents feel guilty about their genetic status, as well as about "neglect" on their part during pregnancy. Parents describe a feeling of emptiness which friends and relatives mistakenly say can be filled by another child. Again, other children in the house need to be helped through the grieving process with careful attempts made to insulate them from feelings of guilt.

Suicide

Suicide has increased to frightening proportions over the last few decades with the mourners often unable to accept the fact that a loved one chose to take his or her own life or that they could not recognize the warning signs and prevent it. It is not uncommon for family members to insist the death was only an accident. Anger at the deceased is common because of his/her "selfish" act. Nevertheless, grief is significant. The murder of a loved one, likewise, brings intense grief.

STAGES OF THE GRIEVING PROCESS

Grieving is a process that helps one to cope with a loss. There are many stages of grief. Researchers acknowledge that mourners progress through these stages at different paces.[2]

Shock and Denial

The first stage is shock and denial. The survivor experiences numbness and feels stunned. The numb feeling dampens the pain and serves as a cushion against the tragedy. As soon as the person comes out of the shock and numbness, he or she is able to regain control and develops the feeling of acceptance of the loss. The sudden death of a close relative usually sinks the survivor into such a stage of shock and numbness.

Mourning

The phase of shock leads us into mourning. This is the period where survivors outwardly display signs of grief. For instance, the survivor may spend time at home and receive visits from relatives and friends. Cultures have different ways of mourning.

Depression, Guilt, Anger and Emotional Upsets

Grief causes depression, creates guilt, angers sufferers and causes them to be emotionally disturbed. The symptoms they experience are summarized below:

- *Physiological Symptoms:* These usually include confusion, loss of concentration, mood swings, restlessness, crying spells, panic, fright, feelings of disbelief, insomnia and anxiety. There is a sea of sorrow, flood of feelings, hurt and a sense of emptiness.

- *Physical Symptoms:* These include nausea, vomiting, a loss of appetite, loss of weight, tightness and heaviness in the chest, a lump in the neck, stomach cramps, diarrhea, heart palpitations, fatigue and exhaustion.
- *Psychosocial Symptoms:* The grievers experience guilt and may blame themselves for doing certain things or failing to do certain things. They are angry at themselves and angry at others. They try to blame God, their doctor, a clergy person and, at times, even the deceased.

Acceptance and Healing

During this phase, the impact of the death sinks in and the survivor accepts the death as a reality. This allows the healing process to begin.

HOW SURVIVORS CAN HELP THEMSELVES HEAL

It is important for the bereaved to recognize the following:

- Recovery from grief can sometimes be a long process. It is advisable to take time to mourn slowly and not to rush oneself.
- It is important to recognize one's physical and emotional limits and to believe that grief is not a sign of weakness.
- It is wise to depend on other family members and friends for support.
- It is good to express one's sadness to others because it allows the reality of death to be accepted.
- Expression of grief is integral in allowing convalescence to begin because denials prolong the grieving process. Speaking at a funeral, Boston minister Father Jack McGinnis was insightful when he observed: "Unrecognized losses and unexpressed grief are at the bottom of much of our unwellness."
- It is wrong to seek solace in alcohol or drugs to cope with grief, as they can intensify depression.
- Those suffering a loss should consider themselves normal. The symptoms of grief have been experienced the same way by others in similar situations.

- Postponing major decisions will help the grieving to cope with smaller issues, and this will promote healing.
- Once one goes through the healing process, they will see hope and regain their power to perform.
- One can survive the process and will eventually be able to say:

  "Grief has changed me,
  But not destroyed me."

HOW TO HELP SURVIVORS

- To help a grieving friend or relative, act promptly to be with him or her.
- Participate by making needed phone calls, attending the door and greeting visitors.
- Take food to the mourner and attend to his or her problems. Be understanding and sympathetic, and express your sorrow.
- Join in the prayers. Show your emotions.
- Help in making funeral arrangements from beginning to end.
- Attend the funeral.
- Be with the mourner after the funeral and focus on his or her needs.
- Recognize the mourner's anger, denial and crying spells as normal, and be patient with him or her.
- Extend invitations after the funeral but allow the mourner time to be alone to think and reflect on personal memories.

EASING GRIEF AFTER THE FUNERAL

Mourning is the external expression of a response to a loss of a loved one, and grief is what one feels within oneself. Grief can be prolonged but it is not permanent. After all of the arrangements around the funeral have been completed, one needs to attend to short-term and long-term matters. To do it right, stick to the fundamentals and work on the jobs to do. The following advice will help you:

1. Get help. Talk to relatives, friends, neighbors, coworkers or anyone you feel comfortable with who cares about you, shares your sorrow and wants to help you. A Swedish proverb says:

Shared joy is double joy; shared sorrow is half sorrow.

2. Accept death, express your feelings, banish self-punishment, surrender your grief, put it down. Pain will lessen as time passes.

3. Maintain a regular schedule for cooking, meeting people and exercising.

4. Make your grief public. Go to church, synagogue and pray and talk to people. Remember the Zen proverb:

   If you free what is inside you, it will make you free;
   if you hold onto what is inside you, it will destroy you.

5. Postpone major decisions, such as selling the house, quitting your job or remarrying, for at least six to twelve months.

6. Spend time in acknowledging the help and sympathies you have received. Work on the selection of grave monuments, settlement of probate, transfer of titles, collection of life insurance, application for Social Security and veteran's benefits.

7. If your pain is deep and too prolonged and unmanageable, seek help from a clergy person, mental health counselor or join a grief support group.

8. If you are able, visit friends, do volunteer work, or take up a new hobby.

9. Stay completely busy, avoid exhaustion and take care of yourself physically by eating right and getting a lot of rest.

10. Be gentle and kind to yourself and forgiving to others.

Finally, by understanding that grief is a natural process, one is able to accept it instead of fighting it. It takes time and also much effort to be able to survive a tragedy. The Theos Foundation, which helps mourners, states:

   Grief is not a sign of weakness...
   but a tribute to the loved one who died
   and a healthy response to our heartache.
   Avoiding grief postpones recovery.
   Clinging to grief prolongs pain.
   Neither approach help us heal.[3]

REFERENCES

1. Wolfelt AD (Preface): *Creating Meaningful Funeral Ceremonies: A Guide for Caregivers.* Center for Loss and Life Transition, 1994.
2. Kubler-Ross E: *On Death and Dying.* New York: Macmillan, 1969.
3. Theos Foundation: "Grief is Not a Sign of Weakness," [Brochure]. Pittsburgh, PA, 1998.

Section III:
What Happens
to the Body?

Chapter 8

EMBALMING

*T*o embalm" is to prepare a dead body for the funeral. The word took origin from the Latin words *em* meaning "in" and *balm* meaning "resinous product." In ancient times, the main objectives of embalming were to improve the appearance and long-term preservation of the body. In more modern times, embalming has been required to protect the public from infection. Some people consider that with HIV and other infectious diseases, the dead body may be a "bacterial bomb" waiting to explode. This is not true, but embalmers do take precautions, such as wearing a face shield. Embalming is done in funeral homes in what are called "prep rooms."

Discussing the vital public health function of embalming, Fredrick remarked, "never before in the entire history of embalming has the hazard of personal and public infection from unembalmed remains been as great as it is today."[1] Recognizing the threats of infection, Reather simply stated, "Embalming is the art of disinfecting dead bodies and thereby slowing the process of decomposition."[2] Altogether, the aims of embalming include sanitation, disinfection, restoration, and preservation.

Embalming has increased in the past two centuries. Today in the United States, a majority of the bodies are embalmed. Although embalming is not mandated by law, it may be necessary under special circumstances:

- If the body has to be transported from the place of death.
- If refrigeration is not available.
- If the body is going to be transported out of state or country.
- If there is going to be an unusual delay in the disposition of the body.

- If death is due to certain infectious diseases.
- If the body of the deceased is donated to science.

   The three main reasons for embalming are:

- Protection of public health from bacteria produced by decomposition.
- Preservation of body by retarding decomposition.
- Maintenance or restoration of the appearances of the body for viewing.

TYPES OF EMBALMING

The embalming process used today consists of the employment of mechanical techniques and the use of chemicals. There are eight types of chemicals used in embalming. These are preservatives, germicides, modifying agents, anticoagulants, surfactants, dyes, perfuming agents and chemical vehicles. The preserving chemicals such as formaldehyde and methyl alcohol retard decomposition, the dyes color the skin, and the anticoagulants prevent blood clotting and therefore make aspiration of the blood easy. Special equipment, including pumps, are used to push these chemicals into the body.

The two common methods of embalming are *arterial* embalming and *cavity* embalming.

Arterial Embalming

Arterial embalming is the most common type of embalming. About three to four gallons of chemicals are injected in a large artery while blood is simultaneously removed from a large vein. The right and left carotids, right axillary and the right femoral arteries are dissected and pulled out. Fluids may then be pushed into these arteries with a metal canula attached to a pump. This method achieves fairly uniform hardening of the body.

Cavity Embalming

Cavity embalming is used as a supplement to arterial embalming. In this process, a trocar (an elongated metal pipe) is introduced into the body through a hole made in the abdominal skin. The trocar is pushed into the abdominal and chest cavities in different directions to remove gases and fluids. Then about 16 ounces of chemical preservative is infused into both the abdominal and chest cavities. After the cavity aspiration and infusion is complete, the abdominal skin hole is sewn closed.

Embalmers can encounter several problems during embalming if the body has been severely traumatized or if the body has been autopsied and the pathologist has cut up the large arteries, especially the carotids. Likewise, it is difficult to autopsy a body after it has been embalmed. Cavity embalming in particular creates a nightmare for the pathologist, because it alters the appearances of internal organs so the interpretation of autopsy findings becomes difficult.

There are several other techniques that embalmers use to supplement arterial and cavity embalming. One is called *hypodermic embalming* and it is frequently used when embalming the bodies of infants or autopsied bodies. In this procedure, the preservative is injected in places such as buttocks, shoulders and the abdominal wall to harden these areas and to create proper contours. An additional technique is called *surface embalming*, in which liquid chemicals and gels are applied with a gauze or a brush onto the eyes, mouth or areas with cuts and bruises.

The embalming of an anatomical donor is somewhat different from the routine embalming done for funeral services. For more information, the article by Griffith and Smith[3] cited at the end of this chapter will be helpful. Two good books discussing embalming include *Principles of Embalming*[4] and *Embalming, History, Theory and Practice.*[5]

HISTORY OF EMBALMING

Mummification

Prior to 3100 B.C., bodies were buried in sand. This led to a form of natural preservation, and so embalming was not needed. Over 45 centuries ago the Egyptians perfected the art of embalming that is called mummification.

Because ancient Egyptians believed that life continues in the after world, they went to great lengths to preserve the body, far beyond our best efforts today. The Egyptian process of mummification took about ten weeks. Mildred Martin Pace describes the procedure of mummification.[6]

When a king or other wealthy individual died, the family members and friends took the body to the "House of Embalming," which was an open-air tent. The process of mummification was started the next day in the dry desert environment. First the body was washed and placed on a table. In the presence of priests, a specialist began the next step, which was to remove the brain. This was done by introducing a long hook-like instrument into the nostril to break the ethmoid, or nasal bone. Then a twisted rod was introduced into the cranial cavity and the brain was removed piecemeal. After that, the cranial cavity was stuffed with strips of linen, the nostrils were plugged with wax, the eyeballs covered with linen and the eyelids were pulled down. The face was then washed and coated with a resinous paste.

All of the organs except the heart were removed from the chest and abdomen through an incision in the side of the body. The heart was left in because the Egyptians believed it was the seat of feeling and intelligence. The incision was closed, the fingernails and toenails were fastened with wires, and the body was then washed a second time.

The body was then covered with a powder called "natron," which is a desiccating agent, and left to dry. The drying process took several days. Once completely dried, the body was bathed a third time and spices, herbs and fragrant oils were rubbed in.

At this point the body was wrapped with strips of cloth of different widths torn out of 150 yards of linen. The legs were wrapped first, then the arms followed by torso and lastly the head. In the twenty-first dynasty (approximately 2600 BC), mummification was very artful; elaborate cosmetic skills were lavished on the outside of the body to make it look like a live person.

Once mummification was complete, the body was taken to the "House of Mourning," and then to the tomb, the "House of Eternity." At the time of burial the mummified body was placed in the tomb with the objects that the person had acquired during life, because it was believed he or she would need them in the afterlife.

Besides the Egyptians, there have been other ancient communities who practiced embalming. Shortly after the time of Christ, the people of the Canary Islands off of the Africa utilized a procedure similar to that used by the Egyptians. They eviscerated the body and left it on the hot sandy beach or placed it in a stone oven for drying. Then they wrapped the body in goatskins.

Mummification of the dead was sometimes practiced in China, and mummification is still performed in Tibet in somewhat of a similar fashion.[7]

Modern Embalming

Modern embalming methods appear to have started in the seventeenth century. William Hunter was the first to describe his method of embalming in 1776.[8] In order to prevent decomposition, he injected the femoral artery with oils of turpentine and lavender. After the injection, all the organs from the chest and abdomen were removed and soaked in palm wines and sweet smelling oils. They were then put back into the body, which was placed on a bed of plaster of Paris to dry. Hunter is truly the father of arterial embalming.

Most of the early "embalmers" in the United States were physicians. Dr. Richard Hardan was the first to provide a written record of embalming. In 1837 he embalmed a body in Philadelphia using chemicals such as wine, arsenic and carmine. This allowed the body to be preserved for about three months, after which period it began to decompose.

It is not surprising that someone would think of rejuvenating the idea of mummification for money. Iserson notes that a company called Summum was founded in 1975 in Salt Lake City to mummify the dead.[9] The process used there is a combination of techniques based on the Egyptian principles. The company charges $40,000 per person, and hundreds have already been mummified or have signed up to be mummified. For an additional $7,000 to $10,000, the body will be covered with gold-leaf veneer, and for $25,000 extra the body will be welded into a bronze molded shell.

Cryonics: Another Form of Embalming

Cryonic preservation is for those who hope to be revived after death. It is a process in which a recently deceased human is frozen and maintained at extremely low temperatures in the hope that the body can be revived, even after several decades, once life extension techniques have been perfected. The writer Ettinger stated, "Most of us now breathing have a good chance of physical life after death: rejuvenation of our frozen bodies."[10] The first body "frozen" in order to be revived in the future was that of Professor James H. Bedford in 1967.[11] Only time will tell whether the project was a success or failure, when they try to revive the professor!

In this process, within fifteen minutes of death the body receives cardiopulmonary resuscitation, is connected to a heart-lung machine and cooled to 59 degrees Fahrenheit. Medications such as calcium channel blockers, blood thinners and free radical inhibitors are injected to reduce any damage that can result from decreased oxygen supply. The body is then submerged in silicone oil for 36 to 48 hours and cooled to -108 degrees F. Next the body is wrapped in two precooled bags and lowered into a unit with liquid nitrogen to cool it to -321 degrees F in 24 hours. Finally it is placed in a storage container.[12]

The Life Extension Foundation, which practices cryonic preservation, has the largest membership with 52,000 members as of November 1998. Application for membership at the time of this printing is $100, plus there is an annual due of $324. Whole body suspension costs $120,000, of which $28,000 is for suspension procedures and the rest for long-term care. The price for neurosuspension, or preservation of the brain, is $50,000, with about $19,000 for procedures and the rest for long-term care.[13]

TIPS FOR THE CONSUMER

- Embalming is done to disinfect the body, prevent decomposition and to maintain or restore body appearance.
- Embalming is generally not required by law, although there are several exceptions, listed earlier.
- Embalming is not required for immediate burials or direct cremation.
- The basic embalming charge should include all body preparation costs.
- The funeral director is required to obtain permission before the body is embalmed.
- The average cost of embalming is $313.
- Consult the funeral director for specific laws, policies or circumstances that may influence your decisions regarding embalming.

Embalming preserves the body, improves the appearance of the remains and makes viewing less traumatic. If there are no religious objections and if there is going to be a delay in burial or cremation, it is advisable to opt for embalming.

REFERENCES

1. Fredrick JF: "The Vital Public Health Function of Embalming, Part 3." *De-De-Co Magazine*, vol. 62; June 1969: 64.
2. Raether HC (ed.): *The Funeral Directors Practice Management Handbook*. Prentice-Hall, 1989. As cited in: MW Kubasak: *Cremation and the Funeral Director: Successfully Meeting the Challenge.*
3. Griffith C, Smith S: "Embalming the Anatomical Donor." *The Director*, June 1997: 22-8.
4. Stubs CG, Frederick LG: *Principles of Embalming*. Dallas, TX: Lawrence Frederick, 1970.
5. Mayer RG: *Embalming, History, Theory and Practice*. Norwalk, CT and San Mateo, CA: Appleton and Lange, 1990.
6. Pace MM. As cited in Puckle BS, *Funeral Customs: Their Origin and Development*. London: T. Werner, Ltd., 1926. Republished by Omnigraphics, Detroit, 1990.
7. "Embalming." *New Encyclopedia Britannica*. Chicago: Encyclopedia Britannica, vol. 4; 1987: 468.
8. Puckle BS: *Funeral Customs: Their Origin and Development*. London: T. Werner, Ltd., 1926. Republished by Omnigraphics, Detroit, 1990.
9. Iserson KV: *Death to Dust: What Happens to Dead Bodies?* Tuscon, AZ: Galen Press Ltd., 1994:185.
10. Ettinger R: *The Prospect of Immortality*. 1964; as cited in Iserson, 1994.
11. Kurtzman J and Gordon P: *No More Dying: The Conquest of Aging and the Extension of Human Life*. Los Angeles: JP Tarcher, 1976: 199-217, as cited in Iserson, 1994.
12. Wowk B, Darwin M: *Cryonics: Reaching for Tomorrow*, 3rd ed. Riverside, CA: Alcor Life Extension Foundation, 1991: 47.
13. Bridge S: "Financial Charges." *Cryonics*, 14 (4); 1993.

Chapter 9

BURIAL

*B*urial is the most common method of disposition of a dead body in the United States. Although it usually involves burying a dead body underground, in modern times the above-ground burial in mausoleums is becoming more popular. Burial is usually done in a dedicated cemetery, but a body can be buried on private property if local law permits.

If you choose burial for the disposition of your own body or that of a loved one, you may need to take the following actions:

- Select a funeral director and discuss with him the transportation and preparation of the body (including, if necessary, embalming of the body); determine the goods and merchandise needed and finalize the details of services. You will find more details about these arrangements in the sections on preneed and at need funeral planning.
- If not done earlier, you must buy the cemetery plot.
- Select casket, vault, and headstone.
- Advise the funeral director about your choice of the type of burial.

There are several kinds of burial, and these include immediate burial,burial after services but without embalming, burial after embalming and services, burial at sea, burial of cremains, and above-ground burial (i.e., in mausoleums).

IMMEDIATE BURIAL

Immediate burial is the fastest way to dispose of the body. When immediate burial is chosen, the funeral director will transport the body from the place of death to the funeral home and prepare the remains for burial as per the wishes of the family. He will coordinate the purchase of the cemetery plot, if it has not been bought before. He will help the survivors to select a casket or buy an alternative container and a vault.

A casket is a more expensive container made of wood or metal. It is not required for an immediate burial. With the choice of immediate burial, the body is generally buried without viewing or embalming, and it is generally placed in an alternative container made of unfinished wood, pressboard, cardboard, or canvas.

BURIAL AFTER SERVICES, WITHOUT EMBALMING

If the family chooses burial after services but without embalming, then the burial must be carried out rapidly before the body starts to deteriorate. A casket is not required, although some funeral homes require embalming if there is to be a viewing. In warm weather, the body may start to deteriorate in a day or two if it is not kept in a cooler.

BURIAL AFTER EMBALMING AND SERVICES

Burial after embalming and services is probably the most popular choice in the United States. If embalming is requested, the funeral director will obtain authorization to embalm the body and prepare it for viewing. A casket may be required if a traditional funeral is chosen.[1]

BURIAL AT SEA

Burial at sea is an uncommon choice, but it is available through the Neptune Society, which specializes in sea burial. However, anyone can obtain the proper documents and may conduct a sea burial. The body must be taken in a small private boat into international waters. The funeral director must get a burial permit, conform to state and federal requirements and complete Environmental Protection Agency documents, and report on the identification of the deceased and the exact location of burial.

Sea burial is much more expensive than burial in ground. The cost of sea burial is about $8,000 to $10,000. It is costly because it is unusual, takes more time to get the proper documents, and requires the use of a boat. Many religions do not specify burial in water as an option. For instance, the Jewish religion prohibits sea burial. Sea burial is an individual choice.

In the past, Hindus in India set bodies afloat in the Ganges River. This caused cholera epidemics and hence the practice was stopped. However, Hindus still scatter ashes and dump bones in the river.

BURIAL OF CREMAINS

Some people prefer to bury the remains of a cremated body in the ground or in a columbarium. Chapter 10 provides details on this practice.

MAUSOLEUMS, THE ABOVE-GROUND BURIAL

Mausoleums are above-ground burial sites. They vary in size and they may be made for one casket or many. The interment of a body in a mausoleum is called *immurement*. Mausolos, the King of Caria, built a 140-foot pyramid to serve as a tomb for his wife. This structure was built in Haliearnassus, Asia Minor, in about 350 B.C. and was the origin of the word "mausoleum."[2] The tomb has since been destroyed by an earthquake.

Because they are upright structures, mausoleums are a means of protecting bodies, especially during times of floods. Modern day structures are built by creating a honeycomb pattern; stacking the vaulted areas as high as desired. These individual crypts may open up into a central room or chapel, or each may have an opening to the outside. A stone plate or plaque is hung over the vault or niche where the casket is placed. The person's name, date of birth and death and perhaps a small epitaph may be included on this.

In practical terms, mausoleums have a nice physical appearance and they can be made as attractive as the buyer wants. They are weather-proof and convenient for visits and visual memorization. The name, year and other information on the front of the mausoleum is readily visible to anyone passing by. Another advantage of mausoleums is that extended families can be buried together. If the body is cremated, the cremains can be put in a mausoleum crypt, with or without an urn. Finally, although ground space may be limited, air space is virtually unlimited.

Historical Mausoleums

Two of the most famous mausoleums in the history of mankind are the Taj Mahal in India and the Pyramids in Egypt. Both were among the original Seven Wonders of the World. The Taj Mahal was built as an expression of love, whereas the Pyramids were built to serve as the final resting places for the pharaohs. Both of these architectural marvels are described in detail in Appendix B.

The Chinese emperors, like the Egyptian pharaohs, also selected their own burial sites and built mausoleums during their lifetimes. They believed that they would continue to reign after death from underground tombs. The rank of the person determined the size of his tomb.

During the Ming Dynasty (1368 to 1644) the princes built twenty-foot-high tombs measuring 100 paces in circumference. They were surrounded by ten-foot-high walls and were decorated with four human statues, two statues of horses, two statues of tigers and two of sheep. On the lower scale, the Noblemen had tombs only six feet high with no statues or extra walls.[3]

In the Chinese city now known as Xian, emperors from the Ming Dynasty built an elaborate underground tomb containing a throne with the Terra Cotta Warriors. These were full-sized figures made of clay, bearing arms and in battle dress, lined up in front of the throne as if to protect it.

Ancient Romans also built large mausoleums for their deceased leaders. Often, these had space for more than 500 soldiers, who were buried with him. The tenet was that a ruler would be of equal status in the afterlife and should go forward accompanied by all of the comforts of the life being left behind. Again, these structures were built during the lifetime of the person and were completed by family members if death occurred early.

Modern Mausoleums

As recently as 1977, Mao Tse Tung was laid to rest in a 112-foot high building in T'in-anmen Square next to the Great Hall of the People in Beijing, China. The structure was built by 70,000 people.[4] Even now, every day hundreds of people visit Mao's tomb.

There are mausoleums of various size. The average mausoleum contains 14 crypts, but sometimes they are built for one person.

There are several extremely large mausoleums in the United States. The Cathedral of Memories in Hartsdale, New York contains 8800 crypts and 250 private family rooms. Other large structures are Forest Lawn's Great Mausoleum and the Woodlawn Mausoleum in Nashville, Tennessee. The latter is 20 stories high and can accommodate 129,000 bodies. It is dubbed as the "Death Hilton." In Rio de Janeiro, Brazil there is a mausoleum that is 39 stories high and was built at a cost of $14,000,000.[5]

Above-ground entombment is the most common method of disposition in New Orleans. This is because the water table is high and many times buried bodies surface from the wet ground. Above-ground tombs became necessary after flooding, fires and epidemic created chaos there in 1788.

To get more information about mausoleum space, you should speak to a few facilities in your area. Arguments can be made both for and against an above-ground burial. A cemetery brochure states, "Entombment in an above-ground mausoleum provides your loved one with a final resting place free from the unfriendly elements of the earth."[6] On the other hand, the satirist Ambrose Bierce (est. 1942-1914) has this to say about mausoleums in his book, *A Devil's Dictionary*:[7]

> *Worm's-meat ...The contents of the Taj Mahal, The Tombeau Napoleon and the Granatarium. Worms-meat is usually outlasted by the structure that houses it, but "this too must pass away." Probably the silliest work in which a human being can engage is construction of a tomb for himself. The solemn purpose cannot dignify, but only accentuates by contrast the foreknown futility.*

He goes on:

> *Ambitious fool! So mad to be a show*
> *How profitless the labor you bestow*
> *upon a dwelling whose significance*
> *The tenant neither can admire nor know*
> *Build deep, build high, build massive as you can*
> *The wanton grass-roots will defeat the plan*

By shouldering asunder all the stones
In what to you would be a moment's span.

COST OF BURIAL

Burial is the most common method for the disposition of dead bodies and it can also be the most expensive. In addition to the general funeral director's fees, there are expenses for the cemetery plot, casket, vault, headstone and the opening and closing of the grave. These costs are discussed in the Chapter 13, "The Economics of Funerals and How to Cut Costs." Opening the grave means digging up the ground to create space to accomodate the vault and casket. Closing refers to placing the body in the casket within the vault and into the ground, and then covering them up.

A single grave would allow only one body per plot, but grave sites can accommodate two or three. Double and triple-depth grave sites cost less. In the case of a double-grave plot, the second body is placed on top of the first one. A triple-depth grave site similarly allows three bodies, each one of which may have a separate stone. In terms of cost, the cemetery owner will charge extra for double and triple-depth opening of the grave, for an outer container (a vault for each body), for moving a head stone foundation and for installing a new one. The savings comes from the lower cost of the real estate.

A casket is frequently the single most expensive funeral item in a traditional funeral with burial. Caskets vary widely in style and price. The caskets sold by the funeral homes are usually marked up two to five times their wholesale price. It is possible to spend over $20,000 for a casket, or one can build a casket using plywood for less than $200. Less expensive caskets and other burial expenses are discussed in detail in Chapter 13.

Family plots can be bought at a discount. You will own the real estate forever. The cemetery may cost a lot more if one chooses an oversized plot. One woman in Florida needed a large plot because she chose to be buried in a grave with her car.

Generally, burial in a mausoleum is more expensive than an underground burial. The cost of a single-body mausoleum can range from $1,500 to $25,000, plus the cost of opening and closing the crypt, which usually amounts to a few hundred dollars. Of course, one can spend much more: producer Irving Thalberg's tomb in Forest Lawn cost $800,000 at the time of his death.[6]

Burial is the most common method of disposition because most cultures accept it as a method of choice. The grave site and the mausoleum allow for visitation and memorialization. In the rare situations when exhumation may be necessary, burial makes it possible.

REFERENCES

1. Funeral and Memorial Societies of America: *Earth Burial: A Tradition in Simplicity*, 1998.
2. Iserson K: *Death to Dust: What Happens to Dead Bodies*. Tucson, AZ: Galen Press Ltd., 1994.
3. Information on display at the Royal Ontario Museum. Canada, 1992.
4. Wakeman F: *Mao's Remains*, cited in Watson JL, Rawski ES, (eds): *Death Ritual in Late Imperial and Modern China*. Berkeley, CA: Univ. of California Press, 1988, 254-88.
5. Dempsey D: *The Way We Die: An Investigation of Death and Dying in America Today*. New York: Macmillan, 1975: 196.
6. Young GW: *The High Cost of Dying*. New York: Prometheus Books, 1994.
7. Bierce A, Huck J (probably fictitious), as quoted in Bierce A: *A Devil's Dictionary*. New York: Dover Pub, 1958: 142-3; as cited in Iserson, 1994.

Chapter 10

CREMATION

"Burn what is left of me and scatter the ashes to the wind
to help the flowers grow.
If you must bury something, let it be my faults, my weaknesses,
and all my prejudice against my fellow man.
Give my soul to God.
If by chance you wish to remember me,
do it with a kind deed or word to someone who needs you.
If you do all I have asked, I will live forever."

—Author Unknown

*C**remation is simply the burning or incineration of dead bodies. In other* words, it is a process of reducing a dead body to ashes by means of an open fire or electric heat.

INCIDENCE

Cremation is the second most common method of disposition of a human body in the United States. The number of cremations and crematories are slowly rising. In 1995, 21.14 percent of people who died were cremated. This percentage increased slightly to 21.25 percent in 1996.[1] Jack Springer, the Executive Director of the Cremation Association of North America (CANA), projects that in the year 2000 there will be 578,800 cremations, a 17.54 percent increase over 1996 figures. The prevalence of burials will decrease by 3.25 percent, to reach a projected figure of 1,877,900. The revised data from CANA[2] indicate that in 2000 the percentage of cremations to deaths will be 26.92, while in 2010 it will be 41.81 percent.

The percentages of cremations to deaths in the top and bottom five states in 1997 (actual) and in 2000 and 2010 (projected) are reflected in Table 10-1, which is reproduced with the kind permission of CANA:

Table 10-1: Highest and Lowest Incidence of Cremation by State		
Percentage of Deaths		
1997	2000 *(est.)*	2010 *(est.)*
States with highest incidence		
Nevada 61.11	62.70	68.01
Alaska 58.54	66.50	93.04
Hawaii 56.66	58.89	66.34
Washington 54.42	58.65	72.74
Arizona 53.03	60.92	87.21
States with lowest incidence		
West Virginia 4.85	5.40	7.25
Mississippi 4.96	6.02	9.56
Alabama 5.14	6.10	6.29
Kentucky 6.25	8.95	9.27
Tennessee 6.67	7.93	12.12

In some countries such as Japan, England, Hong Kong, Denmark, Sweden and India, cremation is the most common method of disposition of the body. Table 10-2, developed by Howard Raether, summarizes available data of percentage of cremations to deaths in different countries.[3] The table is reproduced with kind permission of the National Funeral Directors Association (NFDA).

Table 10-2: 1995 Incidence of Cremation in Countries (Highest and Lowest)[4]		
	Number of Cremations	Percentage of Cremations
Countries with highest incidence		
Japan	964,540	98.55
Hong Kong	29.777	75.90
Czech Republic	85,494	72.50
Great Britain	445,574	70.60
Denmark	43,857	69.38
Switzerland	41,369	65.26
Sweden	60,824	64.74
Australia	65,438	52.00
Countries with lowest incidence		
Italy	11,645	2.12
Ireland	1,179	3.74
Brazil	2,846	3.85
Iceland	171	8.90
South Africa	26,431	9.00
Luxembourg	343	9.03
France	62,212	22.76
Namibia	147	13.57

Although some religions do not permit cremation, many religious and ethnic groups will allow or even prefer it. Cremations are preferred because of various reasons other than religion. Cremation is the most cost-effective method of disposition. The cost of the actual process of cremation without any other expenses is usually around $200. A cardboard container can be bought for less than $100. Direct disposition of the body without any services, called immediate cremation, costs nationwide an average of $1,145. A bulk of the expense of the funeral is derived from the cost of the services and casket before the cremation.

CANA issued a Model Cremation Authorization and Disposition Form and Explanation in 1992.[4] This "Model Form" contains a wealth of pertinent information on cremations for the funeral directors, crematory owners and operators, and the consumers. It can be obtained by writing to: The Cremation Association of North America, 401 N. Michigan Avenue, Chicago, IL 60611, (312) 644-6610.

The advice from CANA contained in the Model Form is presented at later in this chapter.[4]

FUNERAL DIRECTOR AND CREMATION

To reduce cremation-related liability, CANA suggests the crematory obtain the signed representations from funeral director as follows:

By executing this authorization form as a licensed funeral director and agent of the funeral home indicated above, I warrant to the best of my knowledge the following:

- That our funeral home was responsible for making arrangements with the Authorizing Agent for the cremation of the decedent and that we reviewed this authorization form with the Authorizing Agent.

- That no member of our funeral home has any knowledge or information that would lead us to believe that any of the answers provided on this form by the Authorizing Agent are incorrect.

- That the human remains delivered to ABC Crematory and represented as the human remains specified on this form are in fact the human remains that were identified to our funeral home as the decedent.

- That our funeral home obtained all necessary permits authorizing the cremation of the decedent, and that those permits are attached.

- That the representations contained above concerning the decedent's cause of death and regarding any infectious or contagious disease are true.

- That the representations contained above concerning a pacemaker and any other material or implant that may be potentially hazardous are true.

ABC CREMATORY'S REQUIREMENTS FOR CREMATION

(Note: ABC is a fictitious name)

Cremation will take place only after all of the following conditions have been met:

- Any scheduled ceremonies or viewings have been completed.
- _____ hours have transpired since the death occurred.
- Civil and medical authorities have issued all required permits.
- All necessary authorizations have been obtained, and no objections have been raised.
- All cremations are performed individually. ABC Crematory will only place the human remains of one individual in the cremation chamber at a time. Exceptions are only made in the case of close relatives, and then only with the prior written instructions of the Authorizing Agent.

Authorization:

I(we), the undersigned (the "Authorizing Agent" or "AA"), hereby authorize and request ABC Crematory, in accordance with and subject to its rules and regulations, and any applicable state/provincial or local laws or regulations, to cremate the human remains of _____ (the "decedent") and to arrange for the final disposition of the cremated remains, as set forth on this form.

Initials of AA _____

Identification:

Date of Death _____ Place of Death _____ Sex____ Age _____

Did the decedent die of natural causes? Y__ N__

If no, please explain:

_____

Did the decedent have any infectious or contagious disease? Y__ N__

If yes, please explain: _____

Mechanical, silicon implants or other radioactive devices in the decedent may create a hazardous condition when placed in a cremation chamber.

Please Initial One of the Next Three Paragraphs

The decedent's remains do not contain a pacemaker, prosthesis, radioactive implant or any other device that could be explosive. They are safe to cremate. Initials of AA _____

The decedent's remains contain silicon implants. Initials of AA _____

The following list contains all existing devices (including all mechanical and prosthetic devices) which may be implanted in or attached to the decedent, and that should be removed prior to cremation.

I have instructed the funeral home to remove or arrange for the removal of these devices and to properly dispose of them prior to transporting the decedent's remains to ABC Crematory. Initials of AA _____

All such devices must be removed prior to delivering the decedent to abc crematory.

Cremation Process

Cremation is performed to prepare the deceased for memorialization and it is carried out by placing the deceased in a casket or other container and then placing the casket or container into a cremation chamber or retort, where it is subjected to intense heat and flame. Through the use of a suitable fuel, incineration of the container and contents is accomplished by raising the temperature substantially (extreme temperature). After about one and a half hours, all substances are consumed or driven off, except bone fragments (calcium compounds), residue from the container and metal (including dental gold and silver and other nonhuman material) as the temperature is not sufficient to consume them.

Due to the nature of the cremation process, any personal possessions or valuable materials, such as dental gold or jewelry (as well as any body prostheses or dental bridgework), that are left with the decedent and are not removed from the casket or container prior to cremation will be destroyed or will otherwise not be recoverable. As the casket or container will usually not be opened by ABC Crematory (to remove valuables, to allow for a final viewing or for any other reason unless there is leakage or damage), the Authorizing Agent understands that arrangements must be made with the funeral home to remove any such possessions or valuables prior to the time that the decedent is transported to ABC Crematory.

Cremation Process *(continued)*

Following a cooling period, the cremated remains, normally weighing several pounds, are then swept or raked from the cremation chamber. The ABC Crematory makes a reasonable effort to remove all of the cremated remains from the cremation chamber, but it is impossible to remove them entirely, as some dust and other residue from the process are always left behind. In addition, while every effort will be made to avoid co-mingling, the inadvertent or incidental co-mingling of minute particles of cremated remains from the residue of previous cremations is a possibility, and the Authorized Agent understands and accepts this fact.

After the cremated remains are removed from the cremation chamber, all non-combustible materials (insofar as possible), such as bridgework, and the materials from the casket or container, such as hinges, latches, nails, etc., will be separated and removed from the human bone fragments by visible or magnetic selection and will be disposed of by ABC Crematory with similar materials from other cremations in a non-recoverable manner, so that only the human bone fragments will remain.

When the cremated remains are removed from the cremation chamber, the skeletal remains often contain recognizable bone fragments. Unless otherwise specified, after the bone fragments have been separated from the other material, they will then be mechanically processed (pulverized), which includes crushing or grinding and incidental co-mingling of the remains with the residue from the processing of previously cremated remains, into granulated particles of unidentifiable dimensions, virtually unrecognizable as human remains, prior to placement into the designated container.

Urns, Temporary Containers

After the cremated remains have been processed, they will be placed in the designated urn or container. ABC Crematory will make a reasonable effort to put all of the cremated remains in the urn or container, with the exception of dust or other residue that may remain in the processing equipment.

ABC Crematory requires that all urns provided be resistant to deterioration and breakage, and that, in the case of an adult, the urn be minimum size of 200 cubic inches. In the event the urn or other container selected is insufficient to accommodate all of the cremated remains, the excess will be placed in a separate receptacle.

Urns, Temporary Containers (continued)

The separate receptacle will be kept with the primary receptacle and handled according to the disposition instructions on this form.

Unless a suitable urn is provided for the cremated remains, ABC Crematory will place the cremated remains in a container designed for short-term use and not recommended for any type of shipment or permanent storage.

Disposition after Cremation

Cremation is *not* final disposition. The cremation process simply reduces the decedent's body to cremated remains. These cremated remains usually weigh several pounds and the volume usually ranges between 150 to 200 cubic inches. Some provisions must be made for the final disposition of these cremated remains. Placing them in temporary storage at a funeral home is not final disposition. Therefore, ABC Crematory strongly suggests that arrangements for final disposition be made at the time that the cremation arrangements are made and that this form is completed.

After the cremation has taken place, the cremated remains have been processed and the processed cremated remains placed in the designated receptacle, ABC Crematory will arrange for the disposition of the cremated remains as follows, and the Authorizing Agent hereby authorizes ABC Crematory to release, deliver, transport or ship the cremated remains as specified. Check one of the following:

1. Deliver the cremated remains to cemetery, with which arrangements have already been made for the cremated remains to be disposed of.
2. Deliver ____ or Release ____ the cremated remains to the following designated person(s):

    Name _____

    Address _____

    Relationship _____

    Scheduled Date of Delivery or Release _____
3. Deliver the cremated remains to the U.S. Postal Service for shipment by Registered, Return Receipt mail to _____ for permanent disposition.

    (Attach Copy of Post Office Receipt)

Disposition after Cremation (continued)

4. Deliver the cremated remains to (name of carrier) for shipment in my name as cosigner to (name and address of consignee) for permanent disposition.

   (Attach Copy of Carrier Receipt)

5. Return to the funeral home within 10 days.

6. Arrange for the disposition of the cremated remains at the discretion of ABC Crematory. The Authorizing Agent understands that if this option is selected, final disposition may include the co-mingling of the cremated remains with other cremated remains, and that, thereafter, the cremated remains of the decedent shall not be recoverable.

7. Other: _____

The Authorizing Agent understands that the services of ABC Crematory will have been fully completed when the cremated remains are delivered to the Postal Service or common carrier for mailing or transportation, that further handling and delivery are the responsibility of the Postal Service or common carrier, that ABC Crematory is only acting as an agent for accommodation in carrying out these instructions.

The Authorizing Agent understands that if no arrangements for the final disposition, release or transfer of the cremated remains are specified on this form, if ABC Crematory is not subsequently provided with instructions concerning the final disposition, release or transfer of the cremated remains within _____ days of the cremation or if the cremated remains have not been picked up by the designated individual within _____ days of cremation, then ABC Crematory shall be authorized to arrange for the final disposition of the cremated remains in any manner permitted by law. The Authorized Agent understands that such final disposition may include the co-mingling of the cremated remains with other cremated remains, and that thereafter the cremated remains of the decedent will not be recoverable.

The Authorized Agent understands that if the option selected for final disposition includes scattering, that the cremated remains will not be recoverable. The Authorizing Agent also understands that if scattering is performed in a common area, that the cremated remains may be co-mingled with particles of other cremated remains that have been previously scattered.

Reduce Cremation-Related Liability

As the Authorizing Agent(s), I(we) hereby agree to indemnify, defend, and hold harmless ABC Crematory, its officers, agents and employees, of and from any and all claims, demands, causes or causes of action, and suits of every kind, nature and description, in law or equity, including any legal fees, costs and expenses of litigation, arising as a result of, based upon or connected with this authorization, including the failure of the authorizing agent to properly identify the human remains transmitted to ABC Crematory, mistakes in processing, shipping and final disposition of the decedent's cremated remains resulting from the authorization, the failure of the authorizing agent or his designee to take possession of or make proper arrangements for the final disposition of the cremated remains, any damage due to harmful or explodable implants, claims brought by any other persons claiming the right to control the disposition of the decedent or the decedent's cremated remains, or any other action performed by ABC Crematory, its officers, agents or employees, pursuant to this authorization, excepting only acts of willful negligence on the part of ABC Crematory.

SUMMARY

Cremation is the second most common method of disposition of a dead body. It is becoming increasingly acceptable because it is relatively inexpensive. It spares the survivors the extra burden of spending money on the cemetery lot and a casket, and yet cremation allows survivors the option of preserving the memory of the deceased by keeping the ashes in an urn or in a mausoleum.

REFERENCES

1. Raether HL "Deaths and Cremations: 1995, 1996 and Beyond." *The Director*, Nov. 1997: 77-79.

2. Cremation Association of North America: "State Percent Cremations Predictions 2000 and 2010," [Table]. June 18, 1998.

3. Raether HL: "International Cremation Statistics." *The Director*, July 1997: 77.

4. Lapin HI: "Cremation Association of North America Issues, Model Cremation Authorization and Disposition Form." *Funeral Service Business and Legal Guide*, Issue 7-8, 1992.

Chapter 11

THE AUTOPSY

The autopsy is the court of ultimate truth and the
most powerful provider of complete closure.

*A*n autopsy is an examination of a dead body performed by a pathologist. It consists of an external examination of the body, examination of the internal organs, and additional investigation such as microscopic examinations and toxicological analyses for the detection of medications or poisons. The main purpose of the autopsy examination is to determine the cause and manner of death.

Autopsies are divided in two groups, those requested by the relatives of the deceased and hospitals, and those performed by medical examiners. The autopsies requested by the family or the hospital are performed by a private, independent pathologist or by a pathologist on the hospital staff. These are called private autopsies. A medical examiner is also a pathologist, but he or she is employed by the county or state to perform autopies on medico-legal cases, as discussed below.

Hospitals may request autopsies because they have an academic interest in determining the "final diagnosis" and sometimes the cause of death. Right after World War II, about 50 percent of patients who died in hospitals were autopsied. There was in fact a requirement that at least 20 percent of the patients dying in hospitals be autopsied. This requirement was dropped in 1971 and the subsidy that had been provided by the Joint Commission on Accreditation of Hospitals to cover the expense of performing autopsies to meet the requirements dried up. Since then, the number of autopsies has been dropping. Probably less than two percent of deaths are now autopsied.

There are further reasons for a drop in the autopsy numbers:

- There is lack of reimbursement for autopsies by third-party payers, the insurance companies. In rare circumstances, i.e. if the insurance company is involved in a litigation, then it may pay for an autopsy.

- Ironically, most pathologists do not like to do autopsies, because they might become involved in a medico-legal process.

- With the rising rates of litigation, attending physicians hesitate to suggest autopsies for fear of discovering an error in their diagnosis or treatment, which could lead to a malpractice suit.

- Family members may not be interested in requesting an autopsy, feeling that the deceased has suffered enough.

- Funeral directors also tend to discourage autopsies, as the performance of an autopsy makes embalming the body more difficult. It can cause a delay in the process of funeral services and may result in disfigurement of the body.

AUTOPSY AND THE FUNERAL DIRECTOR

The results of a survey published in the March 1993 issue of *The Director*[1] indicates that more than 80 percent of funeral directors believe that autopsies help in determining the cause of death, advancing knowledge and educating the medical profession. However, 46 percent admitted to counseling families not to permit autopsy.

There is no doubt that obtaining the authorization for a private autopsy and getting the pathologist to perform it can hold up funeral services. Also, in many instances embalming becomes more difficult after an autopsy has been performed. Radical procedures such as the removal of a large section of the spine or the removal of all of the neck organs can create embalming nightmares. Some pathologists are not considerate enough to recognize the problems embalmers may have as a result of a disruptive autopsy. In fact, embalmers frequently complain that pathologists make unnecessary incisions that interfere with the embalming process, or that they cut up vessels of importance to the embalmer.

For instance, the carotid arteries, which occur on either side of the neck, are frequently cut, largely due to lack of care. As a pathologist, I always pay special attention not to damage the carotid arteries during an autopsy, because they are necessary to achieving good embalming of the head and face. Funeral directors and embalmers appreciate it when a pathologist considers their job when they perform their own.[2]

Although 46 percent of funeral directors discourage families to authorize an autopsy, it should be pointed out that such advice may result in the family's not discovering the answer to their questions about a loved one's death. In the post-autopsy conferences I conduct with a deceased's family, I invariably receive satisfaction as I am able to witness the lessening of their grief and a observe a resolution of conflicts and doubts.

When handling a case for autopsy, the funeral director may expedite the process by obtaining proper authorization. Proper identification of the body must be made before the autopsy is started. Although the pathologist will be liable for performing an unauthorized autopsy, the funeral director may also be liable if an autopsy has been performed on the wrong body.

When a family orders a private autopsy, the funeral director should make sure that it is not a case that calls for the involvement of the medical examiner. If there is any doubt, the death should be reported to the medical examiner. His ruling should be awaited before an autopsy is performed in the funeral home. The funeral director should also take any steps necessary to prevent injuries to himself such as cuts during the performance of an autopsy. And finally, he should fully comply with the Occupational Safety and Health Administration (OSHA) regulations pertaining to autopsies.

AUTOPSY AND THE FAMILY

Some families object to autopsies based on their religious beliefs. For instance, the Jewish and the Islamic faiths do not ordinarily permit autopsies. However, exceptions may be made when they feel the autopsy is going to contribute to science.

One of the most common reasons the family objects to an autopsy is because they feel it may disfigure the body, making viewing impossible. This need not be true. Most people do not know that the incisions made during an autopsy are impossible to detect when the body is sewn up and dressed. Funeral directors can allay any family members' fears by reassuring them on this concern.

THE FUNERAL DIRECTOR AND THE MEDICAL EXAMINER

A large number of deaths are required under the state laws to be investigated. In most jurisdictions throughout the world, only about 20 percent of all persons die under circumstances that require an official medico-legal investigation by a medical examiner, coroner or police surgeon. The cases that require such investigation fall in the following categories:

- Sudden death of a person in apparent good health.
- Death without medical care.
- Violent or unnatural deaths from criminal violence, accident, suicide, poison, injury.
- Suspicious or unusual death.
- Death while in prison or police custody.
- Death occurring in an operating room.
- Death from diseases that constitute a threat to public health.

The funeral director should be aware of the types of cases that ought to be reported to the investigating authority. In many states, failure to report such a death is a misdemeanor.

THE VERDICT

An autopsy can provide answers as to the cause and manner of death. This serves the process of justice. Similarly, treating physicians may use the autopsy to answer questions regarding unexplained signs and symptoms. Hidden conditions can be detected, and treatment failures can be discovered. Above all, the family wants to find answers to many of their questions, such as: *Could I have prevented my child's crib death? Did my parent have Alzheimer's disease or a genetic condition I should be concerned about? Did the doctor make a mistake? Could I learn something to prevent disease and protect my family? Could I help science?*

REFERENCES

1. Heckerling and Williams MJ: "Attitudes Toward Autopsy." *The Director*, March 1993: 26-30.
2. Fatteh AV: *Handbook of Forensic Pathology*. Philadelphia: J.B. Lippincott Co., 1973.

Chapter 12

DON'T PICK UP A LIVING ONE!

There was a young man at Nunhead
who woke in his coffin of lead;
"It is cozy enough"
He remarked in a huff,
"But I wasn't aware I was dead."

—A. Hallam, *The Burial Reformer*, 1906[1]

*T*he dead have been noted to breathe and swallow, to flicker their eyelids and move their arms. They are heard to knock on the inside of the coffin and to sit upright on the autopsy table—even after being autopsied. Furthermore, it is very common for the dead to be observed belching.

In 1964, I was serving as Forensic Pathologist to Her Majesty the Queen in Belfast, Northern Ireland. As I was getting into my autopsy attire, the morgue attendant placed the "corpse" of a man on the table for my examination. I was about to make my first incision when I realized the man was alive. In my book entitled *Handbook of Forensic Pathology*, I described the case as follows:

> [A] physician was called to examine an elderly man at his home. The doctor saw the man lying on his bed motionless, quickly checked the man's heartbeat by placing his hand on his chest and felt the radial artery. He declared the man dead and authorized the removal of the body to a morgue for autopsy. In the autopsy room, while the remains were being placed on the table, this author heard

a gurgling sound and noticed a slight swallowing movement. The man was rushed to a hospital and lived for two more months.[2]

At the scene of death, one of the first functions of any investigator is to make sure that death has, in fact, taken place. The removal service or the funeral director must be positive that a proper pronouncement of death has been made before they pick up the body. In the case of recent death, care should be exercised before the person is declared dead. The absence of respiration and heartbeat, absence of reflexes, and changes in the eyes —such as a clouding of the cornea and absence of corneal reflexes—are some of the signs that should be checked before making the diagnosis of death. A simple check of the pulse may be misleading, for a person who is in a state of shock, has been electrocuted or is a victim of drowning may be alive with no pulse. The pulse of an elderly person may be feeble and imperceptible, and a casual examination and pronouncement of death could result in an embarrassing situation and a possible malpractice suit.

There are times that a person who is undoubtedly dead appears to be alive. I witnessed another fascinating case when I encountered a 21-year-old woman who was "alive," even after she was autopsied. The woman was brought to the Medical College of Virginia morgue one day in 1967. She had taken a large dose of barbiturates with the intent to commit suicide and was admitted to the hospital in a coma. She received gastric lavage, intravenous fluids, and high pressure oxygen treatments. Unfortunately, all therapeutic measures failed, and she was pronounced dead by a team of doctors. I was a Medical Examiner for the City of Richmond at that time and her body was brought to me for autopsy. Evisceration, sectioning, and examination of all the organs in the chest and abdomen revealed findings consistent with barbiturate overdose. Next came the examination of the head. After reflecting the scalp—i.e., cutting the skin on the head to expose the skull—I began sawing the skull with an electric saw and she started to show signs of life. Each time I sawed, the woman's upper extremities flexed, the spine curved forwards and the head and upper torso rose upwards form the table almost to an angle of 45 degrees. I summoned the Chairman of the department and all of the residents, as well as the photographer with a video camera to witness this extraordinary phenomenon. All watched in amazement each time the corpse rose with the touch of saw gyrations. As I continued sawing, the corpse rose a dozen times with diminishing response and decreasing angle. The responses ceased by the time the sawing of the skull was completed. The brain appeared normal. No one can be sure as to why this phenomenon occurred. However, the consensus of all of the academicians was that some of her brain cells were still alive and functioning, probably due to high pressure oxygen administration.

Humans have immense powers to resist death. While I was a medical student in Bombay, India, I witnessed a demonstration by a man who chose to be buried in a grave-like hole four feet deep. He was fully covered by soil. Thirty minutes later, he was pulled out alive and well. Apparently, he went around staging such demonstrations for donations. Puckle cites a similar case of an Indian fakir (beggar) who was known to be buried for three weeks or longer and came out alive.3

Literature shows there have been many cases of accidental burial of living persons. Iserson notes that in 1742, a Paris physician recorded the mistaken certification of death for 72 people.[4] Iserson also cites a 1842 collection of cases where 46 people in Paris who were declared dead recovered while waiting for burial.

A case was reported in *USA Today*[5] where a woman was pronounced dead by the ambulance personnel and later by an investigator in the Medical Examiner's office. Two hours later, she showed signs of life. She was admitted to the hospital and was recovering well the next day.

Puckle described an extraordinary case of a woman in Rye, Sussex who was thought to be dead after a fainting attack.[3] The "body" was wrapped in a shroud and placed in a coffin. She lay in the unsealed coffin till the morning of her burial. Curiously enough, she woke up, got out of her coffin and walked downstairs. She lived for several years after that.

The "dead" deserve the same respect as the living. Mr. Funeral Director, even if you pick up a living one, don't put him on the autopsy table! Unexpected things might happen, as illustrated by the following case:

In May 1864, a man 'died' suddenly in a hospital in New York. To determine the cause of death an autopsy was ordered. When the doctor performing the autopsy made the first incision, the 'dead' person jumped up and grabbed the doctor's throat. The 'dead man' recovered completely but the doctor performing the autopsy was so frightened that he developed apoplexy and died on the spot.[6]

Let us not forget the "dead" may want to live.

REFERENCES

1. Hallam A (ed.): *The Burial Reformer*. 1906: 32. As cited in Iserson KV: *Death to Dust: What Happens to Dead Bodies?* Tuscon, AZ: Galen Press, Ltd., 1994.

2. Fatteh AV: *Handbook of Forensic Pathology*. Pennsylvania: J.B. Lippincott Co., 1973.

3. Puckle BS: *Funeral Customs: Their Origin and Development*. London: T. Werner Ltd., 1926. Republished by Omnigraphics, Detroit MI, 1990: 24.

4. Iserson KV: *Death to Dust: What Happens to Dead Bodies?* Tuscon, AZ: Galen Press, Ltd., 1994: 29.

5. "Quick Recovery." *USA Today*, June 17, 1993:3A.

6. Hartmann F: *Buried Alive: An Examination into the Occult Causes of Apparent Death*. Boston: Trance and Catalepsy, 1895: 80.

Section IV:
The Price of Death

Chapter 13

ECONOMICS OF FUNERALS

And How to Cut Costs

A funeral can be one of the most expensive purchases in your life. Many times it is our third biggest expense, after the expenses of a home and a car. Surveys from the National Funeral Directors Association (NFDA) indicate that the average cost of a funeral is $4,782.[1] Data provided by the American Association of Retired Persons (AARP) reveal that the cost of a traditional funeral in the United States is $4,300, but some funerals may cost over $10,000.[2]

While we always plan in advance for the purchases of a home and a car, most of us do not preplan for the expense of a funeral. This is due in part to the fact that we are often faced with the expense of a funeral unexpectedly. Frankly, we don't like to think about the possibility that we or our loved ones will die. When death does occur, we are grief-stricken and distraught. Our judgement may be clouded. We may feel helpless, and often end up paying more for a funeral than we need to.

In this chapter, all aspects of funeral costs and itemized prices are discussed. Some suggestions on ways to cut back on the cost of a funeral are also presented. It is possible to save thousands of dollars on a funeral if you follow a few tips.

The prices of various items and services discussed in this chapter are derived principally from two sources: *Product Report Funerals and Buri-*

als: Goods and Services,[2] and funeral price information from the *National Funeral Directors Association 1997 General Price List Survey*.[1]

A FIFTEEN BILLION DOLLAR INDUSTRY

There were 2,311,000 deaths in the United States in 1996. This number is projected to rise to 2,367,000 in 2000.[3] In other words, there are well over two million funerals in the United States every year. It is easy to see how the funeral trade is close to a 15-billion-dollars-per-year industry.

Furthermore, funeral costs have been rising steadily at a rate of five percent per year for the past several years. The data compiled by the NFDA indicate the following average escalation in costs of an adult funeral service:

Table 13-1: Average Cost of Adult Funeral Service	
Year	Average Cost
1957	$ 646
1967	$ 850
1977	$ 1,412
1985	$ 2,737
1996	$ 4,782

These averages include professional services, such as transportation, care of the body, embalming, use of the facilities for viewing and ceremony, and casket. Other items, such as the cost for the cemetery plot, vault markers, flowers, clothes, music and obituary notices, are generally not included in the above figures.

COSTS RELATED TO DEATH

The funeral costs for goods and services may be divided into the following categories, which are described in greater detail:
1. Funeral director's professional services: The "basic" or "minimum" service pays for the funeral director's initial conference, consultations with the family and clergy, completion and delivery of necessary paperwork.

2. *Care of the Body:* Body care usually involves disinfecting, dressing and casketing the remains. These are not optional items. *Embalming* is a part of the care of the body too, and if it is needed or authorized by you, there will be an additional charge.

3. *Transportation:* The basic transportation charges include transferring the body from the place of death to the funeral home and transferring the body to the location of final disposition.

4. *Use of Facilities:* The funeral director's facilities may be required for viewing the body or for the funeral ceremony.

5. *Casket:* This is one of the most expensive items of a funeral. Prices for caskets vary a great deal. A 20-gauge wood or steel casket is used for purposes of comparison. The possibility of renting a casket or purchase it from a third party is discussed below.

6. *Burial:* Immediate burial charges include the interment of the body, without embalming, in an alternative container. There is also no ceremony or viewing.

7. *Cemetery Plot, Mausoleum, Vault, Perpetual Care.*

8. *Opening and closing the grave.* This is the cost of digging the ground to create space for the casket and vault, and for covering the grave when the body is laid to rest.

9. *Grave Markers and Other Items.* For example, head stones, engravings and other writings.

10. *Cremation:* Direct cremation charges generally include the funeral director's fee, cost for transportation of the body to the funeral home and the crematory, and for the care of the body. The cost of alternative containers and the cremation fee are not included.

Table 13-2 analyzes these compares prices for the above, as derived from the surveys conducted by both the AARP and the NFDA.

Table 13-2: Average Cost for In-Ground Funerals According to AARP and NFDA Surveys[1,2]		
Item	AARP	NFDA
Services of the funeral director	$ 1,067	$ 1,079
Care of body	$ 319	$ 134
Embalming	$ 123	$ 133
Transportation	$ 313	$ 370
Use of facilities:		
for viewing	$ 206	$ 305
for funeral services	$ 326	$ 326
Casket	$ 1,658	$ 2,176
Grave liner	$ 497	$ 761
Total	$ 4,509	$ 5,284

SERVICES OF THE FUNERAL DIRECTOR

Whether you are preplanning a funeral or arranging one for an "at need" situation, you should analyze and compare costs. Every funeral director is required to provide prices both over the phone and in writing. First, obtain a general price list as well as a price list for caskets and burial containers. Note, however, that the funeral director is not required to disclose prices for cemetery goods and services. You will need to negotiate these with the owner of the cemetery.

The general price list you receive from a funeral director will contain itemized charges for the following services:

- Initial conference
- Consultations with the family and clergy
- Arranging and supervising the transportation of remains
- Coordinating, supervising and conducting the funeral
- Effecting the burial or cremation
- Receiving and arranging flowers
- Providing advice on music, clothes, etc.
- Telephone communications and correspondence

- Completion and delivery of necessary documents (e.g. death certificate, burial permit, cremation certificate)

Overhead expenses such as maintenance of facility, automobiles, equipment, inventory, insurance, administration and government compliance will be included in the prices.

The fees for the funeral director's services may vary considerably. The location of the funeral home, the quality of the facility and the reputation of the funeral director can cause fluctuations in price. Added costs will be allotted for variables such as transporting the body from overseas or for a non-local burial.

In 1996, the AARP determined the average cost of non-declinable professional services based on a survey of 100 funeral directors. The found the range to be from $350 to $2,295, with an average cost of $1,067. In 1997, the NFDA surveyed 1500 of its members and determined the average cost for these services to be $1,079.

CARE OF THE BODY

The funeral director may perform the following services in caring for the body:

- Sanitary care without embalming
- Bathing and handling of the deceased
- Cosmetology
- Hair dressing
- Restoration of disfigured remains
- Restoration of autopsied body
- Dressing
- Casketing
- Embalming of un-autopsied body
- Embalming of autopsied body
- Refrigeration

Some religions require only sanitary bathing of the body to cleanse the surface. The charge for this is about $100. Cosmetic work can be simple if there are no injuries to the face. The cost of cosmetic application may range from $50 to $150. In the case of an accident victim, the funeral director may have to suture the injuries, apply wax and rebuild the facial features. Restorative work may also be needed in cases where autopsy was necessary. The funeral director may charge $100 to $200 per hour for this type of reconstruction work.

Hair dressing is generally part of the preparation and care of the decedent. The average cost of dressing and casketing of the body is $123.

Clothing for the body can be bought from the funeral director or brought by the family. The current trend is to bring clothes from home. This eliminates the expense of clothing. If the family buys new clothes from a store, they will probably spend less money than if they were to buy them from the funeral home.

TRANSPORTATION

After death, the body must be transported from the place of death to the funeral home and/or to the place of final disposition. The body may have to be taken to a church or a synagogue. Sometimes the body must be transported out of town, state or country. Cars, limousines, a hearse or a plane may be needed for such arrangements. Additional vehicles may be required to carry the family, the clergy and the flowers from the funeral home to the place of burial or cremation. A lead car or motorcycle escort may be desired in some cases.

There might be additional transportation costs for conveying a body to and from the airport, or to a place of autopsy and back.

The cost for transporting the body to the funeral home ranges from $75 to $225, with an average cost of $153. The cost for transporting the body from the funeral home to the site of final disposition ranges from $60 to $400, with an average figure of $166. This cost obviously varies depending on the number of vehicles used and the distance traveled. A limousine for the family and the clergy ranges from $55 to $225 and a motorcycle escort may cost anywhere from $15 to $225. These charges are for distances of less than 25 miles. Longer trips will be charged based on mileage.

By eliminating the limousines and using family cars, the consumer can reduce the costs. The family may ask that donations be made to charities in lieu of flowers or they could transport the flower arrangements themselves to eliminate the fee for handling the flowers and the fee for a flower car. Another way to lower the cost of transportation is to use a van to transport the remains, rather than a more expensive hearse. You can provide your own vehicle to reduce costs.

EMBALMING

Embalming is one important step in the preparation of a body. The cost of embalming ranges from $150 to $500, with an average of $370. The embalming charge generally includes the cost of almost all other body preparation, although some funeral directors charge separately for make-up, hair dressing, cosmetic work, clothing, etc. The funeral director will charge a higher fee for embalming if the body is disfigured or autopsied, as this requires more time and materials.

USE OF FUNERAL HOME FACILITIES

Funeral homes are commonly used for viewing the body, for any funeral ceremony where the body is present, and for memorial services without the body. The average cost of viewing in a funeral home for three hours is $305, and for the funeral ceremony it is $326. If the family wants to reduce the expenses, the viewing and ceremony can be held in a private home, place of worship or some other private facility. Another cost effective choice is a memorial service without the body present.

The funeral home may add charges for the use of the facilities for activities other than viewing and ceremony, such as the use of the preparation room where the embalming and other items for care of the deceased are carried out.

CASKET

The casket is the most expensive item in a traditional funeral with burial. This expense can be reduced if the family chooses an immediate burial or direct cremation, or if the body is donated to science. Also, using an alternative container made of cardboard will cost much less. If cremation is a choice for final disposition and a traditional funeral is desired, the family might opt for a rented casket. This will save a considerable amount of money, as is discussed below.

The average price of an 18-gauge standard steel casket purchased from a funeral home is $1,658 or $2,176, according to AARP and NFDA respectively. The average of these two figures is $1,941. Caskets bought from the funeral homes carry a large mark-up. Therefore, it is much more economical to buy one from a third-party burial and funeral goods provider. Note that if the casket is not bought from the funeral director, he cannot charge the casket handling fee, which will save the family even more money.

Most funeral directors admit to marking up a casket two to two-and-a-half times the wholesale price to cover their own cost and to make a reasonable profit. If the mark-up is assumed to be two times the wholesale price, the consumer will pay $1,917 if he buys the casket from the funeral home, but only half that amount ($958) if he buys directly from a third party. For those buying more expensive caskets, the savings are even greater.

There are many discount retailers and wholesalers. Many of them show 20-gauge non-sealing steel caskets for $600 to $700. The examples provided in Table 13-3 have been taken from the Internet[4] and direct quotes from the companies.

Rented Casket

Renting a casket is another choice, if the remains are to be cremated (see below). The cost of renting a casket is usually one-third the price of buying one.

Table 13-3: Cost of Caskets Purchased Directly		
Company	**Casket**	**Price**
Consumer Casket USA Erie, PA	Caroline 20-gauge imperial white, pink crepe	$975
	Irwin 20-gauge Coppertone, curshed crepe	$975
	Gleason 20-gauge Coppertone, crushed crepe	$860
	Cox 20-gauge, non-sealing, silver, crushed crepe	$660
	Alvin 20-gaugue non-sealing, Coppertone, silver, white or rosetan crepe	$525
Alternative Funeral and Cremation Care Hollywood, FL	Westridge-poplar 4VT wood	$975
	Trindex 20-gauge steel NPS	$850
Gadberry Casket Sales Blytheville, AZ	20-gauge non-sealing steel	$610
Direct Casket New York, NY	20-gauge, non-sealing steel	$596
Brookside Caskets Cypress, CA	20-gauge, non-sealing steel	$699
Dignified, Affordable Caskets Helmet, CA	20-gauge, non-sealing steel	$650
Infinity Caskets Hesperia, CA	20-gauge, non-sealing steel	$595
Casket Outlet Oakland, CA	20-gauge, non-sealing steel	$670

BURIAL CHARGES

It is always a good idea to negotiate the purchase of the cemetery plot in advance. If this is not done, the funeral director will advise you on a burial location. The sale of the cemetery plot does not involve any profits for the funeral director; however, he may profit on the merchandise he provides for the burial.

There are several cost items at the cemetery. These include:

- Cost of grave site
- Perpetual care
- Vault
- Opening and closing of grave
- Immediate burial
- Stone marker
- Mausoleum (if selected)

Cemetery Plot

There is a wide range in prices for grave sites. The costs may vary within a town, and even within the same cemetery. All together, Americans spend over a billion dollars a year on cemetery plots. In most cemeteries the cost of one plot is between $100 and $3,000; however, some places cost much more. For example, the minimum fee in Westwood Village Memorial Park in Los Angeles is $15,000.[5] Another cemetery in Los Angeles, Forest Lawn Memorial Park, is very well known. It contains concert halls, wedding chapels, movie theatres, museums and gift shops. It is described as the "Disneyland for the Dead."[6]

The prices for cemetery plots vary a great deal according to location. By preplanning and comparison-shopping, one can save up to 50 percent of the price of a plot.

Another point to consider is that burial does not have to be in a cemetery. In some states, burial in rural property that you own can be a low-cost option. The selection of a plot in a church or town-owned cemetery may result in substantial savings as well. A cemetery plot that is some distance from town may be a lot less expensive than one within town limits. A plot on your family property may not cost anything. Sometimes advertisements in newspapers offer good prices. Take advantage of these. Veterans and their immediate family receive free plots in the national cemeteries.

To reduce the cost for a plot further, you may solicit the help of your church or a local memorial society. A memorial society is a nonprofit consumer group. Members usually pay small fee to be part of a group that negotiates, either verbally or contractually, with local funeral homes. Because of their large membership, these societies are able to arrange better fees for their members. In addition, members also have a fairly accurate assessment of funeral costs beforehand. In some places you may get a "traditional" funeral for less than $1,000. The memorial societies suggest that in most states you can do some of the arrangements yourself to save money. For instance, you may get the permits and death certificate yourself without the help of a funeral director. Chapter 14 discusses memorial societies in greater depth, and Appendix E offers a list of memorial societies.

Vault

A vault, also called a grave liner or outer burial container, is required by many cemeteries, although they are not mandated in many states. This container surrounds and protects the casket and prevents it from sinking into the ground upon deterioration. Like the casket, funeral homes and cemeteries sell vaults at a much higher price than do manufacturers or wholesalers. The average price for an asphalt-coated concrete vault that is purchased from a funeral home is $761.

Grave liners can also be purchased from the manufacturers at about half the price charged by funeral homes, saving an individual consumer approximately $380. Also, because grave markers and urns are not needed at the time of funeral, often they can be ordered from a third party at substantial savings. However, they may take a few weeks to arrive.

Some cemeteries do not require you to buy the grave liner or vault. You can save the cost of the vault if you find a cemetery that does not insist on vault use.

Perpetual Care

When you do buy a plot, make sure the purchasing contract includes the cost of perpetual care of the grave site. The price of a mid-caliber single grave with perpetual care ranges from $200 to $1,750, with an average price of $689. Visit a few cemeteries in your area to compare prices and to find the one most suited to your needs.

Opening and Closing Grave

In addition to other fees, there are the charges for opening and closing the grave. These range from $250 to $930, with an average of $462.

Grave Marker

The stone marker is not a required item. Markers come in different sizes and shapes, and are made of a variety of materials. The average cost with installation is $479. In the past, the markers usually stood upright, but the current trend is to put them flat on the ground.

Sometimes families wish to place a temporary grave marker at the grave site to help mourners to identify the grave. These cost about $20, depending on size, design and price, and are replaced by the permanent headstone when it is ready.

Alternatives to In-Ground Burial

Other means of burial can be achieved through the use of crypts and mausoleums. They cost much more than burial in below-ground graves. The prices in metropolitan areas may be even higher. Further details on above-ground burial are presented in Chapter 9.

An immediate burial is an inexpensive alternative to a traditional burial with viewing. It is low cost, because the body is not embalmed and is buried in an alternative container. This choice includes transportation of the body to the funeral home and to the cemetery, care of the body, and the funeral director's fee. The average cost of immediate burial without a casket is $1,249.

CREMATION

Cremation is commonly chosen as an alternative to an in-ground burial and it usually costs less. There are two types of expenses incurred with the cremation itself: the fees charged by the funeral director for arranging the cremation, and the charges for the actual cremation process. By dealing with the crematory directly, you can eliminate the funeral director's fee.

The cost of actual cremation with no other fees is usually around $200. However, there will be additional charges, depending on what the family wants. The choices made may include:

- Direct cremation
- Burial of the cremated remains
- Traditional formal funeral followed by cremation.

The average cost of direct cremation is $1,145. This price includes transportation of the body to the funeral home and the crematory, care of the body and the funeral director's fee. It does not include the cost for a container or a casket to transport the body, or for a container for the cremated remains. Direct cremation is the most economical method of disposition of a body.

Some people choose to have a full funeral service before cremation. In this case, the family can rent or buy a casket and pay for additional items and services that they select. A casket is not legally required for cremation.

Urn

When a body is cremated, the cremains are collected in plastic bags and stored in temporary containers made of cardboard. The family may choose to bury the cremains in a family grave, to display them in a mausoleum or to keep them at home. If the cremains are not buried, the ashes are usually kept in a permanent container called a cremation urn. These urns may be made of wood, stone or metal with various decorative designs. They can be purchased from funeral homes or funeral shops. The prices of urns vary considerably, depending on the quality of the product. The general price range is $100 to $1,000.

ADDITIONAL ITEMS

Guest Register Book

This can be an ordinary book or one that is specially designed for funeral services. It is presented at the service for visitors to sign at the funeral home, church, synagogue or home. Estimated cost is only $10 to $30.

Obituary Notices

The funeral director will charge the family for placing any paid death notices to be printed in the newspapers. Prices vary, depending on the size of the notice and the newspaper. Some newspapers do not charge for printing regular obituary notices.

Prayer Cards

These are cards printed with the name, birth date and death date of the deceased, along with a prayer. These are commonly used by Christians and given to each visitor attending the funeral, and may cost from $30 to $60.

Acknowledgement Cards

After the funeral services are completed, the family may want to send "thank you" cards to the friends and relatives who attended the funeral, shared in the grief, provided support and sent flowers or donations. The cost may range from $20 to $30.

Death Certificate

A death certificate is an important document that the funeral director must obtain. It is required to complete the disposition of the body. Copies of the death certificate may be needed to collect life insurance benefits, veteran's benefits and Social Security benefits. They may also be needed to transfer titles of real estate holdings and automobiles as well as for probating a will. Sometimes the funeral director ends up spending a considerable amount of time to get these. Copies of the death certificate can range from $5 to $10 each.

You can obtain additional copies of death certificates yourself from the local Registrar of Death.

Burial and Cremation Permits

Burial and cremation permits are also required for the disposition of the remains. They cost between $5 and $10.

Clergy Honorarium

The clergy honorarium can range from between $50 to $200. Similar amounts are paid for mass offerings. The organist and soloist usually charge $75 each, and hired pallbearers and assistants will charge about $25 each. The funeral director may add a charge for taped music, gratuities, emblems, or name plates, which could cost another $100 to $200.

Miscellaneous Expenses

There are several other expenses incurred in arranging and executing a funeral. Along with the copies of the death certificate, burial and/or cremation permit, and clergy honorarium, the funeral director usually pays for these goods and services with the understanding that he will be reimbursed by the family with no mark up on actual costs. Included in this may be:

- Mass offering
- Gratuities
- Organist
- Soloist
- Taped music
- Pallbearers
- Extra escorts, assistants
- Religious emblems
- Name plates for caskets.

THE NFDA COST SURVEY

A 1997 survey of 1500 members lists the most commonly selected items and their average cost. They are presented in Table 13-4.

Table 13-4: NFDA Survey of Funeral Costs	
Most Commonly Selected Items	**Average Cost**
Non-declinable professional service charges	$ 1,078.98
Embalming	$ 369.51
Other preparations (cosmetology, hair, etc.)	$ 132.92
Visitation/Viewing	$ 304.84
Funeral at funeral home	$ 325.73
Transfer of remains to funeral home	$ 134.17
Hearse (local)	$ 161.24
Service car/van	$ 80.76
Acknowledgement cards	$ 18.74
Casket: 18-gauge steel, sealer, velvet interior	$ 2,175.57
Vault, asphalt coated concrete, sealer	$ 760.79
TOTAL:	$ 5,543.25

SUMMARY OF SAVINGS

Here is a list of suggestions that can help you to save on the costs of a funeral:

- Preplan and prearrange. This will give you opportunity to shop around and negotiate. Do price shopping on the Internet.
- Donate the body for medical research and education.
- Opt for immediate burial or for direct cremation.
- Buy the casket, grave liner, grave marker, urn and other items from third party suppliers.
- Rent a casket or get one built. A local carpenter can build one in just a few days.
- Find a cemetery plot in out-of-town country property, or in a church-owned or town-owned cemetery.
- Obtain the permits and death certificate, and arrange the funeral yourself. These forms can be obtained from the vital statistics section of your local health department.

- Cut back on unnecessary services and goods, such as flowers, limousines, a flower car, escorts, a violinist or soloist, obituary notices, music, guest books, acknowledgement cards and prayer cards.
- Secure help from a church or memorial society in your area (see Chapter 14 for further information).

While the consumer must remember that there are many expenses involved in a funeral, fortunately, with careful selection of the services and goods, the total cost of a funeral can be significantly lowered.

REFERENCES

1. National Funeral Directors Association: "Comparison of Funeral Costs, 1957-96." NFDA: June 19, 1997.
2. American Association of Retired Persons: "Product Report: Funerals and Burials - Goods and Services." AARP, 1996, 2:3.
3. "U.S. Death Statistics." NFDA. Online. Available: *http://www.nfda.org/resources/deathstats.html*, 1998.
4. "Caskets: Everything the Mortician Won't Tell You and Some Better Places to Shop." FAMSA. Online. Available: *http://vbiweb.champlain.edu/famsa/caskets.htm*, 1998.
5. Anderson P: *Affairs in Order*. New York: Macmillan, 1991. As cited in Iserson KV: *Death to Dust: What Happens to Dead Bodies?* Tucson, AZ: Galen Press Ltd., 1994.
6. Waugh E: *The Loved One*. As cited in Iserson KV, 1994.

Chapter 14

MEMORIAL SOCIETIES

*M*emorial societies were first created in an effort to cut costs of funerals. The first memorial society in the United States was founded in 1939 in Seattle, Washington. The option of low-cost cremation was promoted. As a result of the success of the Seattle society, another was organized in Brooklyn, New York. The idea caught on, and now there are over 150 memorial societies in the United States and Canada with thousands of members. Many individual societies have hundreds of members. Despite their increased popularity and growth, many people do not know of the existence of these societies.

Memorial societies are essentially consumer movements. They are nonprofit, function on democratic principles, and work cooperatively to cut costs and regulate the funeral industry.

Anyone can join a memorial society for a nominal fee. Some charge a lifetime membership fee of between $15 and $20, while others charge annual dues. Some memorial societies have contracts with funeral homes. Large memberships make it possible for these societies to negotiate better fares with the undertaker. These preneed contracts by the memorial societies give the consumer a fairly accurate assessment of costs for direct cremation or direct burial.

The publication of the Funeral and Memorial Societies of America, Inc., entitled *A Guide to Funeral Planning*, states, "those who use the information a memorial society offers pay less than one-fifth of the average American funeral."[1]

The average American funeral costs $4,782, and many funerals cost much more than that. Other important goals of these societies are to promote simplicity and dignity in funeral services, as well as to allow individual freedom of choice in selecting the method for disposition of the dead.

Some memorial societies operate without any contracts with funeral homes. They have verbal understanding with the funeral homes about the costs of funeral arrangements. They help members by directing them to the these moderate cost places.

There are other memorial societies who have neither contracts nor verbal agreements with funeral directors. This is because they are not able to get cooperation from funeral directors in their area. They simply render advice to their members.

Many memorial societies in the United States and Canada work cooperatively with their reciprocity agreements.

Information about the memorial societies in the United States can be obtained from:

Funeral and Memorial Societies of America, Inc. (FAMSA)
P.O. Box 10
Hinesburg, VT 05461
(802) 482-3437; Fax: (802) 482-5246

There are also nonprofit societies which provide direct cremation or direct burial. If direct cremation is desired, these societies provide services for a fixed amount that may include picking up of the body, cremation, and completing any necessary paper work. Other services, such as viewing and embalming, are eliminated to minimize expenses.

The Funeral and Memorial Societies of America, Inc., the largest organization of its kind in the United States, provides advice to its members in four different areas: services, burial, cremation, and donation of bodies to medical schools. The funeral services are held soon after death with the body present. The memorial services are held without the body and may be carried out several days or weeks after death to allow family members and friends to arrive on a scheduled day. The advice on burial and cremation is provided by this organization to save unnecessary expenses and to reduce grief for the survivors. They work cooperatively with the National Anatomical Service to handle donation of the body to a medical school. The subjects of burial, cremation and body donation are discussed in detail elsewhere in this book.

The directory of funeral and memorial societies in the United States, updated in May, 1999 is reproduced in Appendix E with the kind permission of FAMSA. The information can also be found on the website *www.funerals.org/famsa*. If there is no memorial society in your area, you can contact FAMSA directly at the above address and phone number.

REFERENCE

1. Funeral and Memorial Societies of America: *A Guide to Funeral Planning*. Hinesburg, VT: FAMSA, 1998.

Chapter 15

FUNERAL FRAUD & THE FUNERAL RULE

*F*or decades, the funeral trade has been accused of being a rip-off industry. Undoubtedly the business was not supervised thoroughly before the inception of the Federal Trade Commission's Funeral Rule, which is described in this chapter. Indeed, there is considerable evidence that there were a lot of abuses and exploitations before this law was passed in 1984.

INCIDENCE OF FUNERAL FRAUDS

The famous expose of the funeral industry depicted by Jessica Mitford in the *American Way of Death*[1] pointed out a number of abuses occuring in the funeral business, including preying on survivors' grief, selling expensive goods, putting huge mark-ups on products and services, and selling vaults when they were not needed. Mitford pointed out that once every decade, magazines and newspapers expose the high cost of dying and how the bereaved are taken advantage of. Ultimately, however, this has no effect on the funeral costs: first, because of lack of organized protests and action by the consumer, and secondly, because there is a lack of hard statistical and economic data with which to work.

The editorial columnist of *Arizona Republic* called mortuaries the "greediest, most rapacious industry" in America and alleged that many mortuaries inflated the wholesale prices of the caskets by up to 900 percent and charged "exorbitant fees for minimal services."[2] In its editorial, "Final

Rip-off Can't Last Forever," the *Miami Herald*[3] landed a seething attack on the funeral industry, charging that there was "no significant movement from within the business. . . to reform what has become a ghoulish, profit-above-all, final rip-off." In a 1995 *Consumers Digest* article, Wasik discussed the subject of fraud in the funeral industry in detail and presented some significant concerns.[4]

Against the background of these attacks, allegations and charges, how is it even possible for the funeral industry to exploit the public as charged above?

The following are some of the ways a funeral director can make consumers spend more:

- By saying, "a final tribute should be good" or "you only have this last chance," "he/she would have wanted that expensive casket," they manipulate survivors into buying a more costly funeral.
- By not presenting the consumer with less expensive caskets options.
- With huge mark-ups. It is alleged that in most mortuaries, the mark-up on goods are 2.5 to 7.5 times the wholesale prices.
- By claiming that a casket has a "protective sealer" or that the vault is "waterproof."
- By prolonging the process of services, viewing, etcetera so that they can charge for the extra days they have to hold the body.
- By providing unnecessary limousines, escorts, flower cars, etc.
- In general, by taking advantage of the consumer's ignorance, grief, inability to make choices and lack of experience.

In addition to the above manipulations, the funeral industry has been attacked with charges of illegal and unethical practices. These charges are presented below.

- Substitution of a cheaper casket.
- Substitution of a cheaper vault.
- Not putting the casket purchased by the consumer in the vault.
- Substitution of a cheaper floral arrangement.
- Charging for services not needed or authorized and yet provided.
- Providing a "flower car" for only two or three floral pieces.

- Charging for "holding" a body for one or more days before services, even though the delay occurred because the funeral director did not have room for services.

- Re-using the grave site again and again.

- Collecting more from the consumer for "cash advance disbursements" than what the funeral director actually paid out.

- Selling traditional full service, more expensive funerals, rather than offering less expensive alternatives.

There are reasons that people are particularly vulnerable to rip-offs. Some of them include:

- Very few people make preneed arrangements.

- Most people at need are too helpless to shop around for a bargain. When they are grieving, they are not in a position to think about money. They are vulnerable.

- Most people are not knowledgeable about the prices of funeral goods and merchandise, because the need is occasional.

- Most people are not aware of the fact that goods such as caskets can be ordered from places other than the funeral home they use.

- The prices of the caskets by the funeral director are not advertised, as are the prices of cars or computers, for instance.

There are frauds in every industry, and the funeral industry is no exception. It is possible that the funeral industry is guilty of huge frauds, excesses, greed and cheating, more than any other industry. Nonetheless, the fact is, consumers should always be wary whenever they buy any large ticket items. Chapter 1, "Preneed Planning," and the tips provided in Chapter 13 will help you to minimize funeral costs and protect yourself from the possibility of being a victim of fraud. In addition to these cautions, the Federal Trade Commission's Funeral Rule also assures some protection for consumers.

THE FUNERAL RULE

The funeral industry practices are closely watched by the Federal Trade Commission (FTC). The FTC's Funeral Rule seeks to offer the consumer considerable protection against the possibility of abuses and frauds. It requires the funeral industry to make disclosures of the prices of funeral goods and merchandise and to advise the consumer on Funeral Rule requirements. The following information updated in May 1998 covers the essential elements of the relationship between the funeral industry and the consumer.[5]

Funerals: A Consumer's Guide

Each year, Americans arrange more than two million funerals for family and friends. Because funerals can cost thousands of dollars, you should be aware of federal regulations that can help protect you from overpaying.

The Funeral Rule, enforced by the Federal Trade Commission, makes it easier for you to choose only those goods and services you want or need and to pay for only those you select. According to the Rule, you can find out the cost of individual items whether you shop by telephone or in person.

If you inquire about funeral arrangements in person, the funeral home must give you a written price list of available goods and services. Keep in mind that when you arrange for a funeral, you can buy a package of goods and services or individual items. If you want to buy a casket, for example, the funeral provider must supply lists that describe the available selections and their prices.

Telephone Price Disclosures

You can shop by phone to compare prices among funeral providers. Getting price information over the phone may help you select a funeral home and the arrangements you want.

When you call a funeral provider to ask about terms, conditions, or prices of funeral goods and services, the funeral provider must give you prices and other information from the price lists to answer your questions reasonably.

General Price List

If you inquire in person about funeral arrangements, the funeral provider will give you a general price list that contains the cost of each funeral item and service offered. Use this information to help select the funeral provider and funeral items you want, need, and can afford.

The price list also must include information about embalming, caskets for cremation, and required purchases.

Embalming Information

The Funeral Rule requires funeral providers to give consumers information about embalming. Under the Rule, a funeral provider:

- May not falsely state that embalming is required by law

- Must disclose in writing that embalming is not required by law, except in certain special cases

- May not charge a fee for unauthorized embalming unless if embalming is required by state law

- Will disclose in writing that you usually have the right to choose a disposition —such as direct cremation or immediate burial —if you do not want embalming

- Will disclose to you in writing that certain funeral arrangements, such as a funeral with viewing, may make embalming a practical necessity and, therefore, a required purchase.

Cash Advance Sales

The Funeral Rule requires funeral providers to disclose in writing if they charge a fee for buying cash advance items —goods or services that funeral providers pay for on your behalf. Examples of cash advance items are flowers, obituary notices, pallbearers, and clergy honoraria. Some funeral providers charge you their cost for these items. Others add a service fee to their cost. The Funeral Rule requires funeral providers to tell you when a service fee is added to the price of cash advance items, or if there are refunds, discounts, or rebates from the supplier on any cash advance item.

Caskets for Cremation

Some consumers may want to select direct cremation—i.e., cremation of the deceased without a viewing or other ceremony where the body is present. If you choose direct cremation, the funeral provider will offer an inexpensive alternative container or an unfinished wood box. An alternative container is a non-metal enclosure (often of pressboard, cardboard, or canvas) to hold the deceased.

Because any container you buy will be destroyed during the cremation, you may wish to use an alternative container or an unfinished wood box. These could lower the funeral cost because they are less expensive than traditional caskets.

Under the Funeral Rule, funeral directors who offer direct cremation:

- May not tell you that state or local law requires a casket for direct cremation,

- Must disclose in writing your right to buy an unfinished wood box (a type of casket) or an alternative container for a direct cremation, and

- Must make an unfinished wood box or alternative container available for direct cremation.

Required Purchases

You do not have to buy goods or services you do not want, or pay any fees as a condition to obtaining the products and services you do want, except one permitted fee for the services of the funeral director and staff, and the fees for the goods and services you select or state law requires. Under the Funeral Rule:

- You have the right to choose the funeral goods and services you want, with some exceptions.

- The funeral provider must disclose this right in writing on the general price list.

- The funeral provider must disclose the specific state law that requires you to purchase any particular item on your itemized statement of goods and services selected.

The funeral provider may not refuse, or charge a fee, to handle a casket you bought elsewhere.

Statement of Funeral Goods and Services Selected

The funeral provider will give you an itemized statement of the total cost of the funeral goods and services you select. This statement also will disclose any legal, cemetery, or crematory requirements that require you to purchase any specific funeral goods or services.

The funeral provider must give you this statement after you select the funeral goods and services that you would like. The statement includes the prices of the individual items you are considering for purchase, as well as the total price, in one place. You can decide whether to add or subtract items. If the cost of cash advance items is not known at this time, the funeral provider must write down a "good faith estimate." The Rule does not require any specific form for this information. Funeral providers may include it in any document they give you at the end of your discussion about funeral arrangements.

Preservation and Protective Claims

The Funeral Rule prohibits funeral providers from telling you a particular funeral item or service can preserve the body of the deceased indefinitely in the grave. For example, funeral providers may not claim that embalming or a particular type of casket will preserve the deceased's body for an unlimited time.

The Rule also prohibits funeral providers from making claims that funeral goods, such as caskets or vaults, will keep out water, dirt, or other grave site substances if that is not true.

Other Considerations

Most decisions about purchasing funeral goods and services are made by people when they are grieving and under time constraints. Thinking ahead may help you make informed and thoughtful decisions about funeral arrangements, allow you to choose the specific items you want and need and compare prices offered by one or more funeral providers.

If you decide to make advance plans about funeral arrangements either for yourself or a loved one, you can choose among several types of dispositions and ceremonies. Your choice will affect the cost. Some people prefer a ceremonial service, religious or secular, with the body present. Others prefer cremation, which may be performed directly or after a ceremony. In addition, the deceased body may be donated (either directly or after a ceremony) to a medical or educational institution. To help ensure that your wishes are carried out, you may want to write down your preferences, and tell relatives and family friends what you decided.

For More Information

Most states have a licensing board that regulates the funeral industry. You may contact the licensing board in your state for information or help. Additional information about how to make funeral arrangements and the options available may be obtained from interested business, professional or consumer groups, such as memorial societies, which were discussed in Chapter 14.

REFERENCES

1. Mitford J: *The American Way of Death*. New York: Simon and Schuster, 1963.

2. "What is the Greediest Most Rapacious Industry in America? ...Mortuaries" [Editorial]. *Arizona Republic*, Dec. 29, 1985.

3. "Final Rip-off Can't Last Forever" [Editorial]. *Miami Herald*, June 20, 1978.

4. Wasik JF: "Fraud in the Funeral Industry." *Consumers Digest*, Sept/Oct., 1995: 53-9.

5. Federal Trade Commission: *Funerals: A Consumer Guide*. Washington, DC: FTC, Dec. 1996.

Chapter 16

PAYING FOR A FUNERAL: FEDERAL HELP

*I*n *certain circumstances, the United States Government will help the* survivors of the those who have died. Financial aid is given to cover the transportation and funeral expenses for deceased personnel of the Air Force, Army, Marine Corps, and Navy. The Federal Government also provides survivors with retiree benefits, veterans benefits, and Social Security benefits. These benefits are detailed here. The information is derived from the publications prepared by the National Funeral Directors Association and is reproduced with their kind permission.[1]

MILITARY FUNERAL POLICY

Care of Deceased Personnel of the Air Force, Army, Marine Corps and Navy

The United States Government provides for the care and disposition of the remains of members of the Armed Forces, active and reserve, who die while on active duty status. In most instances, military authorities will assist with the arrangements for these services within amounts allowed by the government, or the next of kin may make their own arrangements if they choose to and claim reimbursement in the amounts allowed.

The U.S. Government will also provide for the preparation of the remains as well as for casketing (primary expenses) and clothing (if not available in the personal effects of the deceased). In addition, the Government pays for a military escort to accompany the remains to the place of funeral and final disposition, a United States flag to accompany the remains to the place of funeral and final disposition, and for the transportation of the remains to the place designated by the next of kin.

Military authorities will arrange for the preparation and shipment of the remains, if desired. Most likely, a funeral with a U.S. Government contract will be engaged. If no government contract is in effect with a funeral director or service provider and the next of kin chooses to make the arrangements him or herself, the maximum reimbursement for preparation and casketing (primary expenses) will be $1,750. If a government contract is in effect and the next of kin chooses to make the arrangements, reimbursement for preparation and casketing will be the contract price or the actual cost, whichever is less.

Military authorities will make the arrangements and will pay for the transportation of the remains. However, if the next of kin makes such arrangements the reimbursement cannot exceed what it would have cost the government to forward the remains.

The government also allows for interment expenses. If the remains of the service member are to be interred in a private cemetery, reimbursement is limited to $3,100. If the remains are to be forwarded directly to a national cemetery, the maximum reimbursement is $110. Finally, if the remains are consigned to a funeral home which will be responsible for delivery to a national cemetery, the maximum reimbursement is $2,000.

In the event a death has occurred but the remains have not been recovered, the government will provide reimbursement for up to $2,000 to cover a memorial service.

Members of the Reserves of each of the Armed Forces and members of the National Guard who die while on active duty, while performing inactive duty training, or while travelling to and from such training, are authorized to receive the same primary/interment allowances as are active duty personnel. They are also authorized these allowances if they die while being hospitalized or undergoing treatment for an injury, illness, or disease incurred or aggravated while on active duty or while participating in inactive duty training.

Military members who are entitled to retired pay, retainer pay or to the equivalent are also entitled to receive transportation of their remains at the government's expense from the place of death to a place of burial that is no further distant than the decedent's last place of permanent residence. Transportation is authorized to a location in the United States, including territories or possessions of the United States. The amount paid for transportation may not exceed the cost of transportation from the place of death to the decedent's last place of permanent residence in the United States or to territories or possessions of the United States. Any dependents of military personnel who die while properly admitted to a military facility in the United States are also entitled to this provision.

Requests for reimbursement should be made on DD Form 1375 and then mailed to one of the following addresses:

For Air Force Personnel:

To the Mortuary Officer of the installation which provided the DD Form 1375 to the next of kin.

For Army Force Personnel:

To the Mortuary Officer of the installation which provided the DD Form 1375 to the next of kin, or if the next of kin made their own arrangements to: CRD Perscom, Attn: TAPC-PED-D, Alexandria, VA 22331-0482.

For Army National Guard:

To the Chief, National Guard Bureau, Attn: NCB-ARL-LG, Washington, DC 20310-2500.

For Navy and Marine Corps Personnel:

To the Office of Medical/Dental Affairs, Attn: Mortuary Affairs, Great Lakes, IL 60088-5200.

For Coast Guard Personnel:

To the Commandant, U.S. Coast Guard (G-PS-5), Washington, DC 20593-0001.

Funeral homes interested in a "mortuary contract" to serve any camp, post, station or base should contract the Mortuary Officer of the facility.

FEDERAL GOVERNMENT RETIREE BENEFITS[2]

This section contains information for anyone interested in knowing what to do after the death of a federal employee, retiree, or survivor. If you or they have any additional questions, call the United States Office of Personnel Management at (202) 606-0500.

The following information is provided to assist survivors of federal employees or former federal employees about:

- Potential death benefits payable under the Civil Service Retirement System (CSRS) or the Federal Employees' Retirement System (FERS).
- Who to contact to report the death.
- What to do with the retirement payments received after death.

To help make a decision on where to apply for death benefits, use the following.

Decision Factor

1. If the deceased was *currently employed by the federal government*, then contact the agency where the deceased was employed. NFDA can provide the address and phone number of any federal agency.

2. If the deceased was a *federal retiree* who was receiving or had applied to receive a CSRS or FERS benefit, or if the deceased was a former employee but was not eligible to receive a CSRS or FERS benefit; or if the deceased was *the spouse or child of a former federal employee* and receiving a survivor benefit from the CSRS or FERS, then call the Office of Personnel Management at (202) 606-0500. Someone is available to answer questions at this number from 7:30 am to 5:30 p.m. EST. Recorded reports of death may be left at this number 24 hours a day. Or you may send a written report to the Office of Personnel Management, Retirement Operations Center, P.O. Box 45, Boyers, PA 16017-0001. In addition, you can fax a copy of the death certificate with a cover sheet providing the name of the deceased, retirement number,

date of birth, Social Security number, name of survivor and address to send application forms to fax number (412) 794-1263.

Survivor Benefits

If the deceased was a current government employee, the deceased's employing agency will provide assistance and application forms. If the deceased was a former government employee, the Office of Personnel Management will provide application forms and assistance, determine whether any benefits are payable to survivors, and make payments to eligible beneficiaries.

Life Insurance Claims

If the deceased was insured under the Federal Employees' Group Life Insurance Program, notify the U.S. Office of Personnel Management, P.O. Box 45, Boyers, PA 16017. The Office of Personnel Management will supply the proper claim form. The claim form should be filed with the Office of Federal Employees' Group Life Insurance, 4 East 24th Street, New York, NY 10010.

Annuity Checks

Return any uncashed retirement checks payable to the deceased to:
Director, Disbursing Center
United States Treasury Department
P.O. Box 8670
Chicago, IL 60680
Such checks are not legally negotiable.

If retirement checks are received after the payee's date of death and are cashed or deposited in the deceased payee's bank account, the Treasury Department will recover the amount of the checks from the bank or other financial institution. The financial institution will, in turn, recover the money from the negotiator of the check(s). All money due the retiree at the date of death will be paid to the eligible survivors.

Direct Deposit Payments

Direct deposit payments made to a decedent's account after his or her death should not be removed from the account. Please notify the financial institution of the death and whether any payments have been withdrawn.

In all cases in which funds have been placed in an account after the recipient's death, let the Treasury take recovery action. Do not attempt to make direct repayment by personal check or by money order, for this could result in the money involved being collected twice. If the Treasury recovery action does not recover all funds paid after death, the negotiator of the check(s) or the estate will be billed for the amount of any remaining overpayment.

VETERANS BENEFITS[3]

Burial in National Cemeteries

Eligibility for burial in a Veterans Administration (VA) national cemetery is based on the length of time in active military service and on the nature of the veteran's separation from the service.

Members of the United States Armed Forces who died on active duty and veterans who were discharged or separated from active duty under conditions other than dishonorable are eligible for burial in national cemeteries. Limitations to this eligibility began in 1980. Veterans who entered active duty as enlisted personnel after September 7, 1980, and all veterans who entered active duty after October 16, 1981 must meet the following criteria to be eligible for burial in a national cemetery:

- Have served at least 24 months of active duty or for the entire period they were called to active duty, or
- Have received a hardship discharge or a service-connected disability.

Burial in a VA national cemetery is also available to the spouse, widow or widower of any eligible veteran so long as they have not remarried. It is also available to the veteran's dependent minor children.

A pamphlet titled "Interments in National Cemeteries" is available from VA regional offices. It provides detailed information on national cemetery burial arrangements. Applications for burial should be made at the time of death by contacting the director of the national cemetery desired. Funeral directors often provide this service.

Be advised that Arlington National Cemetery is under the jurisdiction of the Department of the Army, not the Department of Veterans Affairs. With the exception of cremated remains, burial is limited to specific categories of military personnel and veterans. For more information, write to the Superintendent, Arlington National Cemetery, Arlington, VA 22211, or call (800) 827-1000.

Burial Benefits and Plot Allowances

A veteran who dies as a result of a service-connected disability is entitled to a maximum of $1,500 for burial and funeral expenses. The costs of transporting the body to the national cemetery nearest the veteran's home may also be paid.

Veterans who die for reasons other than service-connected disabilities on or after October 1, 1981 may be entitled to up to $300 in burial benefits. Eligibility is established if the veteran:

- Was entitled at the time of death to receive a pension or compensation, or:

- Died while hospitalized or domiciled in a VA facility or other facility at VA expense.

Eligibility may also be established in the case of some indigent veterans whose remains are unclaimed.

For deaths occurring on or after November 1, 1990, an additional plot or interment allowance of up to $150 is available to the same categories of veterans eligible for the $300 burial benefits, and to those who are discharged or retired from service because of a disability which was incurred or who retired from service because of a disability which was incurred or aggravated in the line of duty. Veterans of any war who died prior to November 1, 1990 were also eligible for the plot allowance. The plot allowance is provided only for those veterans who are not buried in a national cemetery.

Claims for VA burial benefits must generally be filed within two years of permanent burial or cremation. Additional costs of transporting a body may be allowed if the veteran died at a VA hospital or other facility at VA expense, or if the veteran died in transit at VA expense to or from a medical facility. Members of the reserves or of the national guard who die as a result of active duty for training may also be eligible for burial benefits.

Either the funeral director or the individual paying the burial expenses may claim reimbursement for burial and plot allowances through any VA office.

Headstone or Grave Marker Benefits

Veterans eligible for burial in a national cemetery, buried on or after October 18,1978, are entitled to a government-provided headstone or grave marker, regardless of whether they are buried in a national cemetery. Applications for a government-provided headstone should be made on VA Form 40-1330, and mailed to the Office of Memorial Programs (403A), Department of Veterans Affairs, Washington, DC 20420. For information regarding the status of an application, call this same office at (202) 275-1494 or 275-1495.

For deaths occurring before November 1, 1990, a monetary allowance of up to $100 is available in lieu of the government-provided headstone, for veterans not buried in a national cemetery. This allowance can be applied to the purchase or placement of the headstone, or for an additional engraving of an existing monument. This monetary allowance is not available for deaths occurring on or after November 1, 1990.

Claims for the marker allowance should be filed on VA Form 21-8834, be accompanied by a receipt and mailed to the regional office nearest you.

Other Benefits

Applications for a memorial marker may be filed by the next of kin to commemorate any veteran whose remains were not recovered or identified, who was buried at sea or cremated with all ashes scattered, or whose remains were donated to science.

Memorial markers may be erected in private cemeteries in plots provided by the applicant, or in a memorial section of a national cemetery. Applications for memorial markers should be made on VA Form 40-1330 and mailed to the Office of Memorial Programs at the address given above.

VA regional offices can generally assist with any burial benefit questions. They can also aid in the acquisition of an American flag to be draped on the casket of an eligible veteran, and in obtaining a Presidential Memorial Certificate. VA regional offices also provide assistance with claims for other VA death benefits such as dependency and indemnity compensation, nonservice-connected death pensions, and survivors' and dependents' education. A list of VA regional offices is provided below.

Presidential Memorial Certificate Benefit

The Presidential Memorial Certificate is a parchment certificate with a calligraphic inscription expressing the nation's grateful recognition of the veteran's service. The veteran's name is inscribed and the certificate bears the signature of the President.

Eligible recipients of the certificate include the next of kin, other relatives or friends. A local VA Regional Office generally originates the application for a Presidential Memorial Certificate if a veteran's death is brought to official attention. Requests for additional, replacement or corrected certificates may be made through the local VA Regional Office. For the location of the nearest VA facility, call (800) 827-1000.

SOCIAL SECURITY BENEFITS[4]

Lump-Sum Death Benefits

Survivors of deceased workers who have credit for 18 months to 10 years of work covered by Social Security (depending upon the age of the worker at the time of death) may be entitled to Social Security Administration survivor benefits.

The following individuals may be eligible to receive survivor benefits:

- A widow or widower at age 60 or older (50 if disabled) or at any age if caring for an entitled child who is either under the age of 16 or disabled.
- A divorced widow or widower at age 60 or older (50 if disabled) if the marriage lasted 10 years, or if caring for an entitled child who is either under the age of 16 or disabled.
- Unmarried children up to age 18 (or age 19 if they are attending primary or secondary school full time).

- Children who were disabled before reaching age 22, as long as they remain disabled.
- Dependent parent or parents age 62 or older.

A lump-sum death payment of $255 is paid in addition to monthly cash benefits, in the following order of priority:

- A surviving spouse who lived in the same household as the deceased worker at the time of death.
- A surviving spouse eligible for or entitled to benefits for the month of the death.
- A child or children eligible for or entitled to benefits for the month of the death.

Application for survivor benefits can be made at any Social Security Office, or by phone at (800) 772-1213. The following information is required:

- Applicant's and the deceased worker's social security number.
- Proof of the applicant's age.
- Proof of marriage, if applicant is applying for widow's or widower's benefits.
- Proof of the worker's death.
- Children's birth certificates, if they are to receive benefits.
- Deceased worker's Form W-2, or federal tax return if self-employed, for the most recent tax year.
- Proof of support if applicant is applying for benefits as a dependent parent or grandchild of the deceased worker.

It is also advisable for the applicant to provide the Social Security Administration (SSA) with information on checking or savings accounts so that benefits can be deposited directly into the applicant's bank account. In addition to being convenient and safer than mailing checks, this is SSA's customary method of paying benefits.

SSA strongly encourages funeral directors to routinely file Form SSA-721, "Statement of Death by Funeral Director." The agency contends that the timely notification of death by funeral directors provides leads to people who may be eligible for benefits and results in fewer beneficiaries receiving incorrect payments after death. Form SSA-721 was revised in April 1991 to include a tear-off sheet of benefit information for families and SSA's new toll-free information number, (800) 772-1213.

Supplemental Security Income Eligibility

In determining and maintaining eligibility for Supplemental Security Income (SSI), a countable resource limitation is established for an individual and for a couple. The current limits on countable resources are $2,000 and $3,000, respectively.

The law specifies that burial funds up to $1,500 each for an individual and spouse's funeral as well as all resources set aside for burial space expenses are excluded from an individual's countable resources for SSI eligibility purposes. Income and accruals on burial funds and burial space are also excluded.

Assets to pay for the services defined under "burial fund" and merchandise or property defined under "burial space" must be segregated from a purchaser's other assets. Usually, preneed contracts (which are regulated under 47 different state laws) provide that segregation.

In most situations, one preneed contract covers both the burial fund and the burial space, although separate values are delineated for the various items. Such a breakdown is recommended to show compliance with SSA law.

If an individual has a revocable, prearranged funeral contract, which may or may not include provisions for a repository, that contract constitutes a countable resource unless it is excluded under the provisions of the "burial space" and/or "burial fund" provisions of the law. An irrevocable contract for final disposition, including income from the contract, is not considered a resource.

"Burial funds" are separately identifiable assets which are clearly set aside for burial and may include:

- Revocable burial contracts or trusts.
- Bank accounts clearly designated for burial expenses.
- Life insurance policies that are countable and not excluded by another provision of the Social Security Act.

- Assets with a ready cash value, otherwise countable as resources, that an individual clearly designates as set aside for burial.

The maximum legal limit for exclusion of funds set aside for the burial fund (services) is $1,500 plus future interest and accruals. Therefore, to the extent that the aggregate price of basic services, embalming, other preparations, transportation, visitation, funeral services, other use of facilities and merchandise (other than casket, vault and urn) exceeds $1,500, the excess will not be excluded as a resource. Additionally, the $1,500 maximum limit is subject to the following reductions:

- The face value of any excluded life insurance policy (if total value exceeds $1,500, the cash surrender value must be counted as a resource).
- The amount of any funds held in an irrevocable trust or other irrevocable arrangement which is available for burial expenses.

Interest earned on excluded burial funds and appreciation of the value of excluded burial arrangements is excluded if the interest is also designated for burial.

"Burial space" means burial plots, grave sites, crypts, mausoleums, urns, niches or other customary and traditional repositories for the remains of deceased persons. The term also includes improvements or additions to or upon such spaces, including, but not limited to, vaults, headstones, markers, plaques, or burial containers (i.e. caskets), and the arrangements for opening and closing the grave site. The definition includes burial spaces purchased by contract if paid in full or otherwise held for the individual's use. If an individual owns a repository for the body and the grave site, both are excluded from an individual's resources. Items included in burial space plus future interest and accruals are also excluded from an individual's resources.

State laws and practices are the final determinant regarding the management and accounting of prearranged funeral contracts.

Because SSI applications also serve as Medicaid applications in many states, the SSI exemptions and preneed contract practices just described may not be totally applicable. Some states use more restrictive criteria than that used for SSI in determining Medicaid eligibility, and others make their own Medicaid determinations using SSI criteria.

KNOW YOUR BENEFITS

In the event of a death, the federal government may provide help in several different ways. If you are a federal government worker or if you are in the United States Armed Forces, you should familiarize yourself with the benefits you may be entitled to. Furthermore, your survivors should also be aware of these benefits. Simply call the United States Office of Personnel Management, Treasury Department or any Social Security Office to get further assistance.

REFERENCES

1. National Funeral Directors Association: *Military Funeral Policy*, [Brochure] 1998.
2. NFDA: *Federal Government Retiree Benefits*, [Brochure]1998.
3. NFDA: *Veterans Benefits*, [Brochure] 1998.
4. NFDA: *Social Security Benefits*, [Brochure] 1998.

Chapter 17

DEATH OVERSEAS

From ship to shore
In many a folklore
Around the world, in every town,
At any time, life can come tumbling down.

—Author Unknown

*T*he U.S. State Department indicates that about 6,000 Americans die in foreign countries every year. When a death occurs abroad, many questions are raised and many problems are created. The host country may not be able to take proper steps to handle the remains of a United States citizen because of the lack of knowledge of procedures.

Local laws and religious beliefs sometimes hamper appropriate and rapid action. The family of the deceased may encounter difficulties in getting information about the circumstances of death, or in identification of the deceased, transportation of the deceased, disposition of the remains and the cost involved. The funeral directors involved in handling such a situation might have to face unusual problems because of difficulties of communication, lack of a corresponding funeral director in the country where death occurred and the absence of reciprocity agreements. Despite these seemingly unsolvable problems, if a proper procedure is followed by the funeral director and the family members, many of the problems can be solved fairly easily.

WHEN DEATH OCCURS

When a U.S. citizen dies abroad, the best help comes from the State Department. The State Department has consular officers in every U.S.

embassy or consulate. The consular officer has certain responsibilities mandated by statutes. These responsibilities include:

- Reporting the death to the State Department
- Reporting the death to the deceased person's next-of-kin or legal representative
- Completing of Consular Report of Death
- Helping in identification of the deceased
- Carrying out the wishes of the deceased regarding the disposition of the body if there is no legal representative or next-of-kin, and
- Acting as a provisional conservator of the estate of the deceased until the family or a legal representative arrives, and providing instructions for the disposition of personal effects.

To fulfill his responsibility regarding notifying the proper individuals about the death, the consular officer first tries to contact the relatives by telephone using the name and telephone number in the "emergency contact" section of the decedent's passport. The embassy follows up with a written notification of death. This usually includes an explanation of circumstances of death, a description of options available for disposition of the body, the costs of disposition and advice on obtaining copies of the Consular Report of Death.

The consular officer assists the family member in choosing a funeral home and in transferring the funds needed for the disposition of the body to that funeral home. The funds can be wired to the State Department and they are then transferred to the funeral home through an Overseas Citizens Services Trust.

Identification of the deceased is one of the important and first responsibilities of the consular officer. Visual identification is often made by comparing the deceased with the photograph in the passport. If there are problems in identifying the body, the consular officer often provides the local investigators whatever information that may be needed. This may include finger prints, dental records, DNA evidence, etc.

Disposition of the remains of a U.S. citizen who has died overseas is often complicated. The complication may be created by local laws, difficulties in identifying the dead person, condition of the body and the costs involved. However, the consular officer is always at the center of the affair to provide help to the local authorities, to the funeral directors in the host country and in the United States, and to the relatives of the deceased. He assists the family in the disposition of the body in the host country. If the body is to be shipped to the United States, he assures proper preparation of the documents in accordance with foreign regulations and U.S. federal and local laws. These documents include the Consular Mortuary Certificate, an embalmer's affidavit, a local transit permit and the death certificate.

Some situations further complicate the disposition of the dead. For instance, deaths on cruise ships, in remote places like the Alps or Himalayas, or multiple deaths in plane crashes may delay disposition. In 1978, the mass-suicide by more than 900 Americans in Jonestown, Guyana created the problem of the identification of the remains due to decomposition.

THE OPTIONS

Whereas the consular officer in a U.S. embassy abroad is familiar with his responsibilities and will act rapidly and appropriately when confronted with the news of the death of a U.S. citizen abroad, the funeral director in the United States and the relatives of the deceased may not know what to do right away. They have to make immediate decisions regarding the disposition of the body. The first thing they should do is to call the case officer at the State Department Office of the Overseas Citizens Services and Crisis Management. He or she can be reached at (202) 647-5226, between 8:15 a.m. and 10 p.m. Eastern Standard Time on weekdays, 9 a.m. to 3 p.m. on Saturdays, and at (202) 647-1512 after hours and on Sundays.[1] This office not only keeps close contact with the consular officers abroad, relays messages expeditiously, but it also provides answers to all questions from the funeral directors and the next-of -kin.

Once the initial inquiry is made, the family of the deceased should make quick decisions as to the disposition of the body, and communicate these decisions to the consular officer via Overseas Citizens Services. In most countries the following options are available:

- Return of body to United States
- Burial in host country

- Cremation in host country, and
- Return of the cremated remains to the United States.

It must be understood by the family and the funeral director that the State Department does not pay for preparing and returning the remains or for burial or cremation abroad. No U.S. government funds are available for this, even if the family is indigent. However, there are special benefits for U.S. government employees and their survivors. These are discussed in Chapter 16.

RETURN OF THE BODY TO THE UNITED STATES

Most commonly, the family chooses to have the body of the deceased returned to the United States. In 1996, there were 5831 deaths of United States citizens abroad. Of these, 1931 remains were returned to the United States. The cost of preparing and shipping the remains can be high. It can cost over $5,000 to transfer the body from Europe to the United States, and over $10,000 to transfer the body from Japan. The consular office will help in transferring funds to cover these costs. This may be greatly helpful because the funeral director in the host country may not start providing services until he receives payment.

The body has to be properly prepared before shipment. Preparation of the remains must be done in accordance with local laws and customs. Embalming can be a big problem in some countries.It must be done expeditiously to prevent decomposition. In Brazil, for instance, the law requires that the body has to be buried if it is not embalmed within 24 hours of death. The embalming practices and the quality of embalming vary from country to country. In Nepal, for instance, embalming is not permitted at all. In most countries the facilities and the methods of embalming are poor, and hence the remains that arrive in the United States may not be appropriate for viewing. In such instances, the funeral directors in the United States may have to take further action to restore the appearances of the remains.

BURIAL OF THE BODY IN A HOST COUNTRY

Burying the body in the host country is also a commonly selected option. In this case, the family may fly to the host country and organize the burial. If this is not possible, they might get help from the consular office. Although the consular officer makes arrangements concerning the selection of burial site and burial ceremonies, the family will still have to pay for the costs. If identification of the body is not possible, the host country may order burial. Some countries do not permit burial of foreign nationals in their land.

CREMATION OF THE BODY IN THE HOST COUNTRY

Cremation is a relatively easy and less expensive option. Most foreign countries allow cremation. They are usually carried out in open air. Special cremation facilities like the ones in the United States are difficult to find. The body may have to be transported away from the place of death to a cremation facility. Some Muslim countries and areas with a predominantly Catholic population may forbid cremation of human remains. In Greece and Israel, cremation is prohibited by law, and hence the facilities for cremation are not available.

CREMATION AND RETURN OF CREMAINS TO THE UNITED STATES

If cremation of the remains is to be carried out abroad and the remains are to be brought to the United States, the consular office will provide all assistance but the family will be responsible for paying all expenses.

REFERENCE

1. King K: "State Department Help When Americans Die Overseas." *The Director.* May, 1998: 61-63.

Chapter 18

DEATH ... HERE COME THE LAWYERS

Death is not the end;
there remains the litigation.

—Ambrose Bierce (1842-1914)

We live in a litigious world. Unfortunately death often creates conflicts and controversies resulting in legal actions. It is important to examine death and its consequences in order to reduce the chances of litigation and to minimize grief. In this chapter, a discussion of death-related situations that may lead to legal tangles is first presented. These may take the form of suits against survivors, funeral directors, or medical professionals. This is followed by the discussion of actions that can be taken to prevent or minimize the pains of litigation.

LAWYERS AND SURVIVORS

Lawyers get involved when there are questions about the estate of the deceased. The Federal government may want money from the survivors. The state might come looking to collect taxes, too. The lawyers may be dragged in to resolve the issues of inheritance arising out of fights for money among surviving heirs.

The lawyers will be there whether it is a single death or multiple deaths in mass disasters. They will be there whether it is a criminal case or a civil case. In every homicide death, an attorney is involved. Suicides also raise legal questions. In cases of accidents, there are issues of damages.

Events involving multiple fatalities create elaborate legal fights. For instance, the tobacco companies have given billions of dollars to several states to settle cases involving damages for health problems and deaths from cigarette smoking. On December 3, 1984, a Union Carbide India Ltd. chemical plant in Bhopal, India spewed forth toxic gases killing 1861 people and gravely injuring more than 26,800 others. Within a week a Bhopal gold rush began: the lawyers jumped in and nearly 500,000 people signed retainer agreements. The case settled for hundreds of millions of dollars. Similarly, after a prolonged battle, the survivors of holocaust victims recently received billions of dollars from the German government.

In the past, medical professionals were held in high esteem. Today, the sense that physicians are miracle workers has eroded significantly. Malpractice suits against doctors have been on the rise. Malpractice usually occurs if 1) medications are prescribed in dosages in excess of those recommended, 2) drugs and equipment that have not been approved by the FDA are used, 3) a doctor fails to follow standard procedures and causes misdiagnosis, or 4) nurses fail to follow the doctors' orders. In hospitals, the surgeons have left towels and instruments in the patients' bodies, operated on the wrong patients or amputated wrong extremities.

I was involved in an unusual "malpractice" case myself, some years ago. On May 25, 1968, I was a Medical Examiner for the City of Richmond in Virginia. I authorized the removal of heart from a decedent for the first heart transplant at the Medical College of Virginia. The decedent had sustained severe head injuries in a fall and died as a result of these injuries. About 23 months later, the administrator of the estate of the decedent filed a suit against me and the members of the transplant team. The suit alleged that we pronounced the person dead ahead of his actual death, removed his heart and thus caused his death. The case was tried by a jury.

During the trial it was shown that the decedent had suffered brain death before the heart was removed. The jury returned the verdict in our favor. However, as a consequence of this suit, the General Assembly of Virginia enacted a new definition of death in 1973. This definition included, for the first time, "absence of spontaneous brain function" as a criterion to pronounce death.[1]

It is important to take certain actions in life to prevent legal problems after death. Pre-death planning will reduce grief for the survivors and prevent unnecessary legal bills.

LAWYERS AND FUNERAL DIRECTORS

As in any occupation, errors can occur in the funeral profession. These errors may result from personal failures, system failures, or through accidents. Sometimes these errors create legal actions. The malpractice actions may be legitimate, they may be just nuisance suits or they may be the result of greed. Regardless of whether they are merited, lawsuits always create a nightmare for the funeral director. Whether liability is proven or not, legal actions invariably cost a lot in terms of time, money and aggravation.

Unauthorized Cremations

In one legal dispute,[2] the widow of the deceased brought action against a funeral home, crematory and other parties for cremating the remains of her husband without authorization. She claimed damages for negligent infliction of emotional distress. The trial court dismissed the suit but the appellate court agreed to review the dismissal. An Illinois appeals court found that the plaintiff was not able to show that she suffered physical injury and hence affirmed the dismissal. The dismissal was based on the finding that the plaintiff was not in the "zone of physical danger" and was not a "direct victim" of cremation without authorization.

Despite the fact that the defendants prevailed, they incurred considerable amount of inconvenience and costs of defending at trial and for appeal.

Liability for Accident Incurred While Using the Company Car

A mortuary supervisor used a limousine owned by the funeral home to pick up an employee of that funeral home. On the way, the limousine collided with another car, causing head and face injuries to the passenger in that car. The passenger sued the funeral home for property damage and personal injuries. He was awarded $100,000 in damages. The case was appealed but the Court of Appeals of Georgia (*Randall Memorial Mortuary V. O'Quinn*, 414 S.E. 2d. Ga. App. 1992) upheld the award stating that the claimed "personal use" of funeral home car by a supervisor to pick up an employee was "a business use of the car."[3]

Defective Caskets

There have been some interesting cases pertaining to defective caskets.[4] In one case, the casket started to fall apart while "the body was being carried from the hearse to the grave." In this case, the plaintiff sued the funeral home for emotional distress damages. But the court ruled in favor of the defendant, stating that the plaintiffs cannot recover unless they show "an actual physical impact or touching of themselves by the defendant or his product."

In another case, a defective casket failed to latch at the time of interment. As a result, the relatives saw parts of the deceased through a gap between the lid and bottom of the casket. They sued the funeral home for emotional distress on the basis of breach of contract. The court ruled that the funeral home had breached the contract by providing a "defective" casket.

A casket was bought by another family. It came with a "written warranty stating it had been tested air and weather tight." Yet, the decedent's grave was found sunken and wet about two and one-half months later. The family was distraught and requested the cemetery to disinter the casket. The disinterred casket was found to be full of water. The family sued but the court found that the warranty applied only to the condition of the casket at the time of burial.

Liability Arising out of Mishandling of Remains

In a case discussed in *The Legal Compass*,[5] relatives and friends of over 16,000 decedents sued a funeral home and crematory in Los Angeles area for the negligent and intentional mishandling of their loved one's remains. They alleged that the defendants "removed and harvested without authorization" numerous organs and body parts including corneas, eyes, hearts, lungs and bones, and sold them for profit. The appellate court ruled that all family members and close friends of the deceased could sue if they were claiming intentional mishandling of the remains. On appeal, the State

Supreme Court of California limited the right of those suing and ruled that only close family members had a right to sue.

Burial of the Wrong Body

A Wisconsin case resulted when one deceased person was buried in another person's casket. The next day, the family members of this deceased person discovered that the wrong body was in their decedent's casket. The family sued the funeral home and its insurance company, alleging that they suffered physical and emotional injuries because of the premature burial. However, they were not able to present expert medical testimony to show that their injuries were linked to the substitution of the bodies. The Wisconsin court of appeals dismissed the family's claims.[6]

Failure to Maintain the Grave

If a funeral service agrees to provide continuous care to maintain their clients' graves in proper condition, they cannot afford to neglect them. In New York, the law specifically requires that cemeteries maintain graves in proper condition and maintenance. In one suit against the cemetery, plaintiffs won damages for distress and mental anguish resulting from poor maintenance of the grave of their deceased (*Yochim V. Mount Hope Cemetery Association*, - N.Y.S. 2d - , 1994 WL 762 640, NYC Court).[7]

Autopsy without Authorization

In a case described by T. Scott Gilligan,[8] an autopsy was performed on a deceased individual by Duke University Hospital. The body was returned to the funeral director without the major organs, eyes and spinal column. The family sued Duke University, alleging that the autopsy was unauthorized, done in such a way that it prevented embalming, and that the major organs were not returned with the body. The family was deprived of the opportunity to perform the tradition of an open-casket, final touch and good-bye kiss, and had to opt for closed casket ceremony. The family won the suit. The jury awarded $142,500 in compensation damages and $11.25 million in punitive damages. One of the jurors, however, changed her vote on the amount of punitive damages. After that, the jury could not resolve the dead lock. A new jury will be convened at a later date to decide the punitive damages.

Some religious faiths object to an autopsy. If an autopsy is done over their objections, legal action can arise, as was exemplified by a case in New York.[9] In this case, a partial autopsy was performed on the body of an Orthodox Jew despite the family's objection to the autopsy on religious grounds. The family sued the funeral home. The jury awarded the plaintiff $75,000 in compensatory damages and $1,350,000 in punitive damages. The case was appealed to the New York State Supreme Court because the trial court dismissed the punitive damage award. The Supreme Court ordered a new trial to determine the amount of punitive damages but gave the plaintiff the option to accept $650,000.

Mishandling of Cremated Remains

In Illinois, a woman sued a funeral home because she did not receive all of her daughter's cremated remains from the funeral home as requested. She claimed that she could not fulfill her daughter's burial wishes and suffered physical trauma, mental anguish, loss of sleep, vomiting, and constant worry. She sought damages in excess of $50,000. The U.S. District Court in Illinois ruled that she could bring the action in federal court, because of punitive damage legality.[10]

Incomplete Embalming

In New Mexico, a funeral director failed to perform complete embalming that was "expressly authorized." The family claimed that partial embalming breached the preneed contract and resulted in emotional distress. The widow was awarded $100,000 judgement plus punitive damages.[11]

Unauthorized Embalming

Unauthorized embalming is not an uncommon allegation. However, the damages claimed do not amount to much. Embalming is not required except in some special circumstances, as detailed in the chapter on embalming. The funeral director should not embalm the body without proper authorization. If embalming is performed without authorization, the funeral director must certainly not bill the family for the service.

Miscellaneous Complaints

Some errors on the part of the funeral director do not necessarily result in legal actions. However, they do make the practice of the profession somewhat unpleasant. My own informal surveys show that complaints about poor make-up of the face, lost personal effects, and missing dentures are not uncommon.

PREVENTION OF NIGHTMARE SCENARIOS

In our litigious society, we cannot expect to eliminate all lawsuits. However, here are some steps funeral professionals can take to prevent malpractice actions against them, or at least to minimize the risk.[13]

Steps by Funeral Directors

- Obtain adequate malpractice insurance.
- Educate the staff through continuing education programs to identify and reduce the risks of malpractice.
- Strictly enforce compliance with state laws, and follow the Environmental Protection Agency (EPA) and the Occupational Safety and Health Administration (OSHA) guidelines.
- Require the staff to follow the FTC Funeral Rule rigidly, and insist on consistency.[14]
- Obtain proper authorization for any services to be rendered, such as organ donation, cremation, embalming and autopsy.
- Document the details of any mishaps or errors.
- Be aware of ethnic and cultural differences in the conduct of a funeral.
- Maintain high-caliber public relations policy.
- Seek counsel from a qualified attorney as soon as the need is indicated.

The Consumer's Part

In a broad plan of preparing for a funeral, one of the most important things you can do is to prepare a will and a living will. These wills should be made as early as possible, because accidents can happen any time. Full details about wills and living wills are presented in previous chapters.

The will allows you to have the opportunity to direct the way you want your property distributed. Without a will, your family will be saddled with uncertainty, needless work, a lot of legal expenses and estate tax liabilities. A living will also helps you make a valid directive to your physicians to withhold or withdraw certain treatments when you are suffering from an illness or injury from which you are not expected to recover. Your kin will be spared the agony of making such difficult decisions.

The organization Choice in Dying also recommends completing a document called the Durable Power of Attorney for Health Care.[12] With this you appoint someone in advance to make decisions for you when you cannot make these decisions yourself. This document is important because the living will statutes don't always cover every possible contingency that you may face in a health care crisis.

The documents pertaining to the will should be stored in a place where they can be easily found by your survivors. One copy of the living will should be given to your doctor and another to your family members. All documents related to ownership of real estate, including the cemetery plot, should be easily accessible to your family members. It is advisable to prepare a special file to hold these documents as well as instructions about your funeral, burial (or cremation), body and/or organ donation and all prepaid funeral arrangements.

REFERENCES

1. Fatteh A: "A Lawsuit that Led to the Redefinition of Death." *The Journal of Legal Medicine*. July-Aug 1973: 30-34.
2. "Wrongful Cremation: Surviving Spouse Cannot Claim the Negligent Infliction of Emotional Distress." *Legal Compass*, Dec. 1992, 57:12, 2747.
3. "The Company Car: Personal use Makes Mortuary Liable for $100,000 in Damages." *Legal Compass*, July 1992, 57:7, 2727.
4. Troutman R, Crichton C: "Funeral Firm Liability in Defective Caskets." *The American Funeral Director*. Jan. 1992, 57:1, 20-21.

5. "Dying to Sue: California Supreme Court Limits Right to Sue Funeral Homes, Crematories for Mishandling Remains." *Legal Compass*, Jan. 1992, 57:1, 2703.

6. "Premature Burial: Family Members Denied Emotional Distress Damages for Burial of Wrong Body." *Legal Compass*, May 1994, 59:5, 2815.

7. "Cemetery Must Pay Mental Distress Damages to Family Member for Failure to Provide Grave Maintenance." *Legal Compass*, May/June 1995, 60:5, 2863.

8. Gilligan TS: "Legal Liability for Autopsy and Organ Donation Cases." *The Director*, June 1998: 68-9.

9. "Funeral Home Must Pay Punitive Damages for Initiating Autopsy." *Legal Compass*, Nov. 1996, 61:11, 2935.

10. "Claims for the Mishandling of Cremated Remains Worth at Least $50,000 in Federal Court." *Legal Compass*, 61:8, Aug. 1996: 2923.

11. "Exhumation Reveals Partial Embalming: $100,000 Judgment Plus Punitive Damages." *Legal Compass*, 59:4, Apr. 1994: 2811.

12. Choice in Dying: "Choice in Dying Issues: Background on the Right to Die." Online. Available: *http://www.choices.org/issues.htm*, 1998.

13. Lapin HI: "Avoiding Litigation." *Funeral Service Business and Legal Guide*, issue 6, 1992.

14. Gilligan TS: "Avoiding FTC Funeral Rule Liability." *The Director*, Feb. 1993: 30-31.

Section V:
Regulation of the
Funeral Industry

Chapter 19

ALL FUNERAL DIRECTORS ARE NOT CROOKS!

Being a physician, lawyer and a pathologist, I have worked closely with the medical, legal and funeral profession and have carefully observed the practices and ethics of these three professions. After thirty-nine years of non-biased scrutiny, my conclusion is that the funeral professional should be ranked number one in respectability as compared to any other professional.

WHO WOULD WANT TO BE A FUNERAL DIRECTOR?

Funeral directors deal with death and its survivors. It is a serious business, with no place for humor. Funeral professionals have a heavy burden to counsel the survivors and to care for the grief-stricken. They continually must put aside all of their personal problems to cope with the troubles of others. Death does not always come during business hours, and a funeral director has to respond to a survivor's call immediately, at any time of day or night. These initial calls always pertain to the ultimate loss, and the director must exhibit supreme calm and composure, and must provide appropriate advice. The funeral director not only deals with the survivors' emotions and sorrow, but he also must render counsel on choices and prices. He has to deal with the touchy issues of affordability while the consumer is experiencing the most intense moments of grief. In essence, the funeral director has to combine the good qualities of a businessman, counselor and clergy person. This calls for a sincere dedication, massive sacrifices and deep knowledge of various aspects of life and death.

The general population does not realize that death creates immense deadline pressures for a funeral professional. There is always a rush to pick up the remains of the deceased from the place of death. Frequently there is urgency relating to taking actions to preserve the body. Some religious faiths require that all arrangements for burial be completed within a day or before the next sunset. If the remains are to be transported far, airline schedules have to be observed. Space reservations in prayer and religious facilities have to be made in a timely fashion. All of these activities, together with the necessity of handling any complaints and criticisms, create intense stress on the funeral director. Yet, there are people who are funeral directors, and more who want to be, despite the many challenges they will have to face. They deserve recognition and admiration.

THE IMAGE OF THE FUNERAL DIRECTOR

In September, 1995, a survey of American attitudes about the death care services and the funeral industry trends was carried out by the Wirthlin Group of Mclean, Virginia.[1] It was requested by representatives of the Funeral and Memorial Information Council and NFDA. This survey included 1000 consumers age thirty or older from different ethnic groups and religious beliefs residing in urban, suburban and rural areas of the U.S. The survey showed that an overwhelming majority—86 percent—had a positive or neutral attitude towards the funeral industry.

During my career, I have silently monitored the functions of the funeral directors and reactions of their consumers. The funeral directors are generally perceived by the consumers as helpful, kind, courteous, considerate, compassionate and caring. The total picture of the funeral industry discerned from the consumers' reactions is, by and large, a positive and healthy one. Personally, I have never encountered a dishonorable funeral director in reference to their business dealings, professional manners and ethical standards. I have found most of them to be understanding, supportive and knowledgeable. The people in this profession are able, affable and always available. I salute all of them for the dignity they reflect in an industry that is so sensitive and demanding, in a profession that demands many sacrifices.

One other way to assess the funeral industry and the image of the funeral director is to examine the published pitfalls, mishaps and complaints. It must be noted that the incidence of malpractice, fraud and misrepresentation is not as rampant as it is in some other professions. Cases of neglect, human error and greed have occurred in the funeral industry but, as an outsider, I believe the criticism of the industry has been unduly harsh.

VERY LITTLE ROOM FOR CROOKERY

The funeral industry is more rigidly regulated than many other professions. There are numerous rules and regulations, and several regulatory agencies watching and controlling this industry.

First, the funeral directors have to be licensed by their states. They are required to possess knowledge in the areas of removal of the body from the place of death, preparation for burial or cremation, and final disposition with all the necessary documents. Secondly, there are specific laws governing funerals. These state and federal laws are discussed in detail in the appropriate chapters. Third, there are regulations from the Environmental Protection Agency and the Occupational Safety and Health Administration that must be followed for the safety and health of the funeral industry workers. Finally, the FTC Funeral Rule protects consumers with regards to the funeral industry. Various aspects of this Rule are detailed in another chapter.

A business guide produced by the FTC entitled, *Complying with the Funeral Rule*[2] and an FTC brochure entitled, "Funerals: A Consumer Guide"[3] reflect regulations protecting the consumer. The consumer has rights that leave very little room for crookery on the part of the provider of death care services.

CONSUMER PROTECTION ADVISORY

To secure maximum comfort and protection from possible fraud and to minimize unnecessary costs, consumers should pay special attention to the following tips:

- Do not assume that all funeral directors are crooks.

- Research your options. Talk to relatives, friends, persons, who have had personal experiences of funeral arrangements before you make a final selection of a funeral director.

- Select a funeral director on the basis of your rapport with him and his reputation.

- Request all the information you need and obtain specific prices for all aspects of the services and goods. Demand exact total cost.

- Pay only for services authorized by you, and for goods and merchandise selected by you.

- Be knowledgeable about the rules and regulations required to be followed and the laws to be obeyed by the funeral directors.

- Be particularly aware of the contents of the FTC Funeral Rule. The rule contains a great deal of information about consumer protection.

- Read and understand the contract with the funeral home and sign it only if it is fully acceptable to you.

- If the contract is complex, secure the services of a good attorney.

A funeral arrangement can be less painful when the funeral director has integrity and honesty, and consumer is reasonable and fully knowledgeable of his rights, needs and financial limitations.

REFERENCES

1. Wirthlin Group of Mclean, VA: *American Attitudes about Death Care Services*. NFDA: Brookfield, WI: 1998.
2. Federal Trade Commission: *Complying with the Funeral Rule*. Washington, DC: FTC, Aug. 1995.
3. Federal Trade Commission: "Funerals: A Consumer Guide" [Brochure]. Washington, DC: FTC, Dec. 1996.

Chapter 20

LAWS GOVERNING
FUNERALS

*T*he laws relating to the business and practice of funeral directing in different states are more or less similar. Pertinent information regarding the laws governing funerals in the states of California, Florida and New York is presented in this chapter. For specific information on laws in other states, you are advised to contact their state government or your local Funeral Directors Association.

GENERAL OVERVIEW

All states require that a funeral director be licensed and registered. The laws outline what the practice of funeral directing, embalming, and related professions consist of and, in some cases, what they do not include.

Every state requires that embalmers and funeral directors must be licensed to practice. Licenses must be renewed, and temporary or student embalmers and funeral directors must be registered. Funeral establishments and crematoriums must be licensed, as well.

Bodies are not to be released to anybody other than a licensed funeral director or body disposer, although in some cases if the individual is acting under the supervision of a licensed funeral director, then he or she is allowed to transport the body. A body may not be removed unless the funeral director has appropriate authorization to move it.

In all states, funeral homes must meet certain health and safety standards. Some of these are described in Chapter 21.

Funeral establishments are required to disclose information, and to provide consumers with price lists both over the telephone and on paper, when requested. The list should include the prices of all services and goods.

The funeral director is licensed to sell funeral services, to plan the details of a funeral service with direction of a family member or friend of the decedent, or another with the proper authority. The funeral director manages visitation and viewing, as well as funeral and memorial services. In some states, the funeral director need not be present, but he or she must have direct or indirect supervision over the events.

In Florida, a funeral director's duties do not include phoning or faxing obituary notices, ordering flowers or merchandise, or assisting in the clerical duties regarding the death certificate, insurance forms, etcetera. These services would be extra.

Only a licensed individual may remove and transport remains from place of death, or remove remains from or to a funeral establishment, embalming facility, refrigeration facility, cemetery, crematory, medical examiner's office, common carrier, or other locations. He or she may do it only as authorized.

STATE OF FLORIDA[1]

The business and practice of funeral directing in the state of Florida is regulated by the Florida Department of Business and Professional Regulation (DBPR), Division of Professions, Board of Funeral Directors and Embalmers. The Board is located at Northwood Center, 1940 North Monroe Street, Tallahassee, FL 32399-0754, telephone (904) 488-8690. The laws and rules relating to the business and practice of funeral directing are contained in Chapter 470, Florida Statutes and Rule Chapter 61G8, Florida Administrative Code, July 1996 edition.

Chapter 470 deals with funeral directing, embalming and direct disposition. Section 470.0087 outlines the practice of funeral directing.

The practice of funeral directing shall be construed to consist of the following functions, which may be performed only by a licensed funeral director:

- Selling or offering to sell funeral services on an at-need basis.

- Planning or arranging, on an at-need basis, the details of a funeral service with the family or friends of the decedent or any other person responsible for such service; setting the time of the service; establishing the type of service to be rendered; acquiring the services of the clergy; and obtaining vital information for the filing of death certificates and obtaining of burial transit permits.

- Making, negotiating, or completing the financial arrangements for a funeral service on an at-need basis, provided that unlicensed personnel may assist the funeral director in performing such tasks.

- Directing, being in charge or apparent charge of, or supervising, directly or indirectly, a visitation or viewing. Such functions shall not require that a licensed funeral director be physically present throughout the visitation or viewing, provided that the funeral director is readily available by telephone for consultation.

- Directing, being in charge or apparent charge of, or supervising, directly or indirectly, any funeral service held in a funeral establishment, cemetery or elsewhere.

- Directing, being in charge or apparent charge of, or supervising, directly or indirectly, any memorial service held prior to or within 72 hours of the burial or cremation, if such memorial service is sold or arranged by a certificate holder or registrant.

- Using in connection with one's name or employment the words or terms "funeral director," "funeral establishment," "undertaker," "mortician," or any other word, term , title or picture, or combination of any of the above, that when considered in the context in which used would imply that such person in engaged in the practice of funeral direction or that such person is holding himself or herself out to the public as being engaged in the practice of funeral directing; provided, however, that nothing in this paragraph shall prevent using the name of any owner, officer, or corporate director of a funeral establishment, who is not a licensee, in connection with the name of the funeral establishment with which such individual is affiliated, so long as such individual's affiliation is properly specified.

- Managing or supervising the operation of a funeral establishment, except for administrative matters such as budgeting, accounting, and personnel, maintenance of buildings, equipment and grounds, and routine clerical and record-keeping functions.
- The practice of funeral directing shall *not* be construed to consist of the following functions:
  - The phoning-in or faxing of obituary notices
  - Ordering of flowers or merchandise
  - Delivery of death certificates to attending physicians
  - Clerical preparation of death certificates, insurance forms, and any clerical tasks that record the information compiled by the funeral director or that are incidental to any of the functions specified above.
- Furnishing standard printed price lists and other disclosure information to the public by telephone or by providing such lists to persons making inquiry.
- Removing or transporting human remains from the place of death, or removing or transporting human remains from or to a funeral establishment, centralized embalming facility, refrigeration facility, cemetery, crematory, medical examiner's office, common carrier, or other locations as authorized and provided by law.
- Arranging, coordinating, or employing registered removal services, registered refrigeration facilities, or registered centralized embalming facilities.
- Any aspect of making preneed funeral arrangements or entering into preneed contracts.
- Any functions normally performed by cemetery or crematory personnel.

NEW YORK STATE[2]

Introduction

The business and practice of funeral directing in New York State is regulated by the State Department of Health. With more than 2,000 funeral firms, in excess of 5,000 licensees, more than 100 registered residents and 125 students annually, the Department regulates one of the largest statewide funeral directing industries in the country.

The Department is guided in its regulatory role by state statute and regulatory provisions. Of particular note, Article 34 of the Public Health Law is solely concerned with the business and practice of funeral directing within this state. Together with the State Sanitary code and the Vital Statistics Law, these three pieces represent the major bodies of law addressing the business and practice of funeral directing. In addition, a variety of other statutes contain provisions applicable to the funeral directing. These include the state's Tax and Finance Law, General Business Law, Cemetery Law, Religious Corporations Law, and Workman's Compensation Law.

Through its Bureau of Funeral Directing, the Department is responsible for the licensing of funeral directors, and registration of funeral firms, licensees, students, and residents. In addition, the Department is authorized to approve all funeral directing schools within the state and to insure compliance of mandated academic requirements. Department staff are responsible for the investigation of complaints and alleged violations of Public Health Law and implementing regulations governing the business and practice of funeral directing. In addition, staff conduct inspections of all funeral firms to insure compliance with applicable laws and regulations. The Department administers the state licensing examination, which is given several times per year.

While the statutory provisions address the broad issues of the law, regulatory provisions detail the specific requirements implementing the law. These represent the Commissioner's Administrative Rules and Regulations, and are found at 10NYCRR Parts 77, 78, and 79. Part 77 addresses the licensing and registration aspects of funeral directing professionals and establishments. Part 78 is devoted to the requirements of the written itemization statement to be provided to the person(s) making arrangements for the care and disposition of a deceased person. Lastly, Part 79 details the requirements for price disclosure of funeral services and merchandise.

The Laws and Administrative Rules and Regulations relating to the Business and Practice of Funeral Directing were updated in April 1998.

Part 77 dealing with practice of funeral directing covers details under following sections:

Section 77.0: Definitions of department, commissioner, school, curriculum, accrediting agency, common carrier, customer, customer's designee, casket, outer interment receptacle, actual retail price, direct cremation, direct burial, unfinished wooden box and alternative container.

Section 77.1: Academic requirements for funeral director.

Section 77.2: Examinations.

Section 77.3: Registered residents.

Section 77.4: Funeral service schools.

Section 77.5: Funeral establishments – embalming; embalming and preparation room; business telephone; display of signs; listing; publications and advertising; food and beverages.

Section 77.6: Registration.

Section 77.7: Funeral directing – (a) A funeral director, undertaker or embalmer shall not permit any unlicensed person to engage in or take charge of the activities for which a license to engage in the business or practice of funeral directing, undertaking or embalming is required by the provisions of the Public Health Law.

A licensed funeral director or undertaker shall be present and personally supervise and arrange for the removal or transfer of each dead human body from the place where death occurs, or from the place where it is released to him by the family or other legal authority.

A licensed funeral director or undertaker shall be present and personally supervise the conduct of each funeral service.

Nothing herein shall be construed as prohibiting religious supervision of the funeral service by a member or members of the clergy designated by the family of the deceased person.

A licensed funeral director or undertaker shall be present and personally supervise the interment or cremation, or the pickup from or the delivery to a common carrier, of a dead human body.

No person other than a duly licensed and registered funeral director or undertaker shall make or be permitted to make arrangements on behalf of any funeral director, undertaker or funeral firm with a customer or customer's designee:

- For temporary or final entombment, or cremation, disinterment, reinterment or other lawful disposition of a dead human body;
- For the care, preparation, shipment or transportation of a dead human body; or
- For the purchase, sale or rental of funeral merchandise, services or paraphernalia. The taking of preliminary information over the telephone by an unlicensed person shall not be construed as the making of funeral arrangements under this section.

(b) (1) In no case shall a dead human body be released from any hospital, institution or other place where the death occurred or from the place where the body is held by legal authority to any person not a duly licensed and registered funeral director or undertaker.

(2) Every person, including, although not limited to, a person in charge of a hospital, institution, or place where a person has died, having lawful possession, charge, custody or control of a dead human body, shall request the person seeking to obtain the release of said body and acting as, for, or in behalf of a funeral director or funeral firm, to produce his current certificate of biennial registration, showing that he is personally entitled to practice as a funeral director or undertaker.

(c) Every person, including a person acting lawfully in an emergency, in charge of a cemetery, crematory, vault or other place to which a dead human body is brought for temporary or permanent disposition shall require the person in charge of such body to identify himself as a duly licensed and registered funeral director or undertaker and to produce his current certificate of biennial registration as such.

(d) In the event such burial or other disposition is not in charge of a duly licensed and registered funeral director or undertaker, the person in charge of the cemetery, crematory, vault or other place where dead human bodies are brought for temporary or permanent disposition shall immediately submit to the Department of Health the name and address of the person who had charge of the body at the time of burial or other disposition and the name and address of the funeral director, undertaker or funeral firm for which such person was acting.

(e) In the event that a person other than a duly licensed and registered funeral director or undertaker shall make any arrangements for the purchase, sale or rental or funeral merchandise, service or paraphernalia accompanied by the representative of a decedent at a casket showroom, display room or other facility, the owner or manager of such facility shall immediately notify the Department of Health of the name and address of the person and of the funeral director, undertaker or funeral firm for which such person was acting.

(f) Nothing contained in this section shall be deemed to require that a mere transporter, to whom or to which a dead human body has been duly released for the sole purpose of transportation or transfer, shall be a duly licensed and registered funeral director or undertaker.

(g) A funeral director, undertaker or funeral firm entering another state or a province of the Dominion of Canada, personally or by a agent or employee, pursuant to a reciprocal agreement between the State Commissioner of Health and such state or province, shall not violate any statute, code, rule or regulation of such state or province relating to the practice of funeral directing, undertaking or the equivalent thereof.

Section 77.8: Managers
Section 77.9: Tests prescribed by the commissioner for signs of death.
Section 77.10: Embalming procedure.
77.11: Funeral director business practices.
77.12: Misconduct.

Part 78 deals with statement to be furnished by every funeral director or funeral firm under the following sections:
Section 78.1: Contents of statement.
Section 78.2: Itemization of funeral services and merchandise selected.
Section 78.3: Customer's designation of intentions.

Part 79 covers the following under different sections:

Section 79.1: Telephone price disclosure.

Section 79.2: Casket price list.

Section 79.3: Outer interment receptacle price list.

Section 79.4: General price list.

Section 79.5: Alternative pricing methods.

Section 79.6: Alternative containers.

Section 79.7: Retention of price lists.

Section 79.8: Comprehension of disclosure.

STATE OF CALIFORNIA[3]

The Business and Professions Code:
Funeral Directors and Embalmers Law

Sections 7600 – 7610 deal with functions of the board.

Sections 7615 – 7635 deal with funeral directing laws:

- A funeral director is a person engaged in or conducting, or holding himself or herself out as engaged in any of the following:

- Preparing for the transportation or burial or disposal, or directing and supervising for transportation or burial or disposal of human remains.

- Maintaining an establishment for the preparation for the transportation or disposition or for the care of human remains.

- Using, in connection with his or her name, the words, "funeral director," or "undertaker," or "mortician," or any other title implying that he or she is engaged as a funeral director.

- A licensed funeral establishment is a place of business conducted in a building or separate portion of a building having a specific street address or location and devoted exclusively to those activities as are incident, convenient, or related to the preparation and arrangements, financial and otherwise, for the funeral, transportation, burial or other disposition of human remains and including, but not limited to, either of the following.

- A suitable room for the storage of human remains.

- A preparation room equipped with a sanitary flooring and necessary drainage and ventilation and containing necessary instruments and supplies for the preparation, sanitation, or embalming of human remains for burial or transportation.

- Licensed funeral establishments under common ownership or by contractual agreement within closed geographical proximity of each other shall be deemed to be in compliance with the requirements of paragraph (1) or (2) of subdivision (a) if at least one of the establishments has a room described in those paragraphs.

- Except as provided in Section 7609, and except accredited embalming schools and colleges engaged in teaching students the art of embalming, no person shall operate or maintain or hold himself or herself out as operating or maintaining any of the facilities specified in paragraph (2) of subdivision (a), unless he or she is licensed as a funeral director.

- Nothing in this section shall be construed to require a funeral establishment to conduct its business or financial transactions at the same location as its preparation or storage of human remains.

- Nothing in this chapter shall be deemed to render unlawful the conduct of any ambulance service from the same premises as those on which a licensed funeral establishment is conducted, including the maintenance in connection with the funeral establishment of garages for the ambulances and living quarters for ambulance drivers.

- Every funeral establishment holding a funeral director's license on December 31, 1996, shall, upon application and payment of fees for renewal of its funeral director's license, be issued a funeral establishment license.

Sections 7640 –7671 deal with embalming laws.

Section 7680 deals with law of displaying licenses.

Sections 7685 – 7685.3 deal with price disclosure laws.

Sections 7686 – 7711 deal with disciplinary actions.

Sections 7715 – 7719 deal with other violations of laws.

Sections 7725 – 7729 deal with licensing laws.

Sections 7735 – 7745 deal with preneed contract laws.

No funeral establishment licensed under the laws of the State of California, or the agents or employees of a funeral establishment, shall enter into or solicit any preneed arrangement, contract or plan, hereinafter referred to as "contract," requiring the payment to the licensee of money or the delivery to the licensee of securities to pay for the final disposition of human remains or for funeral services or for the furnishing of personal property or funeral merchandise not immediately required, unless the property or merchandise is not immediately required, unless the contract requires that all money paid directly or indirectly and all securities delivered under that agreement or under any agreement collateral thereto, shall be held in trust for the purpose for which it was paid or delivered until the contract is fulfilled according to its terms; provided, however, that any payment made or securities deposited pursuant to this article shall be released upon the death of the person for whose benefit the trust was established as provided in Section 7737. The income from the corpus may be used to pay for a reasonable annual fee for administering the trust, including a trustee fee, to be determined by the board, and to establish a reserve of not to exceed 10 percent of the corpus as a revocation fee in the event of cancellation on the part of the beneficiary.

None of the trust corpus shall be used for payment of any commission nor shall any of the trust corpus be used for other expenses of trust administration.

Only portions of the pertinent California Funeral Directors and Embalmers Law are reproduced here. Sections 7600 – 7745 of the business and professions code contain complete details.

REFERENCES

1. Florida Department of Business and Professional Regulation: *Division of Professions, Board of Funeral Directors and Embalmers.* Tallahassee, FL, July 1996.
2. New York State Department of Health: *Compilation of Laws and Administrative Rules and Regulations Relating to the Business and Practice of Funeral Directing.* updated, April 1998.

3. "Official California Legislative Information." *California Business and Professions Code, Funeral Directors and Embalmers Law.* Online. Available: *http://www.leginfo.ca.gov/index.html*, October 1998.

Chapter 21

OSHA AND THE
FUNERAL INDUSTRY

The Federal Trade Commission (FTC) functions to protect the funeral industry consumer. The Environmental Protection Agency (EPA) works to safe guard the environment, and the Occupational Safety and Health Administration (OSHA) is concerned about protecting the worker. The funeral industry is regulated directly or indirectly by all three agencies. The role of FTC has been discussed in an earlier chapter. The EPA is primarily concerned about pollution of the areas outside the funeral home. OSHA's role is much more involved. Our government wants to protect you, the consumer. The laws executed by the FTC, EPA and OSHA are very much in your best interests.

Employees in the funeral industry are involved in a variety of tasks. When death occurs, the funeral home employee picks up the body from the place of death, such as a home, hospital, nursing home or sanatorium. If the death was caused by a communicable disease such as tuberculosis, hepatitis or AIDS, the handler of the remains could be exposed to a possible health hazard. In the funeral home, the employees work with bodies and biological waste. They are involved in organ donation procedures, embalming of the body, and the performance of the autopsy, all of which may expose them to harmful diseases. Further, they may be exposed to hazardous chemicals that are commonly used in funeral homes. The OSHA is stringent in enforcing its regulations to protect these workers against all of such risks to their health.

EMPLOYER'S RESPONSIBILITIES

The OSHA requires compliance by the funeral home in the following areas:

1. *Evaluation of work place for the presence of hazardous chemicals and harmful physical agents.*

   The funeral home must maintain a list of all the hazardous chemicals in the funeral home. All of the containers must be marked with the identity of the hazardous substance, hazard warnings and the name and address of the chemical manufacturer. Generally, a hazardous substance is any material that has a Material Safety Data Sheet (MSDS) provided with it. Among the hazardous materials found at a funeral home are formaldehyde, phenol and methanol.

2. *Training of employees who are routinely exposed to hazardous substances or harmful physical agents at work.*

   This training must be given before the workers go into the areas where hazards exist. The training must include specifications about:
   - Functions in work area where hazards exist
   - Requirement of Hazard Communication Standard
   - Location of Material Safety Data Sheets
   - Reading and understanding the Material Safety Data Sheets
   - Dangers of spills and means for recognizing spills
   - Risks from blood borne pathogens such as tuberculosis, hepatitis, and HIV/AIDS
   - Methods to protect themselves from hazards.

3. *Maintenance of Material Safety Data Sheets on the hazardous substances for the employees.*

   These sheets must be available to employees and jurisdictional authorities upon request. If an employee is exposed to a hazardous substance specific written information on the effects of exposure must be obtained.

4. *Updating of records on training and blood borne pathogens as required by the OSHA.*

Employers must comply with the OSHA standards for several reasons:

- The OSHA levies stiff fines and penalties for violations.
- Transmission of hepatitis B, AIDS, tuberculosis and other infections is avoidable.
- If a worker is infected in the funeral home, the employer may face legal liability.
- If the worker becomes infected, the disclosure of his infection will create ethical, legal and financial conflicts for the worker, since he will not be able to continue working in funeral homes or in the health professions.

BLOOD BORNE PATHOGENS

Records Required By OSHA

The employer must maintain the following records:

1. Training records, including:
   - Dates of training
   - Contents of training course
   - Names and qualifications of persons conducting the training
   - Names and job titles of employees attending the training session.
2. Medical records for each employee with occupational exposure details including:
   - Name and Social Security number
   - Hepatitis B vaccination status
   - A copy of all results of examinations, medical tests and follow-up procedures
   - The evaluating health care professional's written opinion as required in the event of an exposure
   - A copy of the information provided to the health care professional as required in the event of an exposure.

Actions and Record Keeping

The following are a few suggestions for the actions and record keeping that will help the funeral home to comply with OSHA standards, avoid citation and penalty in the event of an inspection and to protect the employer:

1. Insist on understanding and following: "Universal Precautions," the Center for Disease Control and Prevention's policy for health care workers regarding blood and fluids of all bodies as potential sources of blood borne pathogens, with special focus on the hepatitis B virus and HIV.

2. Require proper disposal of regulated waste such as human blood, isolation waste, contaminated sharps, contaminated carcasses and pathological wastes like tissues, organs, body parts and body fluids. Prior to disposal, insist that employees place all regulated waste in closeable, leak proof containers or bags that are color-coded or labeled according to the OSHA standard.

3. Establish cleaning and decontaminating guidelines and enforce them strictly.

4. Have a written Exposure Control Plan designed to eliminate or minimize employee exposure. Enlist employee support and monitor compliance.

5. Assign responsibility for record keeping to a single individual, preferably one who will represent the employer and is familiar with the files.

6. Maintain employee file with information on:
    -   Hepatitis B virus vaccination status
    -   Training and education
    -   Exposure incidents
    -   Post-exposure follow-up

7. Update records at least once each year. Establish an annual date for review and update.

8. Keep thorough records of OSHA inspections.

9. Encourage employees to get the hepatitis B vaccinations. Most of the funeral home employees will be dealing with not only dead bodies but

also with infectious agents, blood, pathological waste, excreta, body parts and contaminated sharps. They may deal with these at the place of death such as private home, hospital, nursing home, etc. During their involvement with the remains of the deceased they may be exposed to hepatitis B virus. Therefore, they should receive vaccination against this infection. The employers are required to offer this protection to employees at no cost. The vaccine is given in three doses over a period of 6 months. If the employee declines to receive this vaccination he must sign a declination statement.

Hepatitis B Vaccine Declination Form (Mandatory)

I understand that due to my occupational exposure to blood or other potentially infectious materials, I may be at risk of acquiring hepatitis B virus (HVB) infection. I have been given the opportunity to be vaccinated with hepatitis B vaccine, at no charge to myself. However, I decline hepatitis B vaccination at this time. I understand that by declining this vaccine, I continue to be at risk of acquiring hepatitis B, a serious disease. If in the future I continue to have occupational exposure to blood or other potentially infectious materials and I want to be vaccinated with hepatitis B vaccine, I can receive the vaccination series at no charge to me.

Date _____   Employee Signature _____

Occupational Hazards to Employees and Remedies

Whether the funeral home employee is embalming the body, handling pathological specimens or assisting in autopsies, he may encounter occupational health hazards. These may include infection hazards, chemical hazards from formaldehyde and other chemicals, and physical hazards from cut injuries.

A study by Gershon and colleagues[1] of 130 funeral service practitioners indicates that there is a low rate of occupational exposure to HIV, hepatitis B virus and hepatitis C virus. Nevertheless, proper precautions must be taken.

The handling of human cadavers can create an infection hazard. The infectious conditions in a recently deceased person that present risk include

179

tuberculosis, group A streptococcal infection, gastrointestinal organisms, the agents that cause Creutzfedt-Jacob disease, hepatitis B and C viruses, HIV, and possibly meningitis and septicemia.[2] In such cases the observance of Control of Substances Hazardous to Health regulations and the use of proper clothing will provide protection against infectious hazards.

If the employee is assisting a pathologist in the performance of an autopsy he must take certain precautions. For instance, respiration protection should be worn while performing an autopsy on a deceased person who may have had tuberculosis at the time of death. Gershon and his colleagues studied "Tuberculosis risk in funeral home employees."[3] On the basis of their results they recommend that "funeral home employees who routinely embalm cadavers undergo annual tuberculin skin testing, receive initial training on tuberculosis prevention, and wear respiratory protection when preparing known tuberculosis cases."

OSHA Formaldehyde Standard requires that the clothing, linen and bottles contaminated with formaldehyde be isolated into special containers and the empty bottles be rinsed three times and placed in trash bins.

SUMMARY

The goal of the funeral home must be to protect the health and safety of its employees. This in turn makes the funeral home a safer place for the consumer. The best way to achieve this goal is to comply with the OSHA standard. The important elements in complying are record keeping, training, organization, equipment, practice and common sense.[4]

REFERENCES

1. Gershon RR, Vlahov D, Farzadegan H, Alter NJ: "Occupational Risk of Human Immunodeficiency Virus, Hepatitis B Virus, and Hepatitis C Virus Infections Among Funeral Service Practitioners in Maryland." *Infect Control Hosp Epidemiol* 1995 Apr; 16(4): 194-197.
2. Healing TD, Hoffman PN, Young SE: "The Infection Hazards of Human Cadavers." *Common Dis Rep CDR Rev* 1995 Apr 28;5(5):R61-R68.

3. Gershon RR, Vlahov D, Escamilla-Cejudo JA, *et al*.: "Tuberculosis Risk in Funeral Home Employees." *J Occup Environ Med* 1998 May; 40(5):497-503.

4. "OSHA." *The Director*, Jan. 1994: 81.

Section VI:
Death Rites & Customs
Around the World

Chapter 22

A BRIEF HISTORY OF FUNERALS

Death is beautiful in itself, and the dead have many tales to tell.

*W*hat is death? What are the uses of a dead body? How should we deal with our dead? Our ancestors have answered these questions in a variety of ways. They may have feared death or they may have prepared for it. Some of them ate the dead as food, used their bones for decoration, and treated their departure as an excuse for erecting massive mausoleums. How are we different from our ancestors in dealing with death and the dead? Perhaps a brief peep into the past will serve to stimulate our curiosity about the amazing practices of our ancestors. Subsequent chapters describe the customs of different ethnic and religious groups with regard to death. They reflect much about the culture and world-view of those who practice them.

Evidence of funeral rituals exists in every culture and religion of the world, dating back as far as prehistoric times. Though the methods and beliefs may vary, the general purpose of the funeral always appears to be to respect, honor and remember the dead. Survivors use the funeral to celebrate the life of the one who has died and, at the same time they use funeral and death rites to find ways to reduce their grief and promote healing.

In a fascinating review of the origin and development of funeral customs written in 1926, Bertram S. Puckle described various aspects of dying, death and funerals.[1] He presented a historical perspective that included a discussion of death warnings, preparations for death and the management of the dead. These glimpses into the history of funerals reveal many interesting customs.

BURY THE DEAD –OR EAT THEM?

Today, human remains may be "recycled" by removing undamaged parts from the deceased and transplanting them in living beings, or simply by dissecting them for the study and advancement of medicine and science. Not too many decades ago, our ancestors used the remains for a different purpose. When a person died, his remains were not simply burned or buried, but the flesh of the dead was eaten by fellow humans and the bones were discarded. In fact, in the Stone Age, cannibalism was very common. Puckle cites writer Colonel J. Garnier in the "Worship of the Dead," who described examples where Stone Age humans ate human flesh as a part of religious rites. In Australia, eating the flesh of the deceased was done to associate the living with the virtues of the dead. Some Australian aboriginal tribes practiced the consumption of the dead by the next of kin. Among other peoples, living kin consumed the deceased's body fluids by mixing it in food. Even as late as 1912, after one of the leaders of a rebellion in China was executed, his body was opened and his heart was removed and cooked in accordance with the rites of the Ming Dynasty. This prized organ was eaten by the very soldiers who had executed him, with "the belief that the courage and skill of the chief [would] be passed on to them by this means." Even today, cannibalism is an accepted ritualistic, symbolic activity in some tribal societies.[2,3]

PRESERVATION OF THE BODY

Mummification, which is described in greater detail in Chapter 8, Embalming, is probably the most well known means of preserving the body after death, but there are others as well. The body of King Henry I was salted and sewn into ox hide for preservation before it was brought to England for burial. In pre-Revolutionary France, when a child died the parents prepared a receptacle from chestnut tree bark. This bark was then bound around the child's with slender branches as yet another method of preservation.[1]

DISPOSITION OF THE DEAD

In the past, the most common method for disposing a body was *inhumation*, or burial in the ground. Many African people initially buried the body and later exhumed it after the soft tissues were lost through decomposition. They then re-buried the leftover bones in a final resting place.

While the idea of using the bones of the deceased as eating utensils seems incredible, that is exactly what was done by the Tobriand Islanders of Melanesia, who exhumed the bones after burial and used them for spoons and other utensils. The practice was one way to honor and respect the deceased, for it was believed that using the bones of the dead would transfer the spirit of the deceased into their own bodies.

There were other methods for cleaning the bones besides burial with exhumation. Ancient Australians placed the newly dead bodies in trees until they decomposed completely, while some Polynesian tribes put them on scaffolds until they were dry. The Parsees of India placed their corpses on "towers of silence" for the birds to feed on the flesh. After the corpses were picked clean they were taken down and preserved in ossuaries.[4]

Different Native American Indian tribes practice a variety of methods of disposition in accordance to their religious beliefs, tribal laws and social customs. For example, the Navajo fear death and believe in ghosts. Therefore, they keep the dying isolated and away from home in case the ghost chose to inhabit the place of death. Native American Apaches believe in burying the dead with their possessions and they also place food at the grave site. This is done to pacify the dead so that they do not return to haunt the living. If a mourner has nightmares of death or illness after the deceased has been buried, he believes that his house is being visited by the dead and therefore he must destroy the home and move to a new dwelling.

Native Americans of the north bury bodies in a shallow grave to allow for the easy liberation of the soul. Later they hold a feast and burn the body. The bones are then put in a box or wrapped in an animal skin robe. Some place the body in a special burial tepee and others send the body down a river in a burial canoe.[5]

BURIAL

History has left us with phenomenal monuments to the dead. Two of these are among the ancient wonders of the world. The first, the Taj Mahal in Agra, India was built in the seventeenth century by Mogul emperor Shah Jahan for his beloved wife, Mumtaz Mahal. It took ten years and the labor of more than 20,000 skilled workers to complete. The second, the pyramids, were built during the Fourth Dynasty (2600 to 2500 B.C.) in Giza, Egypt to serve as burial chambers for the pharaohs. The largest was built for the pharaoh Khufu, and two others were constructed for the pharaohs Kahfre and Mankaure. These monuments are discussed in greater detail in Appendix B.

Thousands of years ago in China, the emperors built underground tombs in which they planned to reside and rule from after their death. The tombs contained ceramic figures of warriors in battle dress. Some of these warriors appeared on full-sized replicas of horses, and others were placed in chariots. One Ming emperor built an entire palace underground and was buried there with many treasures.[6] Even Mao Tse Tung's tomb may be considered a modern day example of exotic indulgence in death.

In the past, the horses of dead warriors were sometimes buried with their owners, with the belief that the horses would carry the warriors to victory in the "spirit world." Throughout most of Europe, there was a practice of killing dogs, horses, bulls, goats, cattle and sheep and then burying them with the deceased to accompany the dead and assure a rich afterlife.

Ancient tombs teach us a lot about the traditions of the past. Bodies were sometimes buried with gilded armor, weapons and chariots. Sometimes cooking utensils were placed in the grave so that the deceased could prepare food in the afterlife. Pottery, coins, watches and clothes have also been found in tombs, and toys have been known to accompany the bodies of children. A Swedish custom required burying every unmarried woman with a mirror so that she would be able to arrange her loosely coiled tresses to look better on the Day of Resurrection. All of these items were included in the tombs because of a strong belief that there exists a life after death. They were meant to provide comfort to the spirit of the deceased.

Gifts, wine and food were also provided to the dead. The offerings were given with the belief that the dead needed them in the after life, just as they needed them in life. Egyptian and Roman funeral ceremonies included offerings of wine, sweet beer, cakes, fruits and scented oils for nourishment in the afterlife. As recently as 1926, some Chinese people held a similar belief of making offerings to the dead. In his book *The Story of Primitive Man*, Edward Clodd relates how Solomon Islanders throw food into the fire and set aside a portion of their daily meals for the dead.[7]

While some cultures provided the dead with amenities, followers of the Roman Catholic Church believed in a simple, dignified burial. They wanted the blessed spirit to go to God unencumbered. All they required was that (1) the body be decently laid out, (2) lights be placed beside the body, (3) a cross be laid upon the breast or the hands placed in the form of a cross, (4) the body be sprinkled with holy water and incense, and (5) the body be buried in consecrated ground.

PREPARING FOR DEATH

Historically, preparations for burial were usually well thought out. Many cases have been recorded where people have bought their own coffin and used it as a bed in order to prepare themselves for the "long sleep." The actress Sarah Bernhardt did just this. She even went so far as to photograph herself in the coffin so that she could see for herself how she would look laid out in it for her funeral.

In ancient China, it was not uncommon for a son to give his father an expensive coffin made of fine wood with an outer shell that was up to eight inches thick, a middle shell that was six inches thick, and an inner shell that was four inches thick. The coffin was often given long before the individual's death.

BURIAL GARMENTS

Of course, the funerals of the rich differed from the funerals of the poor. In the early days of England, the poor were buried naked or wrapped in linen. In 1666, to add dignity to burial, the laws required the use of a woolen shroud instead of the linen. In fact, in 1680 the laws were further modified and the family was required to produce a certificate that stated that a woolen shroud was used at the burial of their relative.

In China, one could tell the social rank of the deceased by his clothing upon burial. Those of high social standing wore clothing that was costly and elaborate. For instance, the corpse of the ruler was dressed in up to fifty suits, while those who were well-educated were given a rich assortment of black silk robes. However, in exception to these rules of social-standing, Italians were traditionally buried dressed in their everyday clothing.

There have been no significant changes in the traditional Jewish burial clothes. The seventeenth century Jewish costume for the deceased consisted of two layers of underclothes, a skirt with frill of fine linen, a cloak, a square of ribbons and a white head cap. Even the other Jewish funeral customs have not changed much. In ancient times, as nowadays, a plain wooden coffin without decoration or adornment was used and flowers were forbidden.

BURIED ALIVE? NO WAY!

No one likes the thought of being buried or burned alive. There is a historical exception, however. As late as 1829 in India, when a Hindu died his widow voluntarily jumped into the flames of the funeral pyre. This practice, known as *sati*, was considered to be an honorable act. The tradition was abolished by the British government during their rule of India.

Some individuals have been so obsessed by the fear of being buried alive that they have been known to go to desperate measures to ensure that they are dead before they are buried. Puckle describes two such examples in 19th century England. One lady from Kent asked that she be stabbed in the heart several times post mortem to make sure she was truly dead before her burial. Another wealthy man requested as many medical tests as necessary to verify he was indeed dead, and used the services of two nuns to watch his remains until his body was buried to make sure that his life had, in fact, ended.

CELEBRATION AT DEATH

Feasting at a funeral is not uncommon. Perhaps these party-like customs were designed to help minimize grief. Not too long ago, I attended a wake where alcohol was liberally served and about half of the attendees were intoxicated.

In Scotland, serving intoxicants and pancakes was expected and the wake was to be entertaining. In Ireland, mourners would gather at the grave site after midnight for bread, cheese, whiskey and entertainment. All attending were expected to participate in the events of the evening; for instance, even a non-smoker was expected to smoke in honor of the dead. These traditions continue today in a similar fashion.

THE DEATH BELL

Perhaps the ringing of a bell to announce a death gave origin to the expression "death bell." In Scotland, the death bell was called "mort-bell" or "soul bell." There the bell tolled after a death had taken place. By counting the number of rings, people were able to tell who had died: the bell tolled three times for a man and two times for a woman. After this, there would be a pause, followed by a stroke for each year of the dead person's life.

These different historical accounts show us that the dead can tell tales. There are many acceptable rites and rituals that one can perform when a loved one dies. Although some of them may seem a bit vulgar and inhumane to us, we must keep in mind that the ultimate purpose of all funerals is to respect and to remember a loved one, and to help the living grieve. Whatever funeral customs one may choose for themselves or their family member, religious and personal beliefs must be considered and respected. Death can be beautiful in itself.

REFERENCES

1. Puckle BS: *Funeral Customs: Their Origin and Development.* London: T. Werner, Ltd., 1926. Republished by Omnigraphics, Detroit, 1990.

2. Sanday PR: *Divine Hunger: Cannibalism as a Cultural System.* Cambridge: Cambridge Univ. Press, 1988.

3. Fatteh AV: "Cannibalism and the New Milestones in Medicine." *Virginia Medical Monthly* 97:11, 1970:715.

4. "History of Funerals," in: *The Encyclopedia Americana*, vol. 8. Danbury, CT: Grolier Inc., 1998: 568-9.

5. Maxwell JA (ed.): *America's Fascinating Indian Heritage.* Pleasantville, NY: Reader's Digest Association, Inc., 1978.

6. Blais RE: "A Brief Look at Funerals in China." *The Director*, Nov. 1997:75-6.

7. Clodd E: *The Story of Primitive Man.* As cited in Puckle, 1990.

Chapter 23

THE CHINESE FUNERAL

*T*he *Chinese traditionally highly revere their forefathers and believe* that, at death, one is simply elevated to the world of ancestors. Blessing a departed spirit is a way of showing respect for those who have died. Honoring the dead allows them to remain with the living and to share everything the living have here on earth. Even in death, the ancestors will continue to receive and to give care and support from the living.

FUNERALS IN CHINA

In the past, the Chinese believed that life continued after death. The emperors from the Ming Dynasty built elaborate tombs underground in the belief that they would live after death and would reign from these underground tombs. More recently, in 1977 Mao Tse Tung built a tomb in T'in-anmen Square. His body is displayed encased in a crystal enclosure. However, cremation is actually a much more common means of disposition in China, and only a minority of Chinese bury their dead.

The Chinese funeral homes and crematoriums are owned and operated by the Chinese government.[1] Bodies are embalmed by physicians only if they are to be shipped away. Funeral services may take place before and after cremation. Immediately after death, the body is taken to a funeral facility where it is put in a refrigerated space. It is kept fully clothed. The funeral services are conducted on the seventh day following the death, at which time the body is brought into a large room for viewing.

After viewing and services, the body is taken into a retort, which is a chamber in which the cremation process takes place. Diesel fuel is used to operate the retorts and the cremation process takes only forty minutes.

After cremation, the family places the ashes in an urn and brings it to a garden with fireplaces. Candles are burned and expensive gift offerings are made to the gods at the fireplace. This is done with the belief that it will help the soul of the deceased to enter heaven. The urn is then placed in a columbarium (depository for cinerary urns) rented by the family. In some places, funeral services are conducted every seventh day for seven weeks. Sometimes the ashes are buried on the forty-ninth day.

CHINESE MINORITY GROUPS

Some Chinese minority groups conduct their funerals differently. Blais notes that one group holds the body of the deceased at home for a year prior to burial.[1] Aromatic liquids are poured into the mouth to reduce any odor, and incense is burned continuously around the body.

In Northern China and Tibet, after a person has died, a priest comes to the place of death and washes the body. A procession of relatives takes the body to the top of a mountain where it is undressed. There the body is cut into pieces and the skull is crushed. A strong type of incense is burned to attract hawks, which are considered to be sacred birds. It is believed that when the birds eat up the whole body, the soul then departs to God. In Tibet, only priests and people of highest social standing are allowed to be cremated.

The Yin tribes in China follow an interesting process. Their funeral ceremony lasts three days. During this period, the family of the deceased must feed all the people in the town, as well as all visitors to their town. This custom usually forces thee family to slaughter their cattle.

The Muslims in China follow the funeral rites dictated by Islamic customs. These are detailed later in Chapter 26, which discusses the Muslim Funeral.

CHINESE FUNERALS IN THE UNITED STATES

There are over 1.2 billion Chinese in the world, accounting for 22 percent of the world's population living on 7 percent of the total land on Earth. More than a million Chinese live in the United States. Like most immigrant ethnic groups in the United States, they tend to cluster in large cities.

Most Americanized Chinese have no deep understanding of the funeral practices in China. Those who have had no previous experience of funerals depend heavily on the United States funeral director for guidance and support. In larger communities, however, they conduct the funeral ceremonies in the traditional Chinese fashion. Their observances are well described by Chin in a series of three articles in the *American Funeral Director.*[2-4]

The important elements of the Chinese funerals are respect and honor for the deceased, the family and the community. Whereas in the past the immigrant Chinese reflected reservations and even fear in expressing their wishes, they now feel more free to arrange and practice their native funeral customs in the United States. There is a difference, however. The old fashioned code of ritual grieving was elaborate and momentous, but now the ritual is simple, with an emphasis on respect for the deceased. Yet still the three common characteristics of tradition, pageantry and ethnic values are preserved.

PAI SHOU BANQUET

The traditional Chinese funeral ceremonies start with a banquet. This is a preneed party, arranged when death is imminent. Some Chinese throw this party for a person who is neither sick nor near death. The idea is to celebrate the mortality of an older person and to talk about his or her death freely. Family members, friends and neighbors participate in the banquet preparations once a date is set for the occasion. This celebration, called Pai Shou (meaning "Honor Longevity"), involves the funeral professionals, who help in assessing the budget and other preparations. The banquet aims at celebrating the age of the person for whom it is arranged by showing love for him and honoring his achievements. Some of those participating express gratitude and others use the occasion to show family solidarity and to mend past misunderstandings. Some families spend large amounts of money for this banquet to reflect their financial well-being and social status.

SHOU PAO: THE LONGEVITY ROBE

The Chinese believe that the deceased should be buried in clothes that were worn during their life, and that they must be formal. The formal attire is intended to impress the ancestors in the spiritual world when they receive the deceased.

At the celebration banquet, the guest of honor wears the formal gown. Generally, a woman's gown is made of black brocade embroidered with many beautiful colors. Men are dressed in a black or dark-blue full-length robe made of silk or cotton, sometimes with gold, red or white embroidery. After the banquet, the robe is preserved to be used later when the man dies.

Upon death, the man is dressed in three layers of new burial clothing worn under the longevity robe. These are pajama-type pants and long-sleeved tops. The first layer of clothing is a set of white underpants, next is a blue outfit, and the third a black outfit. To complete burial dressing, socks and shoes are placed on the body, and the head is covered with a hat. The woman's body is also similarly clothed; however, if she is a married woman and has a married son, she also wears a black or blue skirt as a fourth layer.

EMBALMING AND BURIAL

Burial is the most common form of disposition practiced by the Chinese in the United States. However, they do not favor embalming. Cremation is accepted more often by those who cannot afford the high cost of burial.

The Cemetery Plot

The Chinese believe in preneed planning. The Pai Shou banquet is part of that planning. In addition, the family buys cemetery plots before, during or following the banquet. The entire family is consulted on the selection of the plot. A plot large enough for all family members is preferable, however it is not uncommon to bury only one person on the plot. The choice spots have a good view and generally are on slopes or summits with no obstructions. After the plot is selected, the family places a monument at the foot end of the grave. No name or dates appear on the monument.

Another ceremony follows the placement of the monument. The family gathers at the grave site to lay spiritual claim on the plot and to bless the site. Chin notes that "this ceremony can be a simple one with only incense, candles and flowers; or it can be an elaborate clan picnic at the cemetery with roasted pigs, ducks and chicken; piles of noodles for long life; rice wine; 'longevity' cakes; and musicians." Usually, the Chinese do not believe in installment payments for the cemetery plot; they like to pay in full and secure the title.[2-4]

The Casket

The purchase of the casket is also a part of the preneed preparation. The eldest son usually buys it as a gift for his parent when the parent is over 50 years of age. The more expensive the casket is, the more respect it demonstrates. The Chinese prefer good, full-couch, non-defective caskets, because any flaws in the form of cuts or splits are thought to disturb the meaning of wholeness of the ritual. They also prefer to pay in full for the casket. After purchase, the casket is put in storage, and sealed with a red ribbon with the decedent's name on it. Purchasing the casket ahead of time is believed to ward off premature death.

FUNERAL SERVICES

The Chinese do not read prayers at the funeral services. There is no traditional concept of heaven and hell, as is found in many religions. However, there is a lot of mourning before death, at death, and after death. If a person is dying, the entire family gathers near the death bed to bid farewell to him.

As soon as death occurs, the entire family gathers near the deceased and cries together loudly, expressing their grief by wailing in unison. The family members kneel facing east, forming a half circle around a temporary altar with candles and burning incense sticks.

This is when the elaborate funeral services begin and the process of active mourning starts. The family members dress in appropriate mourning garments —i.e., the men wear black arm bands and the women wear ribbons of different colors. At this time, wine libations are offered and the chief mourner, who is usually the oldest son, reads the eulogies. A bowl of water that has been treated with fire from burning paper is blessed and made ready to be used to wash the deceased's face.

The casket is also brought in for the blessing process. The children and grandchildren of the deceased circle around the casket three times. Each hold three pieces of incense. They then put some rice, dried fruits and coins in the casket. The chief mourner places the body in the casket and washes the deceased's face with the blessed water. The body is now considered sanctified for burial.

Everyone in attendance passes by the deceased before the shrouding begins. First the body is covered with solid red cloth, and then a white shroud is tucked tightly around the body. Additional shrouds that may be bought as gifts are also used to cover the body. After the shrouds are put on the body, the casket is sealed. A last meal consisting of a bowl of rice and boiled eggs along with chopsticks are placed at the head of the casket.

The mourners then walk in single file around the casket, the eldest mourner first. In the line of attendees, the eldest grandson is second to the chief mourner and carries an incense stick and a photograph of the deceased. The guests file out of the parlor, followed by escorted family members.

The funeral service takes place the morning after the wake. It usually lasts four to five hours. The mourners always walk into the funeral home in a single file, older ones ahead of the younger family members, as they did for the wake. The family members read eulogies. At the end of the services, before the mourners leave, the funeral director or the master of ceremonies removes an incense stick from the urn and gives it to the chief mourner. The photograph of the deceased is removed and handed to the second mourner in line. The mourners and the relatives form a line and leave the funeral parlor.

After funeral services, a band of hired musicians may perform as the hearse leaves. Rice, coins and paper goods are scattered over the hearse while it takes the deceased to the cemetery for final burial.

In larger towns, it is not unusual for the funeral procession to go through Chinatown on the way to the grave. Food, wine, incense and candles are placed in the casket in front of the deceased's photograph. Eulogies are read again and mourners walk by to pay respect. The casket is then closed and the mourners again put earth, rice, flowers, arm bands, mourning clothing and food. Some place a jar of rice soaked with wine on the vault. This is when the funeral service ends and post-burial mourning begins.

The mourners return home where a small fire is lit and the family members leap over it one by one before going in the house. Once inside the house, the family members stand in a circle, a speech is made, and people help themselves to sweets and drinks. The family changes from their mourning black clothes to new red clothes and join together, crying loudly and wailing to express their grief.

Three days later, the family again dresses in mourning clothes and visits the grave for a private service. On the twenty-first day after the death, the family again conducts a collective mourning dressed in mourning clothes. At this time, two eulogies are read, dirges are sung and crying occurs. After this ritual, many of the material goods are burned for the deceased and a multi-course dinner is served.

These ceremonies help the family to celebrate the dead and to grieve together, and they allow the departed one to join his or her ancestors.

The entire length of the mourning period is determined by the family. It usually commences on the day of the wake and can last from 30 days to 100 days, or even as long as one year. Most often the formal mourning ends when the body is buried. During the formal mourning period, the bereaved are not supposed to venture out in public, nor can they cook, wear jewelry, go to work or handle money. The entrance to their house is draped in a white cloth during the entire mourning period.

In the United States, funeral directors participate a great deal in all aspects of the Chinese funeral services. Some funeral directors that actively serve Chinese communities in the United States include the Wing Fook Funeral Home and J.S. Waterman and Sons in Boston, Bowman Funeral Home in Chicago, and John R. Deady Funeral Home in Philadelphia.

REFERENCES

1. Blais RE: "A Brief Look at Funerals in China." *The Director* Nov. 1997:75-6.

2. Chin FK: "Chinese Funeral Traditions." *The American Funeral Director* Oct. 1995: 52-4, 112-18.

3. Chin FK: "Chinese Funeral Traditions." *The American Funeral Director* Nov. 1995: 39, 75-6.

4. Chin FK: "Chinese Funeral Traditions." *The American Funeral Director*. Dec. 1995: 38-41, 66-71.

Chapter 24

THE JEWISH FUNERAL

It matters not how a man dies, but how he lives.

—Samuel Johnson (1709-1784)

*J*udaism recognizes and preaches that death is part of every life and it must be faced honestly and realistically. The fundamental philosophy is that when death occurs, one must appreciate and be grateful for the life that was lived and one should celebrate that life. Within this philosophy are embedded two noble themes: respect for the dead *(Kavod Hamet)* and support for the family members who are in mourning.

At the time of death, the deceased's family joins together and the community draws closer. This helps the mourners by creating the sense that they are not alone. Psychologically this aids in the expedient relief of grief.

BIKKUR CHOLIM

Judaism stresses pre-death, at-death and post-death readiness. In preparation of death, one of the observances Judaism requires is *Bikkur Cholim*, the *mitzvah* (charitable act) of visiting the sick. In the religious text Talmud Shobbat, 127a notes:

> *These are deeds which yield fruit in the*
> *time to come... visiting the sick.*

The tradition of visiting the sick is an old one. In earlier times, Bikkur Cholim societies were formed. The members of these societies visited the sick. These societies were brought to America from Europe by Jewish immigrants, and in some places they still exist.

Judaism also requires daily repentance for one's failings, "lest you die tomorrow," and promotes the belief that one should put one's house in order when death is imminent. In preparation of death, some Jews write letters to their children expressing their wish that their hopes, desires and values will continue in the future. These are called *ethical wills* and are based on the following belief:

When a person dies all that accompanies that
person are Torah and good deeds. [AVOT 6:9]

Further, Jewish law encourages preplanning for death by way of purchasing a grave site in advance.

AT DEATH

When death occurs, Jews traditionally utter the words:
"Praised be the Righteous Judge."

Many generations ago, there were no funeral homes and it was routine to take the body directly to the cemetery from the place of death. Now, however, because funeral homes and synagogues are more common, when death occurs the rabbi and the funeral home are called to begin the processes of transferring the body, and preparing for the funeral and the interment.

If death occurs on Sabbath (from sundown Friday to sundown on Saturday), the rabbi is notified immediately after the end of Sabbath. In very traditional situations, a *shomer* (watchman) is hired to stay with the body until burial. A candle is placed by the side of the deceased, and Psalms 23 and 91, which relate to death, are recited.

CHEVRA KADDISHA

In the past, an organization called *Chevra Kaddisha* —meaning holy society or burial society— was created to help mourners and to prepare the body for burial. The members of this organization are familiar with funeral practices. They perform the ritual cleansing of the body (*Taharah*) and recite appropriate prayers asking God to receive the soul of the deceased and to grant forgiveness for any sins the deceased may have committed during his or her life. Women members of this society help if the deceased is a female, and male members participate if the deceased was male. In modern times, Chevra Kaddisha is called a Care Committee. The deployment of the Chevra Kaddisha for performing the Taharah is getting less and less common. Most often, the ritual washing of the bodies is done by the funeral directors.

THE FUNERAL

Jewish funerals are short and usually take place within twenty-four hours of death. They are conducted with dignity and simplicity. The funeral service may be carried out in the funeral chapel or at the grave site. The rabbi speaks for the family and some mourners are allowed to speak at the service.

Funerals are not permitted on the following Jewish holidays:

- Rosh Hashanah (New Year) (2 days)
- Yom Kippur (Day of Atonement) (1 day)
- Sukkot (Harvest Festival) (2 days)
- Shemini Atzeret (1 day)
- Simachat Torah (Rejoicing of the Torah) (1 day)
- Passover (Commemoration of Freedom from Slavery) (4 days)
- Shavuot (Giving of the Torah to the Jewish People) (2 days)

Also, funerals are also not permitted when "within-24-hours" would mean the service would occur on the Sabbath.

The service usually takes place in a Jewish funeral home. It may also be performed at the deceased's home, at the cemetery or in a synagogue. If a Jewish funeral home is not available, the services may be held at a gentile funeral home; in that case, all Christian religious symbols such as crosses (as well as the symbols of other religious denominations that might be present) should be removed.

Jewish tradition generally prohibits embalming the body. An exception is made if the death occurs overseas or if close family members cannot arrive in time for the funeral service. Jewish law also recommends avoiding a viewing of the body.

The use of a casket is permitted. The casket, however, must be made entirely of wood; no metal is allowed. This is because the Bible (Genesis 3:19) says:

For you are dirt

and to dirt you will return.

Everything that accompanies he body must be made of materials that will disintegrate and become dirt. The casket must be simple and modest with no adornments. It should not reflect wealth.

Along the same principles, the Jews do not believe in the show of dressing the dead in expensive clothes. They believe that all of us are equal at death. Therefore, the garments for the deceased must be simple. The body is clothed in a simple white shroud made of linen, muslin or cotton; i.e., materials that will disintegrate. This tradition started in the first century when the reputed Rabbi Gammaliel requested that he be buried in a simple garment. He explained this by saying that he had come into this world like everyone else and wished to leave in the same way.

In the seventeenth century, the Jewish dress for the corpse consisted of two layers of underclothes, a skirt with a frill of fine linen, a cloak, a square of ribbons and a white head cap. Modern orthodox Jews dress the deceased in trousers, slip-over blouse, coat, sash, prayer shawl, head covering and large sheet. Using at least three of these shrouds is a basic requirement for both for men and women.

The Jewish faith considers the use of flowers at a funeral inappropriate. Instead, individuals are encouraged to give *tzdakah* (charitable gifts). Donations to a charity are suggested in lieu of flowers and gifts. If flowers are received despite the recommendations, however, they will be displayed to show respect for the individual who sent them. The use of music is also considered inappropriate.

KERIAH

The Jewish tradition also calls for a symbolic act of destruction on the part of a mourner to express anguish and grief. The mourner carries out this symbolic act of destruction prior to the funeral service as an expression of the acceptance of death. The mourner makes a tear in his or her clothing or attaches a ribbon to the clothing. This is called *Keriah*. In the case of the death of a parent, the Keriah is on the left side, close to the heart. For everyone else, the Keriah is on the right side. Just before Keriah the mourner recites this benediction:

Praised are you,
Adonai our God,
Sovereign of the Universe,
the True Judge.

The Hebrew word for funeral, *levayah*, means "to accompany." The friends and relatives attend the funeral to respect and honor the deceased and to provide support to the mourners. When the body is taken to the cemetery, the mourners walk along side or behind the casket carrying the body. Sometimes the pallbearers carry the casket from the funeral chapel or synagogue directly to a hearse or to the grave. The pallbearers customarily make seven stops on the way to the grave. Between each stop, Psalm 91 is recited. Upon arrival at the cemetery, they carry the casket from the hearse to the grave, and lower it into the ground.

Sometimes, to symbolize oneness with Israel and contact with the Holy Land, members of the Chevra Kaddisha put soil from Israel within the casket. Families may also bring soil or stones from Israel for this purpose.

After the casket is lowered, relatives and friends then shovel earth onto the grave to cover it. No one leaves until the coffin is fully covered. Psalm 23 is customarily recited at the cemetery:

The Lord is my shepherd, I shall not want. He makes me
lie down in green pastures. He leads me beside the still
waters. He restores my soul. He guides me in straight paths
for His name's sake. Though I walk in the valley of the
shadow of death, I fear no evil, for You are with me. Your
staff and Your rod comfort me. You prepare a banquet for
me in the presence of my enemies. You anoint my head with
oil; my cup runs over. Surely goodness and mercy shall
follow me all the days of your life. And I shall dwell in the
house of God forever.

Before leaving the grave site, the friends and the relatives form two lines facing one another and recite the following words of comfort:

May the Holy One comfort you
among the other mourners of
Zion and Jerusalem.

The mourners walk away from the grave, passing between the parallel lines of these people listening to these words.

After the burial, a seven-day period of mourning called the *Shiva* begins. This is the time when relatives and friends visit the mourners.

PAST AND PRESENT

Following is a summary of the Jewish laws, standards and recommendations pertaining to the funeral practice as spelled out by the United Synagogue of Conservative Judaism[1]:

- Preplanning is encouraged and the advance purchase of grave sites is considered important and appropriate
- Willing one's organs is permissible
- Routine autopsies are not allowed
- Embalming is not permitted
- Cremation is not permitted
- Burial preferably occurs within 24 hours of death, and the deceased is not to be left alone prior to burial
- Viewing of the body is to be avoided
- Cosmetics on the deceased are not permitted
- Flowers and music are considered inappropriate
- Burial clothes are to be plain white shrouds
- The casket is to be made entirely of wood
- Ostentation is to be avoided at funerals.

Some families and communities still follow the conservative standards of the funeral practices described above. However, over the past centuries, the practices have changed considerably. For example, nowadays, only the orthodox Jews use Chevra Kaddisha. Mausoleums are being used frequently, about 20 percent of the time, instead of ground burials. Only about 65 percent of caskets are made entirely of wood. Pallbearers are used infrequently and the funeral director personnel usually carry the casket. At the grave site, not everyone shovels earth on the casket. Almost no one cuts their clothing before the service as part of Keriah, but they cut only a ribbon attached to the clothing.

Despite these modern day differences, the Jewish funeral still remains a sacred rite with no ostentation and no show. It reflects simplicity, immense dignity, utmost respect for the dead, and infinite compassion for the survivors.

REFERENCE

1. The United Synagogue of Conservative Judaism: *Guide to Jewish Funeral Practice*, 1996.

Chapter 25

THE CHRISTIAN FUNERAL

The Christian Funeral can be most effective when the biblical
teaching of the reality of death and the assurance of resurrection by
the power of God are kept in dynamic tension.

—P.H. Biddle, Jr.[1]

*T*he Catholics and the Protestants, including the Baptists, Methodists and the Lutherans, all have similar philosophies concerning the matters of death and funeral services. The focus is indeed on prayers with the goal of emphasizing the reality of death, the reduction of grief and the reassurance of resurrection. Just as a rabbi plays an important part in the Jewish funeral, a pastor takes charge of the Christian funeral and works closely with the bereaved and the funeral director.

The pastor offers informed counsel to the parishioners regarding the Christian funeral service, including advice on scriptures, hymns, sermons and music. This is why the pastor is usually informed of an impending or actual death. He offers pre-death prayers at the dying person's bed side, no matter where he or she is: at home, in a hospital or in a nursing home. At death, the pastor assists the grieving family in planning the funeral and in worshiping.

In this chapter, the funeral practices of Catholics and Protestants and those of Orthodox Christian Church are discussed separately.

THE CATHOLIC/PROTESTANT FUNERAL

When death occurs, the pastor and the funeral director are called. Jointly they assist the family in all matters of the funeral. The body is moved from the place of death to the funeral home, where the body is prepared for the wake and the funeral service. The preparation of the body may include embalming, cosmetization, and hair dressing. The body is dressed in clothes brought by the family and is placed in a casket selected by the family.

Wake

The wake or prayer service is usually planned for the evening before the funeral service and most often takes place at the funeral home. The casket is frequently kept open for relatives and close friends to view the body. Friends and relatives may send flowers or gifts, or the family may suggest that donations to charity be offered instead. The prayers are led by the pastor.

Funeral Service

The funeral service may take place at the funeral home. Most of the time, the casket is kept closed. The pastor conducts the ceremony and offers prayers and a sermon. Oftentimes, Roman Catholic funeral ceremonies are held in a church where scriptures relating to death are read and the concept of resurrection is discussed. Sermons, prayers and group reading of hymns also occurs. The following is a good prayer for the beginning of a funeral service. It is taken from The Book of Common Order of the Church of Scotland (1940):

> *Almighty God, our heavenly father, who loves us*
> *With an everlasting love, and can turn the darkness*
> *of sorrow into the morning, help us to be open to*
> *you in this hour. Give us reverent and*
> *submissive hearts. Speak to us of eternal things*
> *by your Spirit through Scripture and the*
> *experience of worship. Give us hope, O Lord,*
> *that we may be able to pass safely through*

the light of your presence. Grant us peace,
through Christ we pray. Amen.[2]

The music for the funeral service is selected on the basis of appropriateness for Christian worship. The words express a biblical understanding of God, His power and His mercy. They also express the meaning of life and death.

Cremation and the Roman Catholic Church

The human body is considered sacred by the Catholic Church. For centuries, the only method of disposition of the dead was burial. Cremation was prohibited because it was thought to result in the denial of resurrection and that it would therefore disturb the immortality of the dead. However, on May 8, 1963, the Holy Office issued an instruction to allow cremation in cases of necessity. The 1963 *Code of Canon Law* states:

> The Church earnestly recommends the pious custom of burying the bodies of the dead be observed; it does not, however, forbid cremation unless it has been chosen for reasons which are contrary to Christian teaching.[3]

With this change in Church law, cremation is now accepted and used more frequently as a method of disposition of the dead. The cremated remains of the body are allowed in the Church for Catholic funeral rites with the permission of the local bishop. The Church affirms that, "when extraordinary circumstances make the cremation of a body the only feasible choice, pastoral sensitivity must be exercised by priests, deacons and others who minister to the family of the deceased." The Church insists, however, that the cremated remains be treated with the same respect given to a body. Furthermore, it advises that scattering ashes in the ocean, on the ground or keeping them in the home of a relative is not considered reverent. The cremated remains of the body should be buried or entombed in a cemetery or mausoleum. Burial of the ashes in a common grave is also permissible.

The Cemetery: A Holy Place

The Catholic funeral ritual is concluded at the cemetery where participants join in scripture, verse and prayer. The cemetery and the mausoleum are considered holy places. This is where the bereaved accept the reality of death and bid farewell to the deceased with the prayers. The cemetery is a significant station in the funeral journey. It is a place for burial, worship and grief; an open church for encounter with God; and an eternal resting place until the resurrection.

The committal service at the cemetery is concluded with the placement of a flower on the casket, and after mourners shovel a small amount of dirt on the coffin. This signifies final separation. The ritual includes offering the following prayer at all burials:

> *Lord Jesus Christ, by your own three days in the tomb, you hallowed the graves of all who believe in you and so made the grave a sign of hope that promises resurrection even as it claims our mortal bodies.*
>
> *Grant that our brother/sister may sleep here in peace until you awaken him/her to glory, for you are the resurrection and the life. Then he/she will see you face to face and in your light will see light and know the splendor of God, for you live and reign for ever and ever.*
>
> *Response: Amen.*

If the grave has already been blessed, the following prayer is offered:

> *All praise to you, Lord of all creation. Praise to you, holy and living God. We praise and bless you for your mercy, we praise and bless you for your kindness. Blessed is the Lord, our God.*
>
> *Response: Blessed is the Lord, our God.*
>
> *You sanctify the homes of the living and make holy the places of the dead. You alone open the gates of righteous-ness and lead us to the dwellings of the saints. Blessed is the Lord, our God.*
>
> *Response: Blessed is the Lord, our God.*
>
> *We praise you, our refuge and strength. We bless you our god and Redeemer. Your praise is always in our hearts and on our lips. We remember the might deeds of the covenant. Blessed is the Lord, our God.*
>
> *Response: Blessed is the Lord, our God.*

Services and burials for Protestants are substantially similar to those for Catholics.

THE ORTHODOX CHRISTIAN FUNERAL

Significant differences may be found in the funeral practices of the Catholics and the Orthodox Christians. In this section, the general procedures followed by Orthodox Christians are presented with an emphasis on "special procedures." These procedures are governed by the Council of Bishops and are practiced in Greece, Russia, Eastern Europe and parts of Western Asia.[5]

When death is imminent, the family notifies the priest. He conducts prayers daily until death occurs. The funeral director is informed as soon as the individual dies and the body is moved from the place of death to the funeral home without special ceremony. At the funeral home, the body is prepared consistent with the wishes of the family. Embalming is routine, unless the family objects to this practice. The body is dressed in clothes brought by the family. In Europe, a shroud is still used. The body is put in a casket that has been selected by the family.

The services are divided in four parts: pre-services held at the funeral home the evening before visitation; services and viewing at the funeral home; services at the church; and, finally, the committal services at the cemetery. Orthodox Christians, as well as Catholics and Protestants, do not generally have funerals on Sundays, nor on the Holy Days of Christmas, Easter, Assumption and Ascension.

Funeral Home Services

The open casket is brought out and visitation for all relatives and friends takes place at the funeral home before the services begin. A picture of Jesus is placed near the casket, and a cross is positioned behind it. Candles are lit at each end of the casket and the icon of Jesus is placed at the foot end of the casket for people to kiss as they pass by. *Trisagion*, which are three short prayers lasting about ten minutes, are conducted. These are attended by the family and the pallbearers. The procession then moves to the church.

Church Funeral Services

The casket is brought into the church, and the family enters first. They meet the priest who blesses the casket with holy water. The casket is kept open and is placed in front of the altar with its foot end nearest the altar. When all of the relatives and friends are seated, prayers are offered and hymns are sung. A eulogy delivered by clergy or a close relative may follow. When these preliminaries are complete, the casket is moved so that it lies parallel to the *iconstasis*, which is a solid screen with icons that divides the sanctuary and the body of the church building.

The priest then anoints the body with sand and olive oil. An icon is placed at the foot end of the casket. The people sitting in the right half of the church walk to the casket, view the body, kiss the icon and return to their seats. Then the icon is moved to the head end of the casket and those seated on the left side of the church pass by the casket and kiss the icon.

After this, the friends leave the church and the family does a final viewing. The casket is closed and the procession heads to the cemetery.

Disposition of the Remains

The Orthodox Church objects to cremation. Therefore, the body must be buried or entombed. When the body arrives at the cemetery or the mausoleum, the closing ritual and the committal services take place. The committal service includes appropriate readings and prayers by the priest.

REFERENCES

1. Biddle, PH Jr.: *A Funeral Manual*. Grand Rapids, MI: William B. Eerdmans Publishing Company, 1984.
2. *The Book of the Common Order of the Church of Scotland*. Oxford University Press, 1940.
3. Moroney JP: "Cremation and the Catholic Church." *The Director*, Aug. 1998: 50-1.
4. Curley TP: "Catholic Funeral Ritual Emphasizes Burial Service." *The American Funeral Director*, Feb. 1992: 38-44.
5. National Funeral Directors Association:"The Eastern Orthodox Funeral." NFDA, Nov. 13, 1997.

Chapter 26

THE MUSLIM FUNERAL

We are all from God and
To God is our return.

—The Holy Koran

*T*he Islamic culture views death as a normal and natural part of life. Moslems show a great deal of reverence towards their dead.[1] Crying due to grief is allowed, but no one is allowed to question why the death has occurred, nor is anyone allowed to be angry at God that death has occurred. This is because it is believed that Allah (God) knows all and has a good reason for making the decisions that He makes.

Moslem men are expected to mourn for only three days, while women are expected to mourn for four months and ten days. During this grieving period, mourners dress in plain clothing and are forbidden to participate in any form of entertainment. On the third day after death, the family generally holds a prayer meeting to ask Allah to forgive the sins of the deceased.

Since Islamic communities are generally very close, friends of the family cook for the family of the deceased for three days following death, or longer, if necessary. They also help the family with any arrangements that must be taken care of. This is especially true in the United States, where because of cultural and religious beliefs, people of Islamic faith tend to look out for one another.

BEFORE DEATH

If death is imminent, family members contact the extended family and all come to the home of the dying family member. At the gathering, all recite the "Article of Faith in Islam":

There is no God, but God and Mohammed is His prophet.[2]

If the dying person is incoherent, a close family member takes on the responsibility of praying for the dying person until his or her last breath. It is thought that even though the person is unable to respond, his or her soul understands what is happening. This is why it is important for another Muslim, preferably a family member, to pray on the dying individual's behalf. If possible, an Islamic leader (*Haaji*) is called to lead the family in their prayers. From this point until the death of the person, a close family member sits with the dying person.

AT DEATH

Once the person dies, the family notifies their Haaji as well as the friends and family of the deceased. Everyone gathers at the home of the deceased and preparations for burial begin. In the United States, a funeral director would also be notified. The Koran, the Moslem holy text, instructs the family as to how to position and care for the person after death. The body is positioned with the head to the south and the feet to the north. The face is turned to face Mecca, the birthplace of Mohammed. The mouth and eyes are closed and the face is covered with a clean cloth. The legs and arms are straightened, with both hands to the sides of the body. Again, a close family member sits with the body and reads from the Koran.

Due to laws in the United States pertaining to the handling of the deceased, the body is removed from the place of death and taken to a funeral home. With the family's permission, the body is embalmed. Embalming, however, is not preferred, hence it is not commonly requested.

Once the embalming has taken place (if it is chosen or required), the funeral director permits the immediate family of the deceased to come into the funeral parlor's preparation room so that they may cleanse the body in accordance with Islamic laws and culture. It should be noted that in Islamic countries, the body would be kept at home until the time of burial. Embalming is not customary.

CLEANSING THE BODY FOR BURIAL

Islamic laws and culture have very stringent rules about how the body of the deceased should be prepared for burial. It should always be washed by two members of the deceased's immediate family who are of the same gender as the deceased. This washing ritual is known as *Gusal*.

The following is a list of steps for preparing the body, as indicated in the Koran:

1. The clothing of the deceased is removed.
2. The body is covered by a white muslin cloth.
3. The private parts of the dead are washed three times using a fresh cloth each time.
4. The mouth of the deceased is washed with a piece of unused wet cloth.
5. The nostrils are then cleaned with a fresh wet cloth.
6. The face of the deceased is washed by splashing water on the face three times.
7. The right hand is washed first, followed by the left hand.
8. Then the right foot is washed, followed by the left foot.
9. Finally the entire body is washed from head to foot. This is done three times.

It should be noted that if there is no family member of the same gender available to clean the body, then a representative from the mosque who is of the same gender can fulfill the ritual.

DRESSING AND CASKETING

After the body has been properly cleansed, it is dressed in accordance to Islamic practice. The lower portion of the body from the navel to the ankles is wrapped in a white muslin type cloth. Next, the upper portion of the body is wrapped with a second muslin cloth. Several pieces of cloth are used for each portion of the body. Only the face and the hands of the deceased are left uncovered.

In Islamic countries, the body is then wrapped in three more sheets which would serve as the "coffin." The body is buried this way, without a traditional casket. In the United States, due to burial regulations, the family would choose a very simple wooden casket with no adornment. The body is placed into the casket, which is then positioned with the head to the south, the feet towards the north and the face towards Mecca.

VISITATION AND FUNERAL SERVICES

Traditionally, visitation would be conducted in the home of the deceased. Today, the services are usually conducted in a funeral home. Funeral homes that deal strictly with Muslims are rare in the United States. Since Jewish views on the disposition of the dead are similar to those of Muslims, many Muslims prefer to use Jewish funeral homes.

The ceremony is generally open casket and lasts no more than one hour. During this time the entire family is present. The actual funeral services are carried out at the grave site. The body is transported to the site by the male members of the family and the casket is again placed with the head pointing to the south and the feet to the north, and the head turned to face Mecca.

The funeral service itself is open casket and lasts about twenty minutes. At this point, the funeral prayer called the *Janaazah Namaaz* is recited by male attendees.

BURIAL AND GRAVE SITE

Muslim culture requires that the body be buried as soon after death as possible. An ideal situation would be to bury the body on the same day. Although it is considered acceptable in most Islamic cultures to bury a deceased on a Holy Day, some Muslims prefer to wait.

In a traditional Islamic burial, once the body is wrapped in the burial sheets it is placed into a grave that is four feet deep. The body is covered with wood and then dirt. Generally, the dirt mound is raised above ground level to serve as a marker for the grave. Since there is no actual casket, the people feel that it is acceptable to reuse the grave after 25 years, once the body has "returned to the earth."

Once the body or casket is lowered, a funeral prayer is recited. The ceremony is complete and the mourners leave the grave site.

Although cremation is not permitted by Islam, if it is deemed necessary for some reason, then the male family members of the deceased will place the casket into the retort chamber of the crematorium. Organ donation is also not favored by Islam.

SUMMARY

Islam is the major religion in many regions, including as the Middle East, Turkey, Iran, North Africa, parts of India, Bangladesh, Malaysia, Pakistan, and Indonesia. There are over one million Muslims living in the United States. One should keep in mind that Muslim funerals vary slightly due to the incorporation of local culture into the traditional Islamic service. However, in general, Islamic funeral traditions have changed very little since the origin of the religion.

REFERENCES

1. Daniels S: "Funeral Customs of the Newest Americans." *The Director*, June 1994: 30.
2. National Funeral Directors Association: *The Muslim Funeral*. August 25, 1997.

Chapter 27

THE HINDU FUNERAL

When one man dies, one chapter is not torn out of the book,
But translated into a better language.

—John Donne (1572–1631)

*H*induism *dates back to 4000 B.C. Hindus worship many gods and* goddesses rather than just one god. In fact, there are millions of gods, and each has 1008 Hindu names. However, the main gods are Rama, Krishna, Shiva, Vishnu, Gangesh, Saravati and Lakshmi. These gods and goddesses are in different manifestations, at times appearing in the form of men, women, animals, fire, etcetera.

Hinduism originated in India but its founder has never been identified. The religious theory is collected in the Vedas which are scriptures, or laws of living, which have divine origin. They are written in Sanskrit.

The most important element of the Hindu religion is *karma*, literally meaning "action." Hindus believe that what you do in life is what counts. One's karma is the accumulation of all of one's actions in life.

Hindus strive to do good deeds. Their actions are dictated by the abstract laws governing the universe. The result of all the actions of a Hindu in his lifetime is called *dharma*, and this refers to the sacred laws, duties and ideas of truth and ethics. Hindus believe it is this power that upholds society and the cosmos. A good Hindu works all his life to make his karma fit dharma perfectly.

The Hindus believe in reincarnation and see life as a cycle that is not interrupted, even by death. They believe that their karma from the life they live will determine how will be incarnated in the next life. After each death, a Hindu continues to be reincarnated into a new form until there has been no negative conduct in his life. This is when he achieves *moksha*, the ultimate goal. To a Hindu, reaching this goal means he is liberated from all ties to the material world, karma and the cycle of life and death. If death occurs at this stage, he is led into the afterworld for eternity. This is called Nirvana, an "absolute" place where there are no positives or negatives. Hindus believe that it may take as many as 32 million cycles of life and death before one can achieve this highest achievement of Nirvana.[1]

HINDU PHILOSOPHY OF DEATH

Because they believe in reincarnation, Hindus do not fear death. They know that they have been born and have died before. The belief in reincarnation makes the inevitable death a natural event. Dying is like falling asleep, and waking from that sleep is to be born again. They accept that life is a sacred journey and death is a blissful, light-filled transition from one state to another, very simple and natural. Death and birth are simply two sides of the life cycle.

The body dies, but the soul is immortal, for it is the soul that reincarnates. This is described in the scripture Shukla Yajur Veda, Brihadaran Yaka Upanishad (4.4 5-6) as follows:

> *A man acts according to his desires to which he clings. After death he goes to the next world bearing in his mind the subtle impressions of his deeds; after reaping there the harvest of his deeds, he returns again to this world of action. Thus, he who has desires continues subject to rebirth.*

WHEN DEATH OCCURS

> *Where eternal luster glows, the realm in which the light divine is set, place me, Purifier, in that deathless, imperishable world. Make me immortal in that realm where movement is accordant to wish, in the third region, the third heaven of heavens, where the worlds are resplendent. [Rig Veda, Aitareya Aranyaka 6-11].*

Long before death occurs, the Hindu has prepared for it. He knows that life on earth is temporary and the possessions of power, ego and education will end. He prepares all his life for this liberation. As a Hindu ages, he tries to fulfill his obligations to others, resolve misunderstandings and any misdeeds. If he is ailing, he meets friends and enemies to offer blessings and apologies. To minimize the last minute conflicts, he even distributes his assets among heirs, charities and endowments. He then turns to reading scriptures, attending temple and meditation. To seek further peace he may go on a pilgrimage to a sacred place. To remain pure at death, he refrains from using mind-altering substances.

Hindus prefer to die at home. In India, if a person is near death he is brought home to die. He is positioned in the entryway of the house facing east and encouraged recite mantras and concentrate on a lamp placed nearby. The family members sing hymns, pray and read scripture. At the time of death (the great departure) a family member chants the mantra in his right ear if he is unconscious. The most commonly recited mantra is the Gayatri mantra. In English, this mantra translates to:

> O Supreme Lord, the source of existence, intelligence and bliss, the Creator of the universe. May we prove worthy of your choice and acceptance, may we meet Your Glorious grace. May you vouch a safe and unerring guidance to our intellects and may we follow Your lead unto Righteousness.

The other commonly recited mantra reads:

> O three-eyed Lord Shiva, I meditate on you.
> Please, bless me with perfect health, sever me from the pain, disease and death.[2]

If the family does not remember a mantra, they intone "Aum Nama Maryana" or "Aum Nama Sivaya," recitations remembering God. Relatives in attendance apply sandal paste (tilak) to the forehead, chant Vedic verses and put a few drops of milk or holy water from river Ganga (Ganges) in the dying person's mouth.

As soon as death occurs, the body is put in the entrance way of the home and the head is turned to face south. Incense is kept burning. A cloth is wrapped to go around the top of the deceased's head and his chin to keep his mouth closed. In the house, all the mirrors are covered and any religious pictures are turned to face the wall.

A funeral priest or a Hindu minister (*pandit*) is summoned and with the family he starts the *Homa*, or fire ritual. This ritual is to bless nine brass and one clay water pot (*kumbhas*).

The rites are usually led by the eldest son in the case of the father's death and by the youngest son in the case of mother's death. He performs *Arti*, a ceremony where he passes an oil lamp over the remains and then offers flowers. The preparation of the body for the final journey then follows.

PREPARATION OF BODY

No matter where a Hindu dies, the preparation of the body for cremation is carried out by family members. If death occurs away from home the family members will go to the mortuary to prepare the body, rather than leave the task to strangers. If death occurs at home, the body is moved to the back porch where the clothes of the deceased are removed. The body is bathed with water and sesame oil is applied to the forehead. The water used for this is taken from the nine brass water pots that were blessed before. The bathing of the body is done by male members of the family if the deceased is male, and by female members if the deceased is female. If there is no back porch, the body is sponge-bathed inside the house.

The body is then draped with a white cloth or garment characteristic of the nationality of the deceased. The body is placed on a palanquin, and is then taken to the Homa shelter where the fire ritual is carried out.

A coffin is rarely used, and the Hindu tradition does not permit embalming, nor does it allow the removal of organs from the body for donation. The family and children sing hymns. The children encircle the body with lighted sticks. The women go around the body and place puffed rice into the mouth of the deceased. This represents feeding the corpse so that the deceased will have nourishment for the journey ahead. If her husband has died, the widow places her wedding pendant around the deceased's neck to signify her lasting tie to him. If the deceased is a married woman, her body is dressed in colored clothes and she wears jewelry to show her married status.

After visitation and prayers are completed, the family members serve as pallbearers and lead a procession carrying the body to the cremation site.

CREMATION OF A HINDU IN INDIA

Hindus consider cremation to be a sacrament. The funeral ceremony is considered second only in importance to wedding celebrations. They believe the soul is trapped in the skull and cremation of the body will release it, allowing the liberated soul to go forward to the next life. That is why cremation is an integral part of a Hindu funeral ritual. In India, cremation is achieved by burning the body in the open air.

The body is carried to the cremation site by the male family members. The procession is led by the chief mourner who is often the eldest son.[3] Two pots are carried to the cremation site, one clay kumbha containing water and another containing burning embers from the Homa.

The body of the deceased is carried counter-clockwise around the pyre three times and then placed on the pyre. The male members offer puffed rice as the women did earlier. The body is then covered with wood and sprinkled with incense and *ghee* (a form of butter). Often a distinction between the rich and the poor is made in the type of wood used on the pyre. Those who can afford to use sandalwood, which generates a pleasant aroma when burning. The poor usually use simple tree branches which they have gathered from the area.

The chief mourner walks around the pyre while holding a fire brand behind his back and carrying the clay pot on his left shoulder. As he goes around the pyre, another family member strikes the pot with a knife to make a hole in the pot. Water drains out through this hole, signifying that life is leaving. After completing three turns around the pyre, the chief mourner drops the pot. At this point he looks away from the body and lights the pyre. He then leaves the site followed by the rest of the mourners. As the fire continues to burn, the crowd disperses. The family comes back the next day to gather the cremains and bring the ashes to the Ganga, a sacred river which is said to carry the deceased's spirit.

When the mourners return home, they bathe and help to clean the house. The whole occasion is joyous and there is no public display of mourning. No weeping is allowed near the body, as it is thought to disturb the soul.

HINDU FUNERALS IN THE UNITED STATES

The funeral of a Hindu in the United States is significantly different. In some United States communities, a few of the traditional rituals are carried out by the family members at the place of death. However, this is not common. The general pattern of the funeral is molded to fit an American life style. Since open air burning of the body is not possible here, crematoriums become a necessity.

Just as with a Christian or a Jewish death, when a Hindu dies, a funeral director is called. The family finishes the appropriate rituals before the funeral director responds to the call. The family lets the funeral director move the body to the funeral home for further ceremonies and disposition.

The family advises the funeral director regarding the preparation of the body. The family, in all likelihood, will supply the clothing for the body. Garments will vary from country to country. Traditionally, the clothes for a Hindu from India will be white for a man or colored for a woman, but the family of a Hindu from another country might want to reflect their culture in the choice of clothing.

Although caskets are not generally used in India, in the United States they are necessary for services, viewing and for other reasons. Because the body is going to be cremated, the selected casket is usually an inexpensive one.

The average Hindu funeral ceremony in the United States consists of placing the remains in a casket for viewing at a funeral home. Light facial make-up may be requested. If there is going to be a delay in the final disposition, the family may request that the body be embalmed. Depending on the deceased's social status, a period of time is allotted for funeral services. Typically, the service lasts about two hours, but it could last longer depending upon the number and length of the eulogies.

The ceremony is usually very simple. Immediate family members and close friends deliver eulogies, and then there are prayers, chants and a viewing of the remains. Each guest places a single rose or other flower on the deceased's chest as they lie in the casket.

After all the guests have left, the funeral director moves the body to the crematorium. Generally, only close family members accompany the body to the crematorium and in some cases they may even help to carry the remains. Once at the crematorium, the family members may want to carry the body to the retort chamber. The eldest son or another family member may choose to push the body inside the cremation chamber and may operate the switches to begin cremation himself. If the crematorium is gas-fueled, sacred wood and ghee may be put inside the casket. In some places, the family may be allowed to set a small fire inside the coffin before it is subjected to the fire inside the cremation chamber.

At the end of the cremation process, the family departs. They return in one to four days to collect the deceased's ashes. In the United States, many families take the ashes and scatter them in nearby rivers or oceans. Some families choose to take the ashes back to India and scatter them in the river Ganga.. This has great significance for a Hindu, as reflected in the Hindu text, the Padma Purana:

> *Knowingly or even unknowingly,*
> *Intentionally or even unintentionally,*
> *a mortal, having gone to death*
> *in the Ganga, obtains Heaven and moksha.*

REFERENCES

1. Ellinger H: *Hinduism (Basics, 4)*. Valley Forge, PA: Trinity Press Intl., 1996.
2. "Death and Dying." *Hinduism Today International*.Online. Available: *http://hoohana.aloha.net/~htoday/Jan97.html*, January, 1997.
3. Klostermaier K: *A Survey of Hinduism*, 2nd ed. Albany, NY: State University of NY Press, 1994.

Chapter 28

FUNERALS IN JAPAN

*J*apanese funerals are conducted according to Buddhist rites in 90 percent of cases.[1] Although Buddhist ceremonies and rituals vary in different regions of Japan, certain rites and customs are most common.[2] The Shinto funeral rites are somewhat different.

Buddhism was founded by an Indian philosopher in the sixth century B.C., but most present-day followers of Buddhism live in Japan, Thailand, Burma and Sri Lanka. Approximately 100,000 Buddhists live in the United States. The following discussion relates primarily to Japanese Buddhists.

About 99 percent of Buddhist funerals involve cremation. Since most deaths occur in hospitals and nursing homes, often the funeral homes are selected by these facilities. They have contracts with funeral homes and families usually accept their choice. The funeral homes aid in completion of funeral rites, including dressing the body and making arrangements for the wake, memorial service and cremation. In almost all cases, embalming is not done.

In the United States, the disposition of the body by cremation without embalming costs on an average of only $1,145. In Japan, the lower-to-upper-range funeral costs $30,000 to $40,000, with cemetery fees up to $3,000 and urns costing $100 to $1,000. Some Japanese may even spend upwards of $50,000 for flowers.[3]

IMPENDING DEATH

As death approaches, the dying person receives the "last water" from family members, beginning with the closest kin. The "last water" is given by moistening the dying person's lips with a wet brush. After he or she has died, the deceased is generally washed with hot water and dressed in either white garments or favorite clothing. Since 90 percent of deaths occur in hospitals or nursing homes, it is common practice for doctors and nurses to cleanse the body with rubbing alcohol and for morticians to dress the body. Usually, the funeral homes work with the hospitals and nursing homes by contractual agreement. Often families meet with the funeral home manager and they entrust the wake, funeral service, memorial service and cremation to the funeral director.

ETIQUETTE

For the Japanese, etiquette is culturally important. Even in death, the deceased is placed in the portion of the room that is considered the most honorable. The head is placed toward the north, without a pillow. The body is covered with a white cloth. The hands are clasped together and a knife is put on the chest to drive the spirits away. In Buddhist rites, a screen is placed upside-down near the body and a table is put in front of it. The table holds a vase, a candle holder and an incense burner. Sometimes bowls of water and cooked rice are also placed on this table. An undertaker brings all the articles necessary for the altar, but sweets, vegetables and other food offerings are furnished by the family.[4]

The coffin is usually made of pine, fir or Japanese cypress and is unpainted. It is brought to the family home. Usually it is kept open during visitation, although some families prefer a closed ceremony. Candles are burned throughout the ceremony.

When the day of the funeral is chosen, notices are sent out to family members and friends. A notice of mourning, written on a piece of white paper with a black frame, is posted on the front door or gate of the house throughout *kichu* (the mourning period) , which can last from 7 to 49 days.

THE WAKE

The *tsuya* (wake) is held at the family home. It used to be observed throughout the night to mourn for the dead and to pray for the repose of his soul. More recently, half wakes, or *hantsuya*, are held. A Buddhist priest (monk) wearing a burnt orange robe is invited to the house and recites prayers, or *sutras*. While prayers are being offered, the priest places three candles on the casket and lights them. The priest and family members participate in chants which are accompanied by sounds of a gong-like bell. Incense powder (*shoko*) is burned throughout this ritual. At the end of the wake, a meal of rice, peas and carrots is served.

The mourners bring *koden*, or "incense money," in a white envelope tied with black and white or silver strings. Koden may be brought to the house or to the memorial services. The amount of koden varies according to region.[5] It is also customary in Japan to practice *koden gaeshi*, which is a reply to koden. Here, family members prepare token gifts to give to those who have come to mourn for the dead. Flowers are often sent during the wake and during the funeral services as well. Chrysanthemums are often the flower of choice.

THE FUNERAL SERVICES

The day after the wake, a funeral service is held at home, at the parish temple or at a funeral hall. All funeral services are held under the direction of a priest. The chief mourner is first to pay homage to the deceased, followed by those family members who are closest to the deceased and then by all others in the order of their arrival.

At the funeral home, an altar is prepared with a tablet (*ihai*) inscribed with the posthumous name which is given to the deceased. A picture of the deceased, candleholders, incense burners, flowers and other implements of Buddhist ritual are placed on an altar. The deceased is dressed in a black robe. The guests also wear black clothes. Those who do not have proper attire rent this from the funeral home.

At the start of the funeral service, the family of the deceased sit on the right side of the room and relatives and friends sit on the left, facing the altar. The Buddhist priest starts with the recitation of sutras. He may choose a member of the family, generally the eldest male, to assist him with the rituals. A funeral home staff member reads a history of the deceased, and this is followed by a short eulogy by a friend. The priest then continues the prayers. After the prayers, guests are allowed to pay their respects. They pass by the casket, bow and place a flower on the casket. In the funeral home chapel, a meal of rice, peas and carrots is prepared to be taken to the cemetery.

The funeral rites conclude with family members and relatives burning pinches of incense in turn while the priest recites sutras. Other participants pay their last respects by coming to the altar and burning pinches of incense. The funeral service usually lasts about an hour.

FAREWELL CEREMONY

At the farewell ceremony, the guests present their name card and koden. They advance towards the casket from the left. The guests bow to the friends of the deceased. In front of the coffin, they bow and pray to express sympathy. Following this, the mourners bow again to the relatives and leave.

THE CREMATION

After the funeral rites are completed, the coffin lid is nailed shut. Most often the pallbearers are family members. They wear white gloves as they carry the body. The body is cremated on the day of the funeral. At the conclusion of the cremation, the funeral director says the words, "It's finished." The guests eat in the crematorium.

Immediately after the cremation, the family goes to the retort. There, on a small table, two urns and two pairs of long metal chopsticks are placed.[6] The chopsticks are given to the family and the family uses them to pick up pieces of bone fragments from the foot, arm, neck and head. They place the fragments in a small urn (*kotsutsubo*) to take home.

This urn is placed on an altar at the family home, along with a tablet inscribed with the posthumous name of the deceased, a picture of the deceased and an incense burner. The urn is kept at home for thirty-five days. Incense sticks (*osenko*) are burned around the clock. After this time period, the jar of bones is buried at the family burial site in a Buddhist cemetery.

MOURNING

Family members must abstain from celebrations such as weddings for at least forty-nine days (*kichu*) to a year (*muchu*). From the seventh day until the forty-ninth day, the family, relatives and friends of the deceased gather around the altar. A Buddhist priest recites sutras, incense is offered and food is served.

Most Japanese people continue to pay their respects to the dead and visit their ancestral graves at least four times a year as well as during the Obon Festival, a festival for honoring and remembering those who have died. This festival lasts from August 13 through 16 in most areas of Japan. Families prepare simple altars for the deceased, offer meals three times a day, and place fruits and flowers in front of the altar. In some parts of Japan, little boats made of straw and paper are placed in the water so that the souls may be conveyed to the ancestors.[7]

Some Japanese families honor the deceased by creating a *Batsudan*, which is a small family altar, in front of which they offer daily prayers and meals. Most Japanese people believe that their ancestors are always with them, protecting, watching and guiding them.

SHINTO FUNERAL RITES

Shintoism is a religion practiced by indigenous Japanese. Shinto funeral rites are similar to Buddhist rites, with a few differences. The knife is placed near the head of the deceased, not on his chest as in the Buddhist rite. According to Shinto customs, candles, washed rice, salt, water and food are placed on a table. A rite called *senreisai* is performed before the funeral begins. Senreisai sends the soul of the deceased to a guarding god or ancestral spirits.

Posthumous names are not given in Shinto ceremonies, but a honorific title, *mikoto*, is added after the name of the deceased. After the wake, the funeral rites are conducted in a funeral hall.

The funeral altar in Shinto ceremonies is decorated with bamboo poles and braided ropes (*shimenawa*), as well as branches of evergreen camellia (*sakaki*). The priest performs a Shinto purification ceremony (*oharai*) by rinsing the deceased's mouth and washing the deceased's hands with water.

Then he delivers a funeral address. Traditional musical instruments are played and dirges are sung. The family of the deceased offer branches of camellia decorated with white paper to the altar. Soft clapping occurs as they pray.

JAPANESE FUNERALS IN THE UNITED STATES

The Japanese funeral in the United States is relatively uncomplicated. The religion does not impose any rules or restrictions on the removal of the body. Embalming is widely accepted and practiced. The family usually selects suitable clothing for the deceased. Visitation typically lasts a few hours.

The casket, usually wooden or metal, is kept open at the time of viewing. The monk (priest) places three lit candles on the casket which burn throughout the funeral ceremony. The monk and the family chant prayers and a gong is used periodically. The funeral home provides a meal consisting of rice, peas and carrots, as is traditional. The family members usually serve as pallbearers and wear white gloves while carrying the casket. The committal service at the cemetery or crematorium lasts about thirty minutes and consists of burning incense and chanting by the family and the attending monk.

REFERENCES

1. Itasaka, G (ed.): *Kodansha Encyclopedia of Japan*. Tokyo: Kodansha Ltd., 1983.
2. National Funeral Directors Association: "The Buddhist Funeral." *Funeral Rites and Customs and Types of Funeral Services and Ceremonies*. Information obtained from the Professional Training Schools Publication, 1997.
3. Doody AF: "Cremation Funeral Service in Japan." *The American Funeral Director*. Nov 1997:78-80.
4. The World Fellowship Committee of the Young Women's Christian Association of Tokyo, Japan: *Japanese Etiquette, an Introduction*. Tokyo: The Charles E. Tuttle Co., 1955: 82-93.

5. Japanese customs. Online. Available: *http://www.kt.rim.or.jp/ etshioda/customs.html*, September 10, 1998.

6. "Schauwecker's Guide to Japan Funerals." Online. Available: *http://www.japan-guide.com/e/e2060.html*, June 28, 1998.

7. Puckle BS: *Funeral Customs: Their Origins and Development.* London: T. Werner, Ltd., 1926. Republished by Omnigraphics, Detroit, 1990.

Chapter 29

OTHER FUNERAL
TRADITIONS

No person can sum up the life of another.[1]

THE HUMANIST FUNERAL

Humanism is a multi-faceted philosophy based on naturalism that advocates the methods of reason, science and democracy to provide joyous service for the greater good of all humanity. The humanists believe that human beings are an evolutionary product of Nature, capable of shaping their own destiny and solving their own problems. They believe in "today":

For yesterday is but a dream, and tomorrow only a vision;
but today, well lived, makes every yesterday a dream of
happiness and every tomorrow a vision of hope. Look well,
therefore, to this day![1]

MEANING OF DEATH

To a humanist, death is just change. That change, they believe, should be celebrated. As humanist poet Langston Hughes (1902-1967) put it:

Dear lovely Death
That taketh all things under wing–
Never to kill–
Only to change
Into some other thing
This suffering flesh,

To make it either more or less,
But not again the same–
Dear lovely Death,
Change is thy other name.

The humanists have no fear of death, and in the confrontation with death they say:

In the presence of life, we say no to death.
In the presence of death, we say yes to life![1]

THE FUNERAL

About half of all Americans are not formally religious.[2] The number of persons describing themselves as humanists is very small. These individuals conduct very simple funeral services. A personal communication from humanist counselor Edmund Cannon[3] indicated that humanists generally conduct funeral services in a park, a community center, or, if the family requests it, the service is carried out in a church. A family member or friend usually presides over the ceremony. Sometimes a pastor is asked to conduct the ceremony without the use of religious imagery.

When death occurs, the immediate family members, close friends and the funeral director are informed. The body is taken to the funeral home and prepared for funeral ceremony. There is no objection to embalming. The body is usually dressed in clothes brought by the family. Friends and family members bring flowers and gather for the funeral ceremony to acknowledge death and to support each other.

The funeral ceremony begins with the playing of live or recorded music for about twenty minutes. Suggested music includes Block's Schelomo (First movement), Bach's "Come Sweet Death" and "Air for the G String," Barber's "Adagio for Strings," Massenet's "Meditation and Elegie," and the third part of the second movement to Beethoven's "Seventh Sym-phony."[4,5] Following the music, the pastor or other presiding individual speaks. The following statement is often read:

Let us be honest with death. Let us not pretend that it is
less than it is. It is separation. It is sorrow. It is grief. But
let us neither pretend that death is more than it is. It is not

*annihilation. As long as memory endures, her influence
will be felt. It is not an end to love—humanity's need for
love from each of us is boundless. It is not an end to joy
and laughter—nothing would less honor one so vibrant
than to make our lives drab in counterfeit respect! Let us
be honest with death, for in that honesty we will understand
her better and ourselves more deeply.[1]*

A candle is lit as an expression of honor for the life and living of the
deceased and to indicate that the glow of the flame symbolizes death, and
not defeat. The principal speaker may speak again, including in his speech
comments about the acknowledgement of death, the celebration of the life
that was lived, and a message to ease those who are grieving.

After the address, community singing occurs. Frequently, the Roman
philosopher Seneca is quoted:

*In the presence of death, we must continue to sing the song
of life. We must be able to accept death and go from its
presence better able to bear our burdens and to lighten the
load of others. Out of our sorrows should come understanding. Through our sorrows, we join with all of those
before who have had to suffer and all of those who will yet
have to do so. Let us not be gripped by the fear of death. If
another day be added to our lives, let us joyfully receive it,
but let us not anxiously depend on our tomorrows. Though
we grieve the deaths of our loved ones, we accept them and
hold on to our memories as precious gifts. Let us make the
best of our loved ones while they are with us, and let us not
bury our love with death.[1]*

The ceremony continues with the remembrance of personal achievements of the deceased by an individual who knew the deceased well. He or
she then calls for a one or two-minute period of silence out of reverence
and love for the deceased. The friends and the family may read selections
from poetry or literature.

The final act of the ceremony is the benediction, in which the attendees
are asked to bid farewell to the deceased and to feel profoundly glad that
the deceased lived. The entire ceremony takes less than an hour.

DISPOSITION OF THE REMAINS

The family decides whether the body is going to be buried or cremated. Cremation is more common than burial because it is less costly. If burial is chosen, the families usually select simple, inexpensive caskets. If the body is cremated, the ashes are either scattered in the ocean or preserved in urns.

A SIMPLE TRIBUTE

The humanist funeral is usually simple, inexpensive, disciplined and devoid of showmanship. Death is accepted gracefully and life is saluted. Genuine feelings are expressed. God and eternal life are not discussed.

THE AMISH FUNERAL

The Amish faith had its beginnings in Switzerland. The religion was founded by Jakob Ammon, a Christian who wanted to live a life less worldly than that encouraged by the Mennonite church. The Amish were originally known as "Anabaptists," due to their belief that baptism should occur as an adult, after a confession of faith.

Having formed in the sixteenth century, the Anabaptists came to the United States approximately 250 years ago seeking religious freedom. At the present time, approximately 16,000 to 18,000 Amish live in Pennsylvania.

The original Amish church has split into two branches over time. One of these branches is comprised of the House Amish who hold all of their religious services at home and appoint one of their own as the leader of the community's religious affairs. The other group is known as the Church Amish. This group has the more conventional church services with a preacher.

Despite these differences, the beliefs and the ideals of both branches are relatively the same. Their Amish ideals are spelled out in the Scheitheim Articles, which are interpretations of Bible teachings. In his book *Amish Society,*[6] John Hostetler lists these ideals as follows:

- Adult baptism
- Shunning of members who do not follow the rules and ideals
- Separation of their community from the rest of society, in order to avoid outside evil influences
- Rejection of oaths
- Refusal to bear arms
- Breaking of bread (sharing meals) only with other followers.

With these ideals as their foundation, each society clings to the ways of their founders and forefathers. These beliefs are accompanied by the values of devout religion, an agrarian way of life and a cohesive family and community. Each Amish society also agrees upon the "Ordnung," which delineates the social order for each community.

In an effort to keep in touch with their simple roots and to maintain a separation from the rest of society, the Amish continue to dress in the style of their seventeenth century forefathers. Men generally wear dark colored vests over home-made white shirts and collarless coats. They prefer to use hook and eye fasteners, rather than the more conventional buttons or zippers, although it should be noted that they do make some exceptions in the use of buttons for the coats. Married men grow a beard but no mustache to signify their marital status. Women wear ankle length dresses with black stockings and flat shoes.

Once they have been baptized, the women wear what is known as a kapp. This is a simple white prayer cap, usually made of a white gauzy material with ribbons which are pinned to their dresses. In the winter, the *kapp* can be covered with a conventional black bonnet.

The Amish shun the use of modern devices, such as automobiles, tractors, electricity, telephones, indoor plumbing and radios. Due to all of these restrictions, their main sources of income are from farming and carpentry.

DEATH OF AN AMISH

When a member of the Amish community passes away, a clergyman usually takes over for the family and begins the rites of death. In most instances, death occurs in the home of the deceased. The family immediately begins notifying other relatives and friends. Due to their simple lifestyle, the notification must be done in person, so they go from door to door. In some of the Amish communities an obituary may be placed in the local newspaper.

Once the news spreads throughout the community, mourners begin to arrive at the home of the deceased for an informal viewing. At this point, non-relatives in the community take over the farm work, and a couple who are close to the family takes over any household chores to help relieve the family's burden during the time of mourning.

DRESSING AND CASKETING

Due to state laws that do not make any exceptions based on religious or personal beliefs, the body of the deceased must be handed over to a funeral director for embalming. After the embalming process is completed, the family dresses the deceased in white as is ordained by the "Ordnung."[7] Men are dressed in a white shirt, trousers, vest and socks. The family may choose to dress him in a simple white gown, with a pleated top. The women are dressed in a white shawl and apron or a long white gown with a cape. The dress of the woman is usually whatever she wore on her wedding day. The deceased is dressed by a member of the family of the same gender, usually a son or daughter. The Amish prefer to use a plain pine casket, with little or no adornment. The casket is usually cut and made to fit the measurements of the deceased. The lid is either in a two-part style, with the upper part hinged so that it can easily be opened for viewing, or it can have a lid that slides into place along a groove. This way the lid can be slid down to the waist of the body for viewing. The more conservative Amish insist that there be no cushioning or lining of the interior of the coffin. Other Amish will allow a simple cushion of cotton batting or plain white cotton material. Colored or patterned cloth is never permitted, however.

VISITATION

Visitation for family, friends and neighbors is held for one to two days before the funeral. In the case of House Amish, the visitation takes place at the home of the deceased; while for the Church Amish, visitation may be either in the home or in the church, depending on family preference. In either case, benches are set up for mourners and the room is lit only by two oil-burning lamps. The gathering takes place with little conversation. Mourners simply pay their respects and move on.

THE FUNERAL

The Amish funeral service is very plain; there are no flowers and no singing. If the funeral is at the church, then there is a processional from the home to the church. Generally, the body is moved in a horse-drawn hearse, and the rest of the mourners follow in buggies or on horseback.

Regardless of whether the funeral is held at home or at the church, the ceremony is the same. At the start of the sermon, the men in the audience take off their hats in unison. The mourners sit on the benches and a song leader (*Vorsanger*) leads the congregation in hymns from the Protestant hymnal. These hymns are music-less, meaning they are chanted rather than sung. This is usually preceded and followed by sermons from the Old Testament. The sermons typically focus on the importance of leading a good life on earth in preparation for the eternal afterlife, rather than on a eulogy for the deceased.[8]

BURIAL

On the day of the burial, four pallbearers place the coffin into a horse-drawn hearse and the rest of the mourners follow in their buggies. The procession proceeds at a slow pace to the place of burial. Traditionally, the burials would take place on the family farms, but now there are separate Amish cemeteries. These have enough room to accommodate large family plots, so all the members of a family may be buried side by side. The Amish pay special attention to the maintenance and upkeep of their cemeteries out of respect for their dead.

Upon reaching the cemetery, the pallbearers open the coffin for a last viewing. Some Amish choose to have another short ceremony during this final viewing. The coffin is then screwed shut and lowered into the grave. The grave is then half-filled with dirt, the men remove their hats in unison and a short hymn is read. At this point, the rest of the grave is filled.

When burial is complete, a plain headstone is placed with the deceased's name, date of birth and date of death. The Amish also place a small foot-stone opposite the headstone.

Following the service, the mourners return to the home of the deceased where a complete but simple meal is served. Usually all of the food is provided by friends and neighbors. During and after the meal, the mourners socialize with one another, suggesting that life will move on. Friends and family are an integral part of the societal structure of the Amish. Respect for the dead, the afterlife, simplicity and a focus on living a good life are some of the lessons the Amish carry away from the death of a community member.

THE AFRICAN-AMERICAN FUNERAL TRADITION

African-American people have funeral services based on their particular religious beliefs, cultural and family upbringing, and financial status. Thus, there is no "typical" African-American funeral service. There is usually, however, an embodiment of spirituality related to having ties to the church. Different church affiliations account for variations which are minor. Their roots were established years before in Africa and passed through family lines.

A pastor is the first person called at the time of death. Memorial services may be simple and elegant, or they may be a jubilant party replete with music, singing and dancing. Rejoicing at death has links back to the period of enslavement, as a result of the oppression. Death represented an escape to freedom.

New Orleans jazz funerals are derived from Dahomean and Yourba cultures of West Africa as described by Holland.[9] At such a service, the band accompanies the family, friends and the casket to the funeral home or church, playing solemn music such as "Nearer My God to Thee." When the procession leaves the cemetery, the band picks up a joyous melody and the group begins dancing and celebrating the deceased's life. Rousing music choices would include, "When the Saints Go Marching In." As Eileen Southern said of the music of Black Americans, "For almost every activity in the life of the (African) individual or community there was an appropriate music; it was an integral part of life from the hour of birth to beyond the grave."[10]

The type of casket and style of dress worn at funeral services are representative of the African-American person's heritage. Typically, visitation is at the funeral home or a wake is held at the family's home the evening before the funeral ceremony. This is often celebratory with loud talk, food and music.[11]

Because African-Americans most commonly are of Christian faith, they follow Christian religious ceremonies and rites and prefer burial to cremation. Proper burial is of utmost importance, as the deceased is elevated to the status of Spirit.

THE MORMON FUNERAL

Founded in 1830 by Joseph Smith, the Mormon Church is officially known as the Church of Jesus Christ of Latter-Day Saints. Their beliefs are primarily based on the religious books of the Book of Mormon, as well as on the Bible, the Doctrine and Covenants, and the Pearl of Great Price. A large population of Mormons now live in Utah.

At the time of death, there are no special ceremonies performed and a family may choose to notify a church official to make the death known to other church members.

Although no specific casket is required, dress for the deceased Mormon depends on his relationship with the church during life. If the individual received optional training or completed missionary service, then he has a more active or responsible role in the Church. This instructional process is known as the *Temple Ordinances*, or going "through the temple."

If a man has been "through the temple," then in death he may be dressed in white clothing with a shirt, tie and trousers, and a robe is placed over the right shoulder diagonally across the chest in a straight line to the ankle, front and back. A green apron and white sash are placed over the waist and tied in a bow on the left side. Finally, a white cap is placed on the head of the deceased, and tied with bows to the robe. Clothing is comparable for any deceased woman who has undergone the Temple Ordinances instructional process: white garments with a robe and sash are worn, and a veil that covers the face is used instead of a cap. These adornments are placed by Church members, usually while the body is at the funeral home. If a person has not been "through the temple," clothing choices are chosen at the family's discretion.

Visitation or the viewing of the body takes place either at the deceased's home or at a funeral home, and the funeral service occurs the next day. The actual service is held either at the funeral home, cemetery or in a Mormon ward chapel, where public worship takes place. There are no specific guidelines for a Mormon Church service, but an example of the Order of Service[12] is as follows:

- Prelude
- Invocation
- Eulogy/obituary
- Musical Selection
- Speaker
- Benediction
- Postlude.

Earth burial is preferred, though sometimes mausoleum entombment is chosen. Because of the Mormon belief that the spirit re-enters its physical body at resurrection, nothing should be done to change or destroy the body. For this reason, cremation is discouraged. If cremation is planned, the Church states that "no prayer should be offered during or following a cremation ceremony." One exception is a segment of Mormons known as the Reorganized Church of Mormons which broke off from the Mormon Church. This church feels that cremation is allowable.

At the time of burial, the casket is placed in the ground and a short committal service is held with scripture reading and prayer.

THE HMONG FUNERAL

Hmongs are an ethnic group of Christians or Buddhists from China, Vietnam, Laos, Thailand and Burma. They believe that the spiritual world coexists with the physical world. It is felt that spirits of ancestors, nature and even evil, inhabit the world and influence human life. They believe the ancestor spirits play a significant role in affecting life on earth. As part of their desire to please the ancestors, animals such as pigs or cows are used as ritual sacrifices during ceremonies of birth and death.

There are typically two nights of visitation after family members dress the deceased's body. Regular clothes are used to dress the dead; however, all metal adornments such as zippers, buttons and labels are removed. It is believed that any object which does not disintegrate may prevent the spirit from being reincarnated. The dressing ceremony is performed by six to twenty people, and during the ceremony, wailing or loud crying may take place.

A large empty oil drum, up to 50 gallons in size, may be brought to beat on. The drumming goes from morning until night. The funeral drums are sacred and are passed down through generations. They are thought to have a special spirit in them and are used only at the time of death.

Following the dressing ceremony, there is a ritual dance by an individual who also plays a reed horn. The dance takes place under a tripod structure made of long sticks tied at the top. On the second night, the dance and drum sounding are repeated. The spirit of the deceased is thought to remain in the body until burial, so mourners talk to the body and offer animal sacrifices. In America, funeral homes do not allow slaughtered animals to be brought in; however, some funeral homes will allow live animals.[13] For example, Dean Welkers of Helke Funeral Home in Wausau, Wisconsin serves a large Hmong community and he allows a live chicken to be brought in for a short time, for symbolic reasons. It is then quickly removed.

The funeral service is led by a shaman who is usually also the person who plays the reed horn. This music is said to guide the souls from the world of the living to the world of the spirits. A man who has studied the religious verses of the *Qhuab Kev* text acts as a guide for the spirit to the afterlife. In

247

the verses, he mentions every place the deceased has lived, in order to guide the soul step-by-step back to its birthplace. An older person may also read specially selected verses from the text to the family to provide them comfort in their time of grief.

At the cemetery, the spirit is released when family members open the deceased person's eyes and mouth. An archer fires an arrow symbolizing the spirit being sent away.

Another small ceremony takes place at the cemetery and includes burning Chinese paper money. This represents payment to the spirits for the air the deceased has breathed and the land on which he lived while alive.[14]

A year later, another ceremonial service takes place at the family home when a shirt and hat are placed on the mantle to symbolize the deceased. This final ceremony frees the spirit to be reincarnated.

THE VIETNAMESE FUNERAL

A discussion of other Vietnamese people reveals slightly different practices. In Vietnam, cemeteries may be located near the deceased's home in a rice field. The coffin, chosen by family or friends, is taken to the home. The family puts a portion of rice and wine in the mouth of the body so that the deceased will have some food upon reaching his or her spiritual destination. The body is not embalmed and is not placed in the coffin until the date matches with the astrological animal corresponding to the birth year of the deceased. The body is kept on a platform until this time.

The body is placed in a wooden coffin with the hands crossed over the stomach. The coffin is usually fashioned of plain wood and the interior is undecorated and unstained. It may be lined with grass-filled "pillows." As many as 150 mourners may accompany the body to the burial site. They carry bright colored flags and ribbons.[15]

As with the Hmong, a large dinner is held in honor of the deceased one year after the death. This may continue every year. After two or three years, the coffin is opened and the bones and teeth are placed in a rectangular, cement container and buried elsewhere, permanently.

THE MEXICAN FUNERAL

People from Mexico and Central America place large value on the traditions surrounding funeral ceremonies. A large portion of these population are Roman Catholic and a lesser number are Protestant.

Culturally, Mexicans believe that death is a punishment or curse from God for bad deeds during life, although religiously they see it as a rebirth.

At death, the body of the deceased is central to the service and the deceased is dressed in new clothes. The body is placed in an open casket. Mourners often pay attention to the details and beauty of the casket. Cremation is very rarely practiced.

Visitation takes place for about three days, usually at the deceased's home, and it is a very somber affair that often includes all-night vigils. A body may be held at a funeral home for a few days, allowing time for family who life a distance away to arrive. The funeral ceremony is attended by all family and friends, with the family standing nearest to the grave site. Following the completion of the ceremony, recitation of rosaries may continue for a week or even longer. There are often anniversary celebrations, as with other cultures.

REFERENCES

Humanist Funerals

1. "Humanist Graveside Interment Ceremony." Online. Available: *http://www.infidels.org/org/aha/ceremonies/huminter.html,* 1998.
2. National Funeral Directors Association: "Humanist Ceremonies." NFDA, 1998.

3. Cannon E: Personal communication, Humanist counselor, Oct. 20, 1998.
4. Lamont C: *A Humanist Funeral Service.* New York: Prometheus Books, 1977:13.
5. Irion P: *A Manual and Guide for Those Who Conduct a Humanist Funeral Service.* Baltimore: Waverly Press, Inc., 1971.

Amish Funerals

6. Hostetler JA: *Amish Society.* Baltimore, MD: The Johns Hopkins University Press, 1993.
7. NFDA: "Amish Funeral Rite." Nov. 24, 1997.
8. Meyer C: *Amish People: Plain Living In a Complex World.* New York: Atheneum, Murry Printing Co., 1976.

African-American Funerals

9. Holland E: *Jazz Funerals, African Funeral and Memorial Traditions in America.* Internet, *http://www.libertynet.org/balch/rites/african.html*, 1998.
10. Southern E, as quoted in "The Jazz Funeral." The New Orleans Tourism Morketing Corporation. Online. Available: *http://www.neworleansonline.com/*, 1996.
11. Starks E: "African American Death." *Florida Funeral Director*, 6:3, 1998, p. 18.

Mormon Funerals

12. NFDA: "The Mormon Funeral Rite." Feb. 9, 1998.

Hmong and Vietnamese Funerals

13. Daniels S: "Funeral Customs of the Newest Americans." *The Director*, June 1994:22-27.
14. NFDA: "Funeral Rites of the Hmong." Aug. 25, 1997.
15. Mann R: "Travel Abroad Sheds Light on Vietnamese Burial Customs." *The Director*, Feb. 1995:30-31.

Section VII:
Final Remarks

Chapter 30

ALL THE QUESTIONS
YOU EVER HAD

BUT WERE AFRAID TO ASK

1. What does a funeral director do?

Answer: He makes the arrangements for transportation of the body, completes all necessary paperwork, and implements the choices made by the family regarding the funeral and final disposition of the body.

2. What is the NFDA?

Answer: The National Funeral Director's Association is the largest funeral service organization in the world. Its mission is to enhance the funeral service profession and promote quality service to the consumer.

3. What are some basic funeral facts?

Answer: In the U.S. there are 22,152 funeral homes and 34,588 licensed funeral directors/embalmers as of May 27, 1998 (NFDA).

Of more than 2.2 million deaths in 1995, earth burial or entombment was used in about 78 percent and cremation in 22 percent.

The average cost of an adult funeral per NFDA 1997 General Price List survey is $4,782.46.

4. How can I find out more information on funeral services and NFDA?

Answer: Call or write to:

National Funeral Director's Association
13625 Bishop's Drive
Brookfield, WI 53005

Tel: (800) 228-6332, (414) 789-1880
Fax: (414) 789-6977

5. Should I take a child to the funeral?

Answer: Yes, if the child wants to attend he or she should be taken. If the child is scared or frightened, arrange for child care. The child needs to say good-bye and grieve in his or her own way.

6. Should I discuss a death in the family with children?

Answer: Yes. Tell them " ___ has died, that means has left us, and you won't be able to see ___ after the funeral." Be factual and direct. Discuss death in fair details, answer all questions a child asks and be supportive and affectionate.

7. Should children be kept from grieving?

Answer: It is important not to isolate the child and to allow him or her to grieve while providing support. Allow the child to share your feelings and even suffering. A child should feel a part of what is happening.

8. A friend of mine has had a death in the family. Should I go to the visitation and funeral?

Answer: Yes. Funerals bring together families and friends, who provide support for each other. Grieving friends will greatly appreciate your presence. The personal benefit of attending a funeral is that you are forced to face death as a real event, which may help you prepare for a future death in your own family.

9. What should I say to my grieving friends?

Answer: Extend your sympathies. Just say "I'm sorry." Let them know that you are available whenever they need to talk and that you will help in whatever way they need.

10. Once the funeral is over, how can I continue to help?

Answer: You can provide help in many ways. Visit the bereaved. Help with daily routines. Take food or invite them. Tell them you are available to help.

11. What is OSHA?

Answer: OSHA is the Occupational Safety and Health Administration, created to assure safe and healthful working conditions.

12. Can hepatitis B and hepatitis C be prevented?

Answer: Yes, hepatitis B is preventable. Through vaccination, a majority of people achieve durable immunity to the hepatitis B virus. The current hepatitis B vaccines, received in a series of three shots, provide lasting immunity. There is no vaccine currently available to prevent hepatitis C.

13. Is it true anyone who dies of an AIDS-related illness must be cremated or buried in a sealed casket?

Answer: No. You can choose any method of disposition afforded to anyone else who did not die of AIDS-related illness.

14. Can I become infected with HIV by touching the body of someone who has died of an AIDS-related illness?

Answer: No. Evidence shows that casual contact, such as touching the deceased's face or hands, is perfectly safe.

15. How can I cope with my grief?

Answer: You must recognize that grief is necessary and it is something you must work through. It is important to ventilate your feelings by talking openly about your feelings, taking time to cry, venting your anger and discussing the death with the others.

16. How can I help my staff member's family?

Answer: Go to the visitation and offer your regrets. Do whatever you can to help them with any financial matters involving your company, such as insurance policies, worker's compensation forms and employment records. Give them any personal records that your staff member kept at work.

17. What is the legal definition of a "power of attorney"?

Answer: A power of attorney is a legal document which authorizes one party to act as a legal agent for another.

18. What are memorial societies?

Answer: Mostly staffed by volunteers, these are nonprofit organizations which assist consumers in planning simple, dignified arrangements. They provide information on cremation and burial, organ and body donation and legal requirements for those who wish to handle funeral arrangements themselves.

19. What is an open casket?

Answer: Viewing of the deceased with part of the casket open so that the face of the deceased can be seen. The grieving process cannot occur until there is acceptance of the death. Confronting the death in the form of an open casket helps to bring about that acceptance. Viewing the body of a deceased person who was a significant part of your life, can help the emotional healing to start.

20. Why does a funeral cost so much money?

Answer: A funeral does not have to cost much money. To hold down cost, consider what is really needed and stay away from the "traditional" American funeral with lengthy visiting in the funeral home. Immediate burial or cremation is the least expensive.

21. Why is a will important?

Answer: To maintain peace and prevent financial losses after death. For more information, refer to the chapter, "Protect Your Estate: Don't Leave the Door Open for Uncle Sam."

22. Why is a living will important?

Answer: To execute your wishes properly after your death. For more information refer to Chapter 4.

23. What is embalming?

Answer: The American Board of Funeral Service Education states, "a process of chemically treating the dead human body to reduce the presence and growth of microorganisms, to retard organic decomposition, and to restore an acceptable physical appearance."

24. What is cryonic suspension?

Answer: A process of freezing and maintaining a dead human at an extremely low temperature, in the hope that the body may be resuscitated many years later.

25. What organs and tissues can be donated?

Answer: Vascular organs include the heart, lungs, liver, kidneys and pancreas. Transplantable tissues include bone, skin, connective tissue, heart valves, temporal bones and saphenous veins.

26. Why have an autopsy?

Answer: An autopsy helps to determine the cause and manner of death, verify diagnoses, assess treatment, detect malpractice, address issues of genetics and to provide closure.

27. Is there any disfigurement of the donor from the donation of organs?

Answer: No. Organ and tissue procurement are performed as carefully as any surgical procedure on a living person. Reconstruction of the donor is made and incisions are closed. The family should always be able to conduct an open casketed funeral after anatomical donation if they so desire.

28. Is there any disfigurement of the donor from autopsy?

Answer: No. Autopsy incisions are made in such a way that when the incisions are closed, most times you cannot tell that the autopsy was done.

29. If my family member carries a donor card, will that be sufficient notice for donation to take place?

Answer: No. Anatomical donation will not occur without informed consent from the donor's legal next of kin.

30. Is a casket required for cremation?

Answer: No, a casket is not required for cremation.

31. Do I have to hire a funeral director?

Possibly not. Most states permit religious groups or private citizens to obtain the necessary death certificate and permits for transit and disposition.

32. What are catacombs?

Answer: A series of below-ground chambers and passages to house the dead.

33. What are mausoleums?

Answer: Buildings in which bodies can be buried above ground.

34. How quickly can a body be cremated?

Answer: Most states require the expiration of 48 hours after death for cremation of a body.

35. Does a funeral serve a purpose?

Answer: Yes. It helps to accept death and its finality. It is a ritual that allows paying respect to the dead. It helps the survivors begin the grief process. It helps the community to come together and help each other.

36. What recourse does a consumer have for inadequate service or overcharging?

Answer: Funeral service is regulated by the FTC and state licensing boards. Contact the Funeral Service Consumer Assistance Program for information, disputes and arbitration at (800) 662-7666.

37. Who pays for funerals for the indigent?

Answer: Other than the family, there are veteran, union and other organizational benefits to pay for funerals, including payment from Social Security and allowances from either the state, county, city or a combination.

38. Who should have a copy of my living will?

Answer: Your physician, the person you have chosen as the executor of your will, your clergy and your spouse or other trusted relative.

39. Who should know about my will and its whereabouts?

Answer: The executor of your will, family members and your attorney.

40. How long does a body that is embalmed stay intact?

Answer: Once the body is embalmed, decomposition is halted and it stays well-preserved for a long time.

41. How long before a body that is not embalmed begins to decay?

Answer: If a body is not embalmed, it will decompose after a period of time. If the weather is hot and the body is not refrigerated it can start to decompose –skin color changes, smell emission– within a day or two.

42. What is *rigor mortis* and when does it set in?

Answer: Rigor mortis is the stiffening and shortening of muscles after death. It starts in all muscles of the body at the same time, but becomes detectable earlier in some muscles than in others. The whole body becomes stiff in about 24 hours.

43. What percentage of funeral directors are female?

Answer: In the past, women rarely got into the funeral business. New trends have developed, and more and more women are becoming funeral directors. Exact numbers are not available, however.

44. How long are graves maintained? Is it true that they are re-used after a certain number of years?

Answer: If the preneed or at need contract includes the clause for perpetual care, the grave is supposed to be maintained indefinitely. It is not true that the graves are re-used after a certain numbers of years.

45. Are you allowed to bury a loved one on your own property?

Answer: If you live in a rural area, you can bury a loved one on your property provided there are no restrictions imposed by your city, county or neighborhood association.

46. Where are crematories located?

Answer: Some funeral homes have cremation facilities within their premises. Those who do not, use places that handle cremations exclusively.

47. How many funerals does one funeral home handle in a year?

Answer: This varies a great deal depending on the size and reputation of the funeral home. The numbers can range from 20 to over 1000, with an average of about 200.

48. How can you locate information about deceased ancestors?

Answer: You may be able to obtain the information about the location of burial and the date of death from death certificates, obituaries and funeral home and cemetery records. The office of the Medical Examiner or Coroner will have records about the cause and manner of death if they have investigated the death.

49. How big is a cemetery plot?

Answer: A cemetery plot can be just big enough to accommodate the deceased. However, you can buy as large a piece of real estate as you want.

50. Can I place whatever kind of marker I want to on a grave?

Answer: Generally yes, but some cemeteries have specifications on the size and design. And of course, the writings on the marker must be appropriate.

Chapter 31

THE ULTIMATE CHECKLIST

100 Things to Do for Peace of Mind

*T*his is the consumer's complete planning guide for peace of mind. The checklist covers not only preplanning points but also includes all of the things you will need to do at the time of death of a loved one, and after the funeral. It will help to spare you of unnecessary confusion, grief, pain and expenses.

First make a special note of the following eight fundamental principles and practices to dealing with death:

1. Reach out; do not think you are alone. Call immediate family and close friends and depend on them.

2. Seek help from professionals – doctors, paramedics, funeral directors, clergy persons, attorneys and accountants.

3. Take care of the deceased, and take care of yourself.

4. Don't rush, compose yourself, consult with others.

5. Take active part in making decisions and choices.

6. Act within the limits of your emotional and financial capabilities.

7. Find a few moments to think about everything you need.

8. Organize calmly and execute systematically.

The following list of "100 Things To Do" will help you do just that.

PRENEED PLANNING

A. Collect information on yourself or the person for whom you are planning the funeral

1. Name, current address, telephone number
2. Name of business, address, telephone number
3. Occupation, title
4. Social Security number
5. Date and place of birth
6. Duration of stay in state
7. Citizenship and passport number
8. War veteran's service number
9. Father's name and birth place
10. Mother's maiden name and birth place
11. Complete information brochure (as described in Chapter 1); complete disposition instructions (see Appendix D)

B. Collect other information and document your decisions

12. Preneed wishes
13. Budget for funeral, prepayment plan
14. Telephone numbers and addresses of family members and close friends
15. Names, telephone numbers of family physician, funeral director, clergy person
16. Selection of cemetery plot or crematory, choices of services and goods

C. Collect documents

17. Will
18. Living will, advance directive
19. Birth certificate
20. Passport or immigration and naturalization certificate
21. Social Security card
22. Driver's license

23. Marriage license

24. Insurance policies – health, life, accident, disability, real estate, flood, professional liability

25. Bank books – checking, savings, loan accounts

26. Property deeds – real estate

27. Bills of sales, registration – car, boat, other

28. Tax returns, canceled checks, payment receipts

29. Certificate of ownership, contracts – cemetery plot, mausoleum

30. Veteran's discharge certificate

31. Claims documents – disability, workman's compensation

32. Credit cards

33. Keys – house, office, cars, safe deposits

34. Information brochure (see item 11)

D. Document payments and debts

35. Taxes – federal, state, local

36. Credit cards

37. Mortgages, rents – home, office, apartments, condominiums

38. Loans – car, boat

39. Cemetery plot, mausoleum, memorials

40. Casket, vault, grave marker

41. Interment services – opening, closing of grave

42. Funeral services, goods

43. Clergy honoraria

44. Florist

45. Telephones, telegraphs, express mail

46. Doctors, pharmacists, hospitals, dentists

47. Insurance – health, others

48. Yardman, pool man, veterinarian

AT NEED ACTIONS

A. Notify necessary people

49. Immediate family, close friends (see item 14)
50. Family physician, paramedics
51. Medical examiner – if death from accident, suicide, murder or from unexplained cause
52. Funeral director
53. Pastor, rabbi, your religious clergyperson
54. Cemetery representative
55. Employer of deceased
56. Pallbearers
57. Musicians
58. Insurance agents
59. Veterans Administration, religion, fraternity, civic, union representatives
60. Accountant, attorney
61. Executor of estate
62. Banks, creditors
63. Newspapers

B. Decide and arrange

64. Informing relatives, friends, coworkers
65. Assignment of relaying notification, assignment of phone/door take turn duties
66. Meeting with funeral director, visiting funeral home
67. Selection of cemetery, plot, crematorium
68. Memorial type, inscription
69. Embalming, autopsy, cosmetics
70. Casket, vault, grave marker
71. Mausoleum, crypt
72. Clothing for deceased, family, children
73. Clergy person – priest, rabbi, other

74. Time, place of service – home, church, synagogue

75. Type of service – religious, military, fraternal

76. Scriptures, music – soloist, organist

77. Flowers

78. Charitable organization for donations

79. Eulogies, prayers

80. Pallbearers

81. Food, transportation for family, guests

82. Death certificate, burial or cremation permit

83. Children, pets

84. Lodging for out of town guests

85. Information for newspapers

86. Responding to e-mails, telegrams, letters

87. Responding to persons sending tributes, flowers

88. Invitations, guest book, printed order of service, printed prayer and thank you cards

89. Funeral protocol – viewing, visitation, seating, procession, cars, flower car, limousines, drivers

90. Audio-video recording

91. Disposition of flowers

92. Gifts to church, honoraria for clergy, out of pocket expenses.

93. Shipping of remains, if necessary

94. Notification to landlord, utilities, post office, if deceased lived alone

95. Cleaning service or help from relatives, friends

AFTER THE FUNERAL

Take Care of the Rest of the Checklist

96. Copies of death certificate and application for death benefits

97. Cremains disposal; choosing headstone or marker to memorialize; selection of mausoleum

98. Meetings with attorney to handle probate, insurance agent to settle policies

99. Debts, installment payments; notifying bank if Social Security payments are automatically deposited

100. Counseling for grief management.

Section VIII:
Appendices

Appendix A

FAMOUS FUNERALS

I. The Funeral of President John F. Kennedy

Life levels all men. Death reveals the eminent.

—George Bernard Shaw (1856-1950)

*N*ovember 22, 1963 marked the emergence of "collective memory," for on that day the 35th president of the United States of America, John Fitzgerald Kennedy, was brutally assassinated. JFK had brought to the presidency youth, energy and vitality, and suddenly on a clear, sunny Dallas day his life was ended. The suddenness and recklessness of his death brought the country to a halt.

JFK had been elected as a president with an agenda called the New Frontier, and in the early days of his presidency he was tackling a broad range of issues from racial segregation, civil rights, communism and promotion of the space race. Other presidents have also had agendas, but JFK's presidency ushered in a new era, that of television, for he had used television to address the nation five days after taking office.[1] And TV would help define and shape the collective memory and emotions Americans and millions around the world would experience at the time of his assassination and during the days that led to his burial.

JFK was the youngest president elected, the first Roman Catholic president, from an old established Irish–American Bostonian family. On

269

November 22, 1963 he arrived with his wife Jacqueline Kennedy to Love Field, Dallas. In Dallas the president was scheduled to speak at a meeting of the Citizens Council. The presidential motorcade left Love Field for a 45 minute trip to downtown Dallas. The President, along with his wife and then-Texas governor, John B. Connolly and his wife, were in an open top limousine.[2]

As the motorcade approached Elm Street in downtown Dallas under a triple underpass, shots were heard, one, two, three, the first struck the President in the back, the second in his head, mortally wounding him. At the time the President was struck by the bullet, the first lady was looking away from him towards her left and did not realize gunshots were fired until she heard John Connolly yell, "Oh no, no, no." Then she turned to her right. In the midst of thousands of people converging at the site of the assassination the President and other injured parties were rushed to Parkland Hospital where fifteen doctors valiantly tried to save his life, but to no avail. JFK was pronounced dead at 1 p.m.

The events that followed immediately after the president died were mainly those of state. Aboard Air-Force One, Vice-President Lyndon B. Johnson, with Mrs. Kennedy at his side (still in her suit stained with the president's blood) was sworn in as the new President. Mrs. Kennedy then retired to the rear of the plane to sit with her husband's coffin. When Air Force One landed at Andrews Air Force Base, MD, President Johnson addressed the nation with these words, ". . . I ask for your help and God's."

While JFK's body underwent autopsy at Bethesda Naval Hospital, plans for a state funeral with full military honors at Arlington National Cemetery were arranged. Indeed, details for the funeral were modeled after the one held for Abraham Lincoln upon his assassination almost a century before in 1865. On November 11, 1963 President Kennedy had attended a ceremony at the Tomb of the Unknowns at Arlington National Cemetery. After a 21-gun salute honoring the war dead, he had told the then Secretary of State, Robert McNamara, "This is rally one of the beautiful places on earth. I think, maybe, someday this is where I'd like to be."[3] Ironically, barely two weeks later he would be laid to rest there.

At the completion of the autopsy, the president's closed casket, draped in black, was taken to the East Room of the White House, where the

President's wife, daughter Caroline, son John Jr., and brother Robert Kennedy among others were present to receive him. Catholic priests were present and intoned prayers for the president. The following day, the family held a private mass.

On Sunday the 24th of November 1963, the body left the White House to go to the Capitol Rotunda for public viewing. The funeral cortege began its journey to the Capitol, marching to muffled drums. The formal parade included marching units from the U.S. Marines, Army, Coast Guard and Air Force. Six gray horses pulled the black draped caisson, the same one that had carried President Franklin D. Roosevelt's casket in 1945. A riderless black horse named Black Jack followed behind symbolizing a nation's loss of its leader.

Thousands of people lined Pennsylvania Avenue and joined in the march to the Capitol. En route, cannons fired a 21-gun salute and both "Hail to the Chief" and "Naval Hymn" were played. Once the coffin reached the Capitol rotunda it was placed in a catafalque which had once held the coffin of Abraham Lincoln. Tributes were read and President Johnson placed a huge wreath on the bier. Mrs. Kennedy, with her daughter Caroline, walked over and knelt at the casket and Mrs. Kennedy kissed the coffin, etching one of the most poignant scenes of the day. The bier was kept on view to the public until Monday, the 25th of November 1963, the day of official mourning and burial of the slain president. More than 250,000 people came to pay their last respects.

The state funeral was a grand affair conducted with pomp and ceremony. More than 7,000 members of the military were involved and hundreds of foreign heads of state arrived in Washington to pay a final tribute. The planned procession of the cortege began at the White House and proceeded to St. Matthews Cathedral for a funeral mass and then made its final trip to Arlington National Cemetery where the body was to be interned.

The caisson carrying the president was brought to the White House and the march began. Mrs. Kennedy opted to walk, and flanked by the president's two brothers, Robert and Edward, led the march. President Johnson and other dignitaries including visiting heads of state followed close behind. Throughout Washington D.C., church bells tolled and bagpipes played until the body arrived to St. Matthew's Cathedral where Cardinal John Cushing came to bless the casket. Ten years before, Cardinal Cushing had officiated the marriage of John and Jacqueline Kennedy.

In the church, the ceremony was conducted with regal dignity. At each pew a card from Mrs. Kennedy read, "Dear God please take care of your servant John Fitzgerald Kennedy."

During the mass, delivered in Latin, prayers and excerpts from the president's writings were read. Cardinal Cushing concluded his service in English, with the blessing, "May the angels, dear Jack, lead you into Paradise."

When the mass was finished, Mrs. Kennedy, along with her children, left the cathedral to the tune of "Hail to the Chief" and as the casket moved past, young John Jr. stepped forward and saluted his father, embedding in viewers yet another poignant moment in the ceremonies.

The procession took nearly one hour before arriving at Arlington National Cemetery, passing streets lined with over one million people silently weeping and sharing in the first family's grief. At the ceremony, soldiers lowered the casket into the grave which was set up on a hill, while a band played "Star Spangled Banner" and the Air Force bagpipes tuned "Mist Covered Mountain." Fifty military jets staged a V-formation fly-by and Air Force One swooped down to pay its tribute. The Irish Black Watch performed a silent drill.

After the final service prayers were said, cannons again fired a 21-gun salute and soldiers fired rifles in volleys of three. A bugle played "Taps" followed by the band's repeat refrain of "Naval Hymn." The United States flag draping the casket was folded and presented to Mrs. Kennedy. Holding it close to her, she took a lighted taper and lit an eternal flame placed at her husband's grave. At 3:15 p.m., the funeral was over with quiet dignity.

The entire funeral was shown live on television except for the internment. These televised memorial services were viewed by millions of people around the United States and the world. For days, everyone had followed the day-to-day events on television and through magazine and newspaper reports. The burial of the president gave some sense of closure to a catharsis that wrapped the nation. The country could move forward with Lyndon B. Johnson heading state affairs.

The legacy John F. Kennedy left behind has been detailed in numerous books, television stories and movies. After his assassination, his presidential years were referred to as "Camelot." In his preface to "A Question of Character,"[4] author Thomas Reeves writes, "In flesh and blood rather than as King Arthur in Camelot, Jack Kennedy deserves our sympathy and praise as well as our critical judgements." Although his political legacy will be debated for many years to come, one thing became very evident at the time of his death and funeral services was how greatly loved he was by the people. With its regality, pomp and ceremony, the memorial services were fit for a king.

II. The Funeral of a Princess

Death brings greater stature to some,
for we fail to measure them right in life.

*O*n September 6th, 1997, the world laid to rest the woman known as the "People's Princess." In life, Diana, Princess of Wales, was surrounded by pomp and circumstance wherever she went. Out of respect for her, those planning her funeral felt that it should match the spectacular nature of her life.

The funeral was viewed on television by 2.1 billion people around the world. It took place in London, with the largest gathering on the procession route since the end of World War II. The funeral congregation consisted of 2000 people and included political dignitaries, celebrities and representatives of the charitable organizations in which Princess Diana was involved.

As a result of her divorce from Prince Charles, Diana was no longer part of England's Royal Family. Therefore, her funeral represented a combination of Royal Family traditions and honors bestowed simply by the people who loved her as the mother of the future king and as a humanitarian.[5] As quoted by a spokesman for Buckingham Palace, it would be "a unique funeral for a unique person." Lieutenant-Colonel Malcolm Ross, comptroller of the Lord Chamberlain's office at Buckingham Palace, was responsible for organizing the funeral, taking suggestions from Diana's family, the Royal Family, the Prime Minister and the Anglican Church.

Princess Diana died on August 31, 1997, as a result of a car crash at the now famous site in a tunnel in Paris. She was 36 years old. After physicians at the Paris Hospital pronounced her dead, her body was viewed by her sisters, Lady Sarah McCorquodale and Lady Jane Fellows, as well as Prince Charles. Full military honors from the French Republic Guard were extended by President Jacques Chiroc.[6] Later that day, her body was transported to St. James Palace in London. She was placed in a lead-lined coffin that had been specially prepared for the Royal Family in London. The members of the Welsh Guard who carried her coffin during the funeral services had practiced on a 560 pound coffin in preparation. Her body remained at St. James Palace until the eve of the funeral, September 5th, when it was moved to Kensington Palace, Diana's home. Outside St. James Palace, mourners stood in line to pay their respects by signing more than 40 condolence books.[7] Massive floral tributes with cards and letters were placed outside of St. James and Buckingham Palaces.

The funeral ceremonies began at 9 a.m. on September 6th, with a minute of silence followed by the ringing of the muffled bells of Westminster Abbey. The bell tolling continued at one minute intervals until the cortege arrived at the Abbey more than two hours later. The coffin holding the body of the princess was taken from her apartment at Kensington Palace and placed by the Welsh Guard onto a gun carriage. The cortege was pulled by the King's Troop, Royal Horse Artillery to the Abbey, passing through areas such as the Wellington Arch, previously reserved for the funeral processions of the monarch, Royal Family or the Household Cavalry. The funeral procession proceeded through the hushed crowds where the only sounds were muffled sobs and the clip-clop of horse hooves.

For the last one mile to Westminster Abbey, Princess Diana's children, William and Harry, followed the cortege on foot. They were accompanied by Prince Charles, Diana's brother Earl Spencer, and Prince Phillip, the boys' grandfather. Upon reaching the Abbey, the Welsh Guard carried the coffin in for the funeral services.

The cortege proceeded to the quire and sacrarium of the Abbey with all standing in respect. Organ music was played accompanied by the Westminster Abbey choir.[8] The service was led by the Dean of Westminster, the Very Reverend Dr. Wesley Carr, whose first statement was:

> *We are gathered here in Westminster Abbey to give thanks for the life of Diana, Princess of Wales; to commend her soul to almighty God, and to seek His comfort for all who mourn. We particularly pray for God's restoring peace and loving presence with her children, the Princes William and Harry, and for all her family. In her life, Diana profoundly influenced this nation and the world. Although a Princess, she was someone for whom, from afar, we dared to feel affection, and by whom we were all intrigued. She kept company with kings and queens, with princes and presidents, but we specifically remember her human concerns and how she met individuals and made them feel significant. In her death she commands the sympathy of millions. Whatever our beliefs and faith, let us with thanksgiving remember her life and enjoyment of it; let us rededicate to God the work of those many charities that she supported; let us commit ourselves anew to caring for others; and let us offer to Him and for His service our own mortality and vulnerability.*

A hymn sung by Cecil Spring-Rice was followed by Diana's sister, Lady Sarah McCorquodale, leading the congregation in the first biblical reading:

> *If I should die and leave you here awhile,*
> *Be not like others, sore undone, who keep*
> *Long vigils by the silent dust, and weep.*
> *For my sake - turn again to life and smile,*
> *Nerving thy heart and trembling hand to do*
> *Something to comfort other hearts than thine.*
> *Complete those dear unfinished tasks of mine*
> *And I, perchance, may therein comfort you.*

Soprano performer Lynne Dawson then performed an extract from Verdi's Requiem, followed by Lady Jane Fellows' biblical reading:

Time is too slow for those who wait,
too swift for those who fear,
too long for those who grieve,
too short for those who rejoice,
but for those who love, time is eternity.

Further revealing Diana's ability to touch all people, the Prime Minister of England, Tony Blair, read from the Bible, and pop singer Elton John performed a special arrangement of his popular song, "Candle in the Wind." Fighting back tears he performed the special tribute to Diana, calling her "England's rose."

This was followed by a tribute to Diana by her brother Earl Spencer. Finally, the Archbishop of Canterbury, Dr. George Carey, led the congregation in prayers, and the Dean of Westminster Abbey, Dr. Wesley Carr, spoke the Commendation:

Let us commend our sister Diana to the mercy of God, our Maker and Redeemer. Diana, our companion in faith and sister in Christ, we entrust you to God. Go forth from this world in the love of the Father who created you; In the mercy of Jesus Christ, who died for you; in the power of the Holy Spirit, who strengthened you. As one with all the faithful, living and departed, may you rest in peace and rise in glory, where grief and misery are banished and light and joy evermore abide. Amen.

The cortege made its way out of the Abbey, halting at the exit for a one minute silence, observed by the world. The bells again began to ring.

Her coffin was placed in a hearse which then traveled two hours to Althrop, Diana's ancestral home. The route was lined by mourners who threw flowers at the hearse. The burial of Diana was attended by her immediate family. Her final resting spot was chosen to be a small island in the center of a lake at Althrop. This was done to preserve the sanctity and privacy of her burial site.

It was estimated that the flowers left in memory of Diana weighed 10 thousand tons.[9] This alone signifies the impact her death had on so many people. Details of her funeral reveal how much effort went into the service. Although organized by one man, it was made into a true tribute to her life by the emotions of the people who may not have known her, but loved her all the same. Her funeral was watched by billions of people and her loss felt by even more. It was presented with the enormity, grandeur, love and honor, befitting only the "People's Princess." She is gone but she will never die because, as poet Thomas Campbell (1777-1844) said,

> *To live in the hearts*
> *We leave behind is not to die.*

REFERENCES

The Funeral of President John F. Kennedy

1. Hunt C: *JFK for a New Generation.* Dallas, Texas: The Sixth Floor Museum and Southern Methodist University Press, 1996.
2. Groden RJ: *The Killing of a President: The Complete Photographic Record of the JFK Assassination, the Conspiracy and the Cover-Up.* New York: Penguin Books, 1993.
3. Reeves R: *President Kennedy: Profile of Power.* New York: Simon and Schuster, 1993.
4. Reeves TC: *A Question of Character: A Life of John F. Kennedy.* New York: Forum, An Imprint of Prima Publishing, 1991.

The Funeral of a Princess

1. Buskin R: *Princess Diana, Her Life Story 1961-1997.* Lincolnwood, IL: New American Library, 1997.
2. Spoto D: *Diana, The Last Year.* New York: Harmony Books, 1997.
3. Finchner J and Wade J: *Portrait of a Princess.* New York: Simon and Schuster, 1998.
4. "Westminster Abbey Home Page, Funeral of Diana, Princess of Wales, Order of Funeral Service," Online. Available: *http://www.westminster-abbey.org/funeral_of_diana.htm*, 1997.
5. Raether H and Keith R: "The Funeral of Princess Diana: A Review." *The Director*, Dec. 1997: 72, 78.

Appendix B

FAMOUS BURIAL MONUMENTS

I. The Egyptian Pyramids

The tap'ring pyramid, the Egyptian's pride, and wonder of the world
whose spiky top Has wounded the thick cloud.

—Robert Blair, *The Grave*

*E*gyptian culture placed great importance on the housing and protection of the dead. This resulted in the creation of the most expensive and extensive tombs: the pyramids. By definition, pyramids are structures with square bases and four triangle-shaped sides that meet at a point at the top. The most famous pyramids are the tombs of Egyptian kings (pharaohs) built around 4500 years ago. The Egyptian pyramids, graves of the aristocracy, are among the seven wonders of the world.

The Egyptians believed that a person's body must be protected and preserved to allow the soul to live forever; that is, to be assured of eternal afterlife. Everyone—from the farmer and his wife to the pharaoh and his queen—believed in the continuation of life after death. Therefore, extraordinary measures were taken to preserve the remains, especially the royal remains. To accomplish this the body was dried and embalmed, a process called mummification. The Egyptians knew that by drying the body thoroughly and wrapping it, it could be preserved life-like for a long time after death. This process of mummification took about ten weeks and is fully described in Chapter 8.

From 2700 to 1700 B.C., the mummified bodies (i.e., mummies) of kings were buried inside the pyramids in secret chambers with many precious treasures such as gold. The first pyramid was built in 2650 B.C. for King Zoser to serve as a tomb when he died.[1] The burial chamber was hidden far below the pyramid at the bottom of a deep shaft cut in a limestone plateau to prevent theft of the valuables buried in with the remains. There was ample space in this chamber for all the things Zoser felt he would need in the next world, including furniture, chests of clothing, vessels for food and drink, lamps and lamp oil, to make his afterlife as full and comfortable as it was on earth.

Many times a smaller pyramid was built next to the king's pyramid for the body of his queen. There were also two temples connected to the main pyramid and were used for the funeral service.

The most famous pyramids are the Pyramids of Giza found on the banks of the Nile, near Cairo. Three of the largest and best preserved pyramids are among the ten pyramids at Giza. They were built between the years 2600 and 2500 BC.

The largest pyramid, known as the Great Pyramid, was built for King Khufu (Cheops). It took thousands of slaves and 20 years to complete.[2] Stones were dragged from the Nile, cut into blocks with copper chisels and saws, and placed onto inclines. Each block weighed about 2.3 metric tons. The Great Pyramid contains more than two million stone blocks, covers an area of fourteen acres and was originally 481 feet tall. For more than 4300 years, it was the tallest structure on earth. Over time it has lost about 30 feet off its top.[3] The precise construction of the Great Pyramid continues to astound engineers, architects and archaeologists.

Even Napoleon was amazed by the pyramids when he conquered Egypt in 1798. He is quoted as saying, "Soldiers! From the top of these Pyramids, 40 centuries are looking at us." Many believe that even with today's technology it would be extremely difficult to build such astonishing monuments. An Arab proverb says it all:

> *Man fears time,*
> *yet Time fears the Pyramids.*

The study of the Egyptian culture and the pyramids reveals two pertinent links between the ancient times and today. First, the concept of preneed planning of funerals not only existed, but also was well thought out by the Egyptians. The pharaoh Zoser picked an architect named Imhotep and asked him to prepare a tomb for his burial many years before his death. This was not only to prearrange his funeral, but also to create an everlasting monument to his life and to satisfy his longing for a rich afterlife. He even picked out pink granite for his burial chamber. Secondly, the process of embalming as we know it was highly sophisticated and fully developed at that time.

II. The Taj Mahal

thou soul at peace
Return thou unto thy Lord, well pleased
and well pleasing unto Him!
Enter thou among My servants-
And Enter thou My Paradise!

-Inscription from the Koran, found on
the gateway to the Taj Mahal

The Taj Mahal is situated along the banks of the Yamuna River in Agra, India. It was built from 1631 to 1643 to serve as a final resting place for the Mogul queen of Shah Jahan, Mumtaz Mahal. It is not just the splendor and opulence of the mausoleum itself that leaves a lasting impression, but also the story that led to its conception.

Shah Jahan was said to be 15 years old when he first laid eyes on his queen-to-be. In Agra, India there was a private marketplace within the palace walls known as the Muna Bazaar. Here ladies of the royal harem and ladies of court would have stalls where they could sell their fancy wares. One day of each month the doors of the Bazaar were opened to the public and the normally docile women were permitted to act as noisy shopkeepers. It was on one of these days that Shah Jahan, then a prince, saw and fell in love with Arjumand Banu Begam, the daughter of the prime minister. It is said that he asked for her hand in marriage the very next day, though it would be another four years before they were married. On the day of their marriage, Arjumand Banu Begam was given the name Mumtaz Mahal, which means "chosen one of the palace."

From that day on, the two were inseparable; they were never more than one room apart. She even accompanied the emperor on his many military campaigns. They had been together for 19 years when she accompanied him to Burhanpur on one of his military campaigns. It was on that very trip Mumtaz Mahal passed away on June 7, 1631 due to complications related to the birth of their fourteenth child.

As the story goes in David Carroll's *The Taj Mahal: India under the Moguls*, while she lay dying, Mumtaz Mahal whispered a final wish into the emperor's ears, "She asked that he build for her a monument of such perfect proportions and of such purity that no one could be in its presence without sensing somewhere within himself the eternal wonder of the power of love and the inevitability of its passing with death."[4]

After the death of his beloved wife, Shah Jahan retreated into his chambers for a week of mourning. Upon his return from personal exile, he dressed only in simple white robes and devoted the majority of his attention to the planning and construction of the Taj Mahal.

The site he chose for this wondrous monument was said to be none other than the very same site on which the Muna Bazaar had once stood, so that the place where he first fell in love with his queen would also be the place where he laid her to rest for eternity. Upon acquiring the land from its owner in exchange for four other plots of land in Agra, Shah Jahan set out to find an architect.

Although there are no official records identifying the true architect of the Taj Mahal, many stories circulate as to who the architect could have been. One of the most common stories is that after rejecting many plans, Shah Jahan came upon an architect who had recently lost his wife as well. Due to his own feelings of grief and loss he was able to empathize with the ruler. Together they came up with a monument that embodied the love of a man for a woman. The Taj Mahal design was also Shah Jahan's way of recreating the Islamic concept of paradise; the idealization of an Islamic "heaven."

Six months after her death, the body of Mumtaz Mahal was brought to Agra and placed into a temporary grave. In accordance with Islamic practice, it was covered with a dome so that her corpse, that of a chaste lady, could remain concealed from the public eye.

It took 12 years to complete the construction of the Taj Mahal. The mausoleum itself was constructed of pure white marble which was inlaid with intricate carvings, floral motifs, inlays and inscriptions from the Koran. The use of white marble was to symbolize the purity of Mumtaz's soul. And the little details were added in such a way as to enhance the marble rather than to take away from its splendor.

The Taj Mahal is actually part of a large funerary complex. The tomb itself is encompassed by a lush 42 acre garden. And the grounds are encompassed by a large red sandstone wall with gates at both the north and south ends. The wall itself is also made up of many galleries, pavilions, and multi-story towers.

Shah Jahan and other members of nobility traveled to the tomb by boat, while the more common visitors entered through the *jilokhana*, a large courtyard on the south that led to the main gateway. The jilokhana was said to have been bordered by bazaars and other courtyards and to have had 128 rooms for servants' quarters located within its boundaries. There were once tombs of other noblemen bordering the far end of the jilokhana, but they have all but disappeared over the years.[5]

The Taj Mahal and its grounds were designed to be meticulously symmetrical, as is the tradition of Islam. The gateways to the Taj Mahal are more than 100 feet high and are made of richly embellished red sandstone. The spandrels of the arches are decorated with gemstones inlaid in floral patterns into white marble. The central vaulted portals were inlaid with black marble inscriptions from the Koran. These sacred verses and the emphatic manner in which they are displayed emphasize the scale and grandeur of the Taj Mahal.

Once inside the gates, one enters the landscaped grounds leading to the actual building. The grounds on either side of the mausoleum are quartered by intersecting water channels and each of these sections is further quartered. This symmetry again symbolizes the Islamic concept of paradise.

The main buildings are located 900 feet from each entrance. There is a red sandstone platform upon which the tomb stands on its own marble plinth. The platform also holds two red sandstone buildings which flank the marble tomb. These buildings are identical in form though not in function: one is a mosque and the other a rest house.

Although unique in its exterior, the tomb still follows the basic organization of other Islamic tombs of its era. The interior design is that of eight chambers surrounding a large central chamber. This design was known as *hasht behisht*, or eight paradises. The bodies of Mumtaz Mahal and Shah Jahan lie north to south in the main chamber as required by Islamic law. There is also a six foot octagonal screen of marble in which two cenotaphs mark the remains of the emperor and his queen.

Although the Moguls will long be remembered as warriors and conquerors, it is obvious that no expense was spared in building the Taj Mahal; a monument that shows their artistic sense and love of true beauty. Though their mighty empire and reign of power is forever lost, they have left their mark on history and in our hearts and minds with a monument to love and romance that continues to astound us.

Shah Jahan's love defeated death, and could be a message for all mankind:

> *Let love not be buried with death,*
> *Let love devour death.*

REFERENCES

The Egyptian Pyramids

1. Fischer LE: *Pyramid of the Sun, Pyramid of the Moon.* New York: Macmillan, 1988.
2. Ashmawy A: "The Great Pyramid of Giza." Online. Available: *http://pharos.bu.edu/Egypt/Wonders/pyramid.html*, 1998.
3. Pace MM: *Pyramids: Tombs for Eternity.* New York: McGraw Hill Book Company, 1981.

The Taj Mahal

4. Carroll D: *The Taj Mahal: India Under the Moguls.* New York: Newsweek Book Division, 1972.
5. Pratapaditya P, Leoshko J, Dye JM, Markel S: *Romance of the Taj Mahal.* New York: Thames and Hudson Inc., 1989.

Appendix C

WORDS OF COMFORT

*T*his chapter is filled with beautiful words, meaningful messages and prayers. It represents a heartfelt communication between us and the loved ones we lost; the words from them, and the words for them from us.

I. Eulogies, Prayers and Poems

GENERAL EULOGIES

We Come Together Today

We come together today to talk to John/Jane.

We come together today, John/Jane, to admit that your life is beyond comprehension; there is not anyone here capable of summing up your precious life, it cannot be passed over with words.

We come together today to accept your passing; we acknowledge you are not here but your memories will last forever.

We come together today to honor you, for you dedicated your life to love and joy for all of us. You made us happy.

We come together today to touch you, for in life you touched us and brought us together. We come together today to establish a hold on the privilege of remembering you, for your memories will keep us together forever.

We come together today to appreciate what you did in life, for that will kindle courage and infuse hope in us.

We come together today to tell you that God always takes the good ones first; we know you are in good hands, your virtuous journey is just beginning and you will be supremely happy.

We are together today to express our gratefulness for the fact that your life was a gift to this world and your living and love will be eternal sources of joy and strength.

We come together today to let you know that the world will be poorer without you.

We come together today to thank you for your life and bid you goodbye. May you rest in peace.

* * * * *

We come together today to talk to you, the loved ones John/Jane left behind.

We come together today to say God bless you and comfort you in this difficult and painful time, and to let you know we stand beside you in your time of sorrow to share your grief. Let not this death overwhelm you, isolate you. We will not let you do that. We will always be with you, for you.

We come together today knowing that you are severely tested by this death, your pain is deep, you are shocked, saddened and stunned. We will not say how you feel for words will pale in the shadow of your sorrow. But we want you to know that his/her memories will give you courage and strength.

We come together today to give him/her peace; he/she made us laugh, he/she does not want us to weep; he/she made us rejoice, he/she does not want us to mourn.

We come together today to acknowledge his/her death and celebrate his/her life.

We come together today to light a candle of love to honor John/Jane's life, for by living he/she has defeated death and has not died.

PRAYERS

Preface of the Dead

Father, all-powerful and ever-living God,
we do well always and everywhere to give you thanks
through Jesus Christ our Lord.
In him, who rose from the dead,
our hope of resurrection dawned.
The sadness of death gives way
to the bright promise of immortality.
Lord, for your faithful people life is changed, not ended.
When the body of our earthly dwelling lies in death
we gain an everlasting dwelling place in heaven.
And so, with all the choirs of angels in heaven
we proclaim your glory
and join in their unending hymn of praise.

Final Commendation and Farewell

With faith in Jesus Christ,
we reverently bring the body of our brother/sister
to be buried in its human imperfection.
Let us pray with confidence to God,
who gives life to all things,
that he will raise up this mortal body
to the perfection and the company of the saints.
May God give him/her a merciful judgement
and forgive all of his/her sins.
May Christ, the Good Shepherd,
lead him/her safely home
to be at peace with God our Father.
And may he/she be happy forever
with all the saints
in the presence of the eternal King.

A Blameless Life Is a Ripe Old Age

The just man, though he die early, shall be at rest.
For the age that is honorable comes not with the passing
    of time, nor can it be measured in terms of years.
Rather, understanding is the hoary crown for men,
    and an unsullied life, the attainment of old age.
He who pleased God was loved;
    he who lived among sinners was transported –
Snatched away, lest wickedness pervert his mind
    or deceit beguile his soul;
For the witchery of paltry things obscures what is right
    and the whirl of desire transforms the innocent mind.
Having become perfect in a short while, he
    reached the fullness of a long career;
    for his soul was pleasing to the Lord,
    therefore he sped him out of the midst of wickedness.
But the people saw and did not understand,
    nor did they take this in to account.
        This is the Word of the Lord.

MESSAGES FROM THE ONES WHO HAVE DEPARTED

To All My Loved Ones

Do not stand by my grave and weep;
I am not there. I do not sleep.
I am a thousand winds that blow
I am the diamond glints on snow
I am the sunlight on ripened grain
I am the gentle autumn's rain
When you awaken in the morning's hush
I am the swift uplifting rush
of quiet birds in circled flight;

I am the soft stars that shine at night.
Do not stand at my grave and cry;
I am not there
I did not die.

—Author Unknown

For Those I Love and Those Who Love Me

When I am gone, release me, let me go.
I have so many things to see and do,
You mustn't tie yourself to me with tears,
Be thankful for our beautiful years.
I gave to you my love, you can only guess
how much you gave to me in happiness.
I thank you for the love you each have shown,
But now it's time I traveled on alone!
So grieve awhile for me, if grieve you must,
Then let your grief be comforted by trust.
It's only for a time that we must part,
so bless the memories that are within your heart.
I won't be far away, for life goes on.
So if you need me, call and I will come,
Though you can't see or touch me, I'll be near.
And if you listen with your heart, you'll hear
All my love around you soft and clear.
And then, when you must come this way alone...
I'll greet you with a smile and the words,
"Welcome Home!"

—Author Unknown

Miss Me But Let Me Go

When I come to the end of the road
And the sun has set for me
I want no rites in a gloom filled room
Why cry for a soul set free?
Miss me a little, but not for long
and not with your head bowed low.
Remember the love that we once shared
Miss me but let me go.
For this is a journey
That we all must take
And each must go alone
It's all part of the master's plan
A step on the road to home
When you are lonely and sick of heart
Go to the friends we know
And hurry your sorrow in doing deeds
Miss me but let me go.

—Author Unknown

Behind a Veil

And if I go
While you're still here. . .
Know that I live on,
Vibrating to a different measure
behind a veil you cannot see through.
You will not see me, so you must have faith.
I wait for the time when we can be together again—
both aware of each other.
Until then, live your life to its fullest and when you need me,
Just whisper my name in your heart
. . . I will be there.

—Author Unknown

WORDS FOR THE LOVED ONES WE LOST

For a Brother, Husband, Father, Friend

The loved and loving brother, husband, father, friend, died where manhood's morning almost touches noon, and while the shadows still were falling toward the west.

He had not passed on life's highway the stone that marks the highest point, but being weary for a moment, he lay down by the wayside and, using his burden for a pillow, fell into that dreamless sleep that kisses down his eyelids still. While yet in love with life and raptured with the world, he passed to silence and pathetic dust.

This brave and tender man in every storm of life was oak and rock, but in the sunshine he was vine and flower. He was the friend of all heroic souls. He climbed the heights and left all superstitions far below, while on his forehead fell the golden dawning of the grander day.

He loved the beautiful, and was with color, form and music touched to tears. He sided with the weak and with a willing hand gave alms; with loyal heart and with purest hands he faithfully discharged all public trusts.

And now to you who have been chosen, from among the many men he loved, to do the last sad office for the dead, we give this sacred dust. Speech cannot contain our love. There was, there is, no greater, stronger, manlier man.

—for Clark Ingersoll (d. 1879), by
Robert Green Ingersoll (1833–1899)

For a Father:
Do Not Go Gentle Into That Goodnight

Do not go gentle into that goodnight.
Old age should burn and rave at close of day;
Rage, rage against the dying of the light
Wise men, who at their end know dark is right,
Because their words had forked no lightning they
Do not go gentle into that goodnight.
Good men, the last wave by, crying how bright
Their frail deeds might have danced in the fragile day
Rage, rage against the dying of the light.
Wild men, who caught and sang the Sun in flight
And learned too late they grieved it on its way,
Do not go gentle into that goodnight.
Grave men, near death, who see with blinding sight,
Blind eyes should blaze like meteors and be gay,
Rage, rage against the dying of the light.
And you, my father, there on the sad height,
Curse, bless, me now with your fierce tears, I pray.
Do not go gentle into that goodnight.
Rage, rage against the dying of the light!

—Dylan Thomas (1914-1953)

Dear Father. . .

Judge a man not only by how he may appear
Look deep inside, into his soul you must peer;
In my father I saw a warm, ever bright light
In life his spirit, this man was always in flight.
Soaring high above us, not all of us could even see
But I always knew, this man he was not like you and me.
A brilliant man, with fierce determination and courage
With a fire inside him that always led him to encourage.
Comforting those in pain, those in need
With love for all and words of wisdom for all to heed.

I am grieved beyond words to say goodbye to this man not like you and I,
Only comforted that he touched so many in life and that he will watch
over me from the Heavens in the sky.
He lived so many lifetimes in one, his dreams, his wishes will further be
done.
I carry his spirit forth, I will do for him what he did for me.
I will shine so bright,
So that from Heaven he can see me, he will see my light.

—Naaz Fatteh

For A Sister:
A Grand Life

Here I stand today,
not knowing quite what to say,
She is gone . . . the words repeated in my head,
Yet I cannot believe, my sweet angel, my sister, is dead.
I have wept, I have not slept,
I do not understand how she could have just left,
But now as I speak of her, I think of her life,
How beautiful and grand it was;
she was a sister, a mother, a daughter and a wife.
How lucky we were, to know her, see her, watch her spirit shine
The glimmer of that life will last in our hearts for a lifetime.
My sister was kind, pure inside, not a harsh word to say, always bringing
family together
on every special day,
Never a thought without thinking of others first,
An angel on earth, for what more could I pray?
We feel her in Heaven, know that is where she will be,
We will love her while she is in Heaven,
And can't wait until that day when again we will meet,
this time, for eternity.
We miss you my sister, We love you too,

I will not say goodbye now, because in my heart I feel you with me,
And when I finally see you again, what a glorious day that will be!

—Naaz Fatteh

All You Were

Like fireflies lighting the path on a warm summer night,
Like a lighthouse helping a lost ship through a fierce
   stormy flight,
The soft speak of a mother
Guiding a child, holding their hand, teaching the meanings of life,
Looking for a peaceful way, whenever there was strife.
Like a religious source bringing the comfort of God,
Like the marching men guarding against the enemy who would come
    upon us to trod.
You were all of these things to us, dear sister,
the teacher, the protector, the comforter, with words ever wise to say.
Your loss we feel from dusk to dawn,
but your love, your spirit, will never be gone.
The light of your life,
Lit the way for all of us, and now it is dark.
Your guidance and love for an eternity will last,
As an angel you watch over us, from the Heavens so vast.
Like a light burning bright, in our hearts you will stay . . .
Until we meet again one day.

—Naaz Fatteh

For a Child

We are hurting, Lord. With our child's death went all our hopes
our dreams, our future.
But in our grief we can now fully appreciate the little things in life.
We are thankful for even the short time we had with our child.
We realize how fragile and brief life can be. We now take nothing
for granted.

Thank you for being with us in our time of sadness and grief.
We look to you for strength.

—Burial service for Benjamin Matthew Jones

For One Who Was in Pain:
The Day God Called You Home

He put his arms around you, And lifted you to rest.
God's garden must be beautiful, He always takes the best.
He knew that you were suffering, He knew you were in pain.
He knew that you would never, Get well on this earth again.
He saw the road was getting rough, And the hills were hard to climb.
So he closed your weary eyelids, And whispered "Peace be thine."
It broke our hearts to lose you, But you didn't go alone
For part of us went with you, The day God called you home.

—Author Unknown

For One Who Has an Incurable Disease
The Best

God saw you getting tired
and a cure was not to be,
So he put His arms around you
and whispered "Come to Me."
With tearful eyes we watched you,
and saw you pass away.
Although we loved you dearly,
we could not make you stay.
A Golden Heart stopped beating,
hard working hands at rest,
God broke our hearts to prove to us,
He only takes the best.

—Author Unknown

For a Neighbor

I have got my leave. Bid me farewell,
my brothers!
I bow to you all and take my departure.
Here I give back the keys of my
door – and I give up
all claims to my house. I only ask for
last kind words from you.
We were neighbors for long,
but I received more
than I could give. Now the day has
dawned and the lamp that lit
my dark corner is out. A
summons has come and I am ready
for my journey.

—*Rabindranath Tagore*

For All:
An Irish Blessing

May the road rise to meet you.
May the wind be always at your back.
May the sunshine warm upon your face.
May the rains fall upon your fields.
And until we meet again,
May God hold you in the hollow of His hand.

For Burial Committal Services

Fall softly, O thou coat of winter snow, and keep our loved one warm;
Kiss him gently, sun and rain, in the quiet of his rest;
Watch over him, wind and stars, in the silence of the night;
Grow thou to cover him, grass and flowers, and make beautiful his couch,
And thou, Great Spirit of Love and Peace, take him into thine arms
and lull him to rest forever. Amen.

—*Rev. John G. MacKinnon*

For Cremation Committal Service
Fruit-Gathering: XL

O Fire, my brother, I sing victory to you.

You are the bright red image of fearful freedom.

You swing your arms in the sky, you sweep your impetuous
    fingers

Across the harp-string, your dance music is beautiful.

When my days are ended and the gates are opened you will
    burn to

Ashes this cordage of hands and feet.

My body will be one with you, my heart will be caught
    in the

Whirls of your frenzy, and the burning heat that was my

Life will flash up and mingle itself in your flame.

—Rabindranath Tagore

II. Notable Reflections On Death

1. To die will be an awfully big adventure.

   —*J.M. Barrie (1860–1937)*

2. I feel no pain dear mother now,
   But oh, I am so dry!
   O take me to a brewery
   And leave me there to die.

   —*Anonymous 19th century*

3. Death is nothing to us,
   since when we are,
   death has not come,
   and when death has come,
   we are not.

   —*Epicurus (341-270 B.C.)* Diogenes Lacrius, *Book 10, sec. 125*

4. Drink and dance and laugh and lie
   Love, the reeling midnight through
   For tomorrow we shall die!

   —*Dorothy Parker (1893-1967)*

5. I still go up my 44 steps two at
   a time, but that is in hopes
   of dropping dead at the top.

   —*A.E. Housman (1859-1936)*

6. He'd make a lovely corpse.

   —*Charles Dickens (1812-1870)*

7. I read the Times and if my name
   is not in the obits
   I proceed to enjoy the day.

   —*Noel Coward (1899-1973)*

8. Six feet of earth make all men of one size.

   —*Old American Proverb*

Appendix D

DISPOSITION INSTRUCTIONS & OTHER FORMS

DISPOSITION INSTRUCTIONS

I. IMPORTANT INFORMATION

Name: _____

Address: _____

Telephone number: _____

Date_____ Place of death: _____

Social Security number: _____

Spouse

Name, Address, Telephone number:

_____

Executor of Estate

Name, Address, Telephone number:

_____

II. WHO TO NOTIFY UPON DEATH

Relatives

Name, Telephone number:

1. _____

2. _____

3. _____

Close Friends

Name/Telphone number:

1. _____

2. _____

3. _____

Attorney

Name/Telephone number:

_____

Insurance Agent

Name/Telephone number:

_____

Executor of Estate

Name/Telephone number:

_____

Funeral Director

Name/Telephone number:

_____

III. DISPOSITION OF BODY

A. Cremation

__ Direct without viewing, ceremony, embalming

__ After viewing, without embalming

__ After embalming, viewing and services

__ After removal of donated organs

__ After removal of organs and viewing

__ After removal of organs, embalming, viewing

__ After study of donated body

__ Disposition of cremains:

   ☐ Urn
   ☐ Sea
   ☐ River
   ☐ Earth

   ☐ Mausoleum

   ☐ Columbarium

   ☐ Home

   ☐ Burial in ground

     Location of crematory: _____

B. Donation

Donation of whole body to:

_____

(Name of Medical School or Educational Institution)

___ Donation of whole body after death

___ Donation of whole body after services

___ Donation of following organs:

   ☐ Corneas

   ☐ Heart

   ☐ Lungs

   ☐ Liver

   ☐ Pancreas

   ☐ Skin

   ☐ Bone

   ☐ Other (specify) _____

Location of organ donor card or sticker on motor vehicle license:

_____

Body donated to: _____

Organs donated to: _____

C. Burial

___ Immediate, without viewing

___ Embalming (unless required by law)

___ After viewing, without embalming

___ After embalming and viewing

___ After embalming, viewing and service

Cemetery Address: _____

Plot location: _____

Cemetery plot deed location: _____

__ Burial in mausoleum

Address: _____

__ Grave marker:

   ☐ Flat

   ☐ Erect

__ Epitaph to read: _____

D. Funeral

__ Wake at (address): _____

__ Funeral Services at (address): _____

   ☐ Church

   ☐ Synagogue

   ☐ Funeral home

   ☐ Home

__ Wake, Service:

   ☐ Open Casket

   ☐ Closed Casket

   ☐ Flowers

   ☐ Charities

__ Memorial Service without body at (address):

_____

__ Service at Mausoleum (address): _____

__ Service at Cemetery (address): _____

__ Cremation at (address): _____

ANATOMICAL GIFT BY A LIVING DONOR

I am of sound mind and 18 years or more of age.

I hereby make this anatomical gift to take effect upon my death. The marks in the appropriate blanks and words filled into the blanks below indicate my desires.

I give:

__ My body

__ Any needed organs or parts

__ The following organs or parts:

_____

To the following person or institution:

__ The physician in attendance at my death

__ The hospital in which I die

__ The following named physician, hospital storage bank or other medical institution: _____

For the following purposes:

__ Any purpose authorized by law

__ Transplantation

__ Therapy

__ Research

__ Medical education

Dated: _____ City and State: _____

Signed by the Donor In the presence of the following who sign as witnesses:

_____	_____
Witness	*Signature of Donor*
_____	_____
Witness	*Address of Donor*

ANATOMICAL GIFT BY A RELATIVE
OR GUARDIAN OF THE PERSON OF THE DECEDENT

I hereby make this anatomical gift from the body of:_____

On: _____   in: _____

     (Date)   *(City and State)*

     The marks in the appropriate blanks and the words filled into the blanks below indicate my relationship to the decedent and my desires respecting the anatomical gift.

I survive the decedent as:

__ Spouse   __ Adult son or daughter

__ Parent   __ Adult brother or sister

__ Grandparent   __ Guardian

__ Person authorized to dispose of the body: _____

I hereby give the following body parts:

__ Heart   __ Liver

__ Skin   __ Middle ear

__ Kidneys   __ Lung

__ Heart Valves   __ Pancreas

__ Eyes   __ Bone/Ligament

__ Other: _____

For:

__ Any purpose authorized by law   __ Transplantation

__ Therapy   __ Medical research/education

     After the donated organs, tissues, or eyes are removed, the remains of the body shall be disposed of in the following manner:

_____

at the expense of the following person:_____

Dated: _____ City and State: _____

_____	_____
Witness	*Signature of Donor*
_____	_____
Witness	*Address of Donor*

UNIFORM DONOR CARD

Uniform Donor Card

Of: _____

Print or type name of donor

    In the hope that I may help others, I hereby make this anatomical gift, if medically acceptable, to take effect upon my death. The words and marks below indicate my desires. I give:

___ Any needed organs and tissues

___ Only the following organs: _____

For the purpose of transplantation, therapy, medical research or education.

Limited or special wishes, if any:

_____

Uniform Donor Card: Front

Uniform Donor Card

Signed by the donor and the following two witnesses in the presence of each other:

_____   _____
       Signature of Donor   *Date of Birth of Donor*

Date: _____   City and State: _____

_____   _____
          Witness I   *Witness II*

This is a legal document under the Uniform Anatomical Gift Act or similar laws.

Uniform Donor Card: Back

AUTHORIZATION FOR PERMISSION TO USE EYES

Date_____

I, _____ residing at: _____

_____ ,

bearing relationship of _____

to _(Name of the Deceased)_ , do hearby give permission to _(Name of
Funeral Director)_ and/or to _(Name of Eyebank)_ to remove either or
both eyes from said deceased to be used for such purposes that the Eye
Bank may deem necessary.

_____   _____

Signature of person giving   *Witness*
permission

Eye Bank Phone, Day or Night: _____

Appendix E

FUNERAL AND MEMORIAL SOCIETIES

Alaska

Cook Inlet Memorial
907-566-3732
P.O. Box 102414
Anchorage AK 99510

Arizona

Phoenix Valley Memorial Society
602-929-9659
Box 0423
Chandler AZ 85244-0423

Memorial Society of Prescott
520-778-3000
P.O. Box 1090
Prescott AZ 86302-1090

Memorial Society of So. Arizona
520 721-0230
P.O. Box 12661
Tucson AZ 85732-2661

Arkansas

NW Arkansas Memorial Society
501-582-1631
P.O. Box 3055
Fayetteville AR 72702-3055

California

Humbolt Funeral Society
707-822-8599
P.O. Box 856
Arcata CA 95518

Kern Memorial Society
661-854-5689
661-366-7266
P.O. Box 1202
Bakersfield CA 93302-1202

Fresno Valley Memorial Society
559-268-2181
P.O. Box 101
Fresno CA 93707

Bay Area Funeral Society
510-841-6653
P.O. Box 264
Berkeley CA 94701-0264

Valley Memorial Society
559-268-2181
P.O. Box 101
Fresno CA 93707-0101

Los Angeles Funeral Society
626-683-3545
626-683-3751
P.O. Box 92313
Pasadena CA 91109-2313

Stanislaus Memorial Society
209-521-7690
P.O. Box 4252
Modesta CA 95352-4252

Funeral & Memorial Planning
  Society
650-321-2109
888-775-5553
P.O. Box 60448
Palo Alto CA 94306-0448

Sacramento Valley Memorial
Society
916-451-4641
P.O. Box 161688
Sacramento CA 95816-1688

San Diego Memorial Society
619-923-0926
460 Olive St., #C
San Diego, CA 92176
http://www.funerals.org/famsa/
sandiego.htm

Central Coast Memorial Society
805-543-6133
P.O. Box 679
San Luis Obispo CA 93406-0679

Channel Cities Memorial Society
805-640-0109
800-520-PLAN
P.O. Box 1778
Ojai CA 93024-1778

Funeral & Memorial Society of
  Monterey Bay
831-426-3308
P.O. Box 2900
Santa Cruz CA 95063-2900

Redwood Funeral Society
707-824-8360
P.O. Box 7501
Cotati CA 94931
http://www.funeral.org/

San Joaquin Memorial Society
209-465-2741
P.O. Box 4832
Stockton CA 95204-4832

Colorado

Funeral Consumer Society of
  Colorado
303-759-2800
888-438-6431
4101 E. Hampden Ave.
Denver CO 80222
http://www.funerals.org/famsa/
colorado.htm

Connecticut

*Funeral Consumer Information
    Society of Connecticut*
860-350-4197
800-607-2801
P.O. Box 34
Bridgewater CT 06752

District of Columbia

*Memorial Society of Metropolitan
    Washington*
202-234-7777
500 Harvard St. NW
Washington DC 20009

Florida

*Funeral & Memorial Society of
    Brevard County*
407-453-4109
P.O. Box 276
Cocoa FL 32923-0276

Funeral Society of Mid-Florida
904-789-1682
P.O. Box 392
DeBary FL 32713-0392

*Funeral & Memorial Society of
    Southwest Florida*
941-573-0507
P.O. Box 7756
Fort Myers FL 33911-7756

Memorial Society of Alachua Co.
352-378-3432
Box 14662
Gainesville FL 32604-4662

*Memorial & Funeral Society of
    Greater Orlando*
407-677-5009
P.O. Box 953
Goldenrod FL 32733-0953

*Palm Beach Gardens
    Funeral Society*
561-659-4881
P.O. Box 31982
Palm Beach FL 33420

*Funeral & Memorial Society of
    Pensacola & West Florida*
850-477-9085

Memorial Society of Sarasota
941-953-3740
P.O. Box 15833
Sarasota FL 34277-5833

*Suncoast-Tampa Bay Memorial
    Society*
727-895-1442
719 Arlington Ave. N.
St. Petersburg FL 33701

Funeral & Memorial Society of
Leon County
850-224-2082
1006 Buena Vista Dr.
Tallahassee FL 32304
http://www.applicom.com/
humanist/funeral/fmsindex.htm

Memorial Society of Tampa Bay
800-765-0107
18902 Arbor Dr.
Lutz FL 33549-5051
http://www.funerals.org/famsa/
tampabay.htm

Georgia

Memorial Society of Georgia
404-634-2896
800-840-4339
1911 Cliff Valley Way NE
Atlanta GA 30329
http://www.mindspring.com/
~memsoc/memsoc.htm

Middle Georgia Chapter
800-840-4339
5276 Zebulon Rd.
Macon, GA 31210

Hawaii

Memorial Society of Hawaii
808-946-6822
2510 Bingham St. Room A
Honolulu HI 96826

Idaho

Idaho Memorial Association
208-343-4581
P.O. Box 1919
Boise, ID 83701-1919
http://www.funerals.org/famsa/
idaho.htm

Illinois

Chicago Memorial Association
773-238-3746
Box 2923
Chicago, IL 60690-2923

Champaign County Memorial
Society
217-384-8862
309 W. Green St.
Urbana, IL 61801
http://www.prairienet.org/
ccmemsoc/

Indiana

Bloomington Memorial Society
812-332-3695
2120 N. Fee Lane
Bloomington IN 47408

Indianapolis Memorial Society
317-545-6005
5805 E. 56th St.
Indianapolis IN 46226

Memorial Society of Northwest
Indiana
219-464-5483
P.O. Box 329
Valparaiso IN 46384-0329

Iowa

Memorial Society of Iowa River
Valley
319-338-2637
120 N. Dubuque St.
Iowa City IA 52245

Other areas of Iowa:
call FAMSA at 800-765-2637

Kentucky

Memorial Society of Greater
Louisville
502-585-5110
P.O. Box 5326
Louisville KY 40255-5326

Louisiana

Memorial Society of Greater
Baton Rouge
8470 Goodwood Ave.
Baton Rouge, LA 70806

Maine

Memorial Society of Maine
207-786-4323
800-218-9885
Box 3122
Auburn, ME 04212-3122
http://www.funerals.org/famsa/ms
maine.htm

Maryland

Memorial Society of Maryland
and Environs
800-564-0017
9601 Cedar Lane
Bethesda MD 20814
http://www.funerals.org/famsa/
msme.htm

Massachusetts

The Memorial Society
617-859-7990
888-666-7990
66 Marlborough St.
Boston, MA 02116

Memorial Society of Cape Cod
508-862-2522
800-976-9552
P.O. Box 1375
East Orleans MA 02643-1375

Memorial Society of Southeast
Massachusetts
71 8th St.
New Bedford MA 02740

Memorial Society of Western
  Massachusetts
413-783-7987
P.O. Box 2821
Springfield MA 01101-2821
http://community.masslive.com/cc/
memorialsociety/

Michigan

Memorial Advisory & Planning
  Society
734-665-9516
2030 Chaucer Dr.
Ann Arbor MI 48103
http://community.mlive.com/cc/
funeralsociety/

Greater Detroit Memorial Society
313-886-0998
P.O. Box 24054
Detroit MI 48224-4054
http://www.geocities.com/Athens/
Aegean/6858/

Memorial Society of Flint
810-239-2596
P.O. Box 4315
Flint MI 48504-4315

Minnesota

Minnesota Funeral & Memorial
  Society
612-374-1515
717 Riverside Dr. SE
St. Cloud MN 56304

Missouri

Funeral & Memorial Society of
  Greater Kansas City
816-561-6322
4500 Warwick Blvd.
Kansas City MO 64111

Funeral Consumer Information
  Society
314-997-9819
216 E. Argonne Ave.
St Louis, MO 63122-4310

Montana

Memorial Society of Montana
406-252-5065
1024 Princeton Ave.
Billings MT 59102

Five Valleys Burial Memorial
  Association
405 University Ave.
Missoula MT 59801

Nevada

Memorial Society of Nevada
702-329-7705
Box 8413, Univ. Sta.
Reno, NV 89507-8413

New Hampshire

Memorial Society of
  New Hampshire
603-679-5721
P.O. Box 941
Epping, NH 03042-0941

New Jersey

Memorial Society of South Jersey
401 Kings Highway N.
Cherry Hill NJ 08034

Raritan Valley Memorial Society
732-572-1470
176 Tices Lane
East Brunswick NJ 08816

Memorial Association of
Monmouth County
1475 W. Front St.
Lincroft NJ 07738

Morris Memorial Society
973-540-9140
Box 509
Madison NJ 07940-0509

Memorial Society of Essex
973-783-1145
P.O. Box 1327
Montclair NJ 07042-1327

Central Memorial Society
201-385-4153
156 Forest
Paramus NJ 07652

Memorial Society of Plainfield
908-889-5377
520 William St.
Scotch Plains NJ 07076-1910

Princeton Memorial Association
609-924-5525
609-924-1604
48 Roper Rd.
Princeton NJ 08540
http://www.princetonol.com/
groups/pms/

New Mexico

Funeral Consumer Information
Society of Northern New Mexico
505-296-5902
P.O. Box 15164
Rio Rancho, NM 87174

Memorial & Funeral Society of
Southern New Mexico
505-526-7761
P.O. Box 6531
Las Cruces NM 88006-6531

New York

Memorial Society of
Hudson-Mohawk Region
518-465-9664
405 Washington Ave.
Albany NY 12206-2604

Southern Tier Memorial Society
183 Riverside Dr.
Binghamton NY 13905

Greater Buffalo Memorial Society
716-837-8636
695 Elmwood Ave.
Buffalo NY 14222-1601

*Memorial Society of
  Greater Corning*
607-962-7132
607-936-6563
P.O. Box 23
Painted Post NY 14870-0023

Memorial Society of Long Island
516-541-6587
Box 3495
Farmingdale NY 11735-0694
*http://www.funerals.org/famsa/
l-island.htm*

Ithaca Memorial Society
607-273-8316
Box 134
Ithaca NY 14851-0134

Mohawk Valley Memorial Society
315-797-2396
315-735-6268
P.O. Box 322
New Hartford NY 13413-0322

*Memorial Society of
  Riverside Church*
212-870-6785
490 Riverside Dr., Room 537
New York NY 10027

*Community Church of New York
  Funeral Society*
212-683-4988
40 East 35th St.
New York NY 10016

Mid-Hudson Memorial Society
914-229-0241
249 Hooker Ave.
Poughkeepsie NY 12603

Rochester Memorial Society
716-461-1620
220 Winston Rd. South
Rochester NY 14610

Syracuse Memorial Society
315-446-0557
315-478-7258
P.O. Box 67
DeWitt, NY 13214-0067

*Funeral Planning Association
  of Westchester*
460 York Ct.
Yorktown Heights NY 10598-3726

North Carolina

Blue Ridge Memorial Society
828-669-2587
P.O. Box 2601
Asheville NC 28802-2601

Memorial Society of the Triangle
919-834-6898
P.O. Box 1223
Chapel Hill NC 27514-1223
*http://www.sitewest.com/memorial
society/*

*Memorial Society of the Coastal
  Carolinas*
P.O. Box 4262
Wilmington NC 28406-4262

Ohio

Memorial Society of
  Akron-Canton Area
330-836-4418
330-849-1030
3300 Morewood Rd.
Akron OH 44333

Memorial Society of Greater
  Cincinnati
536 Linton St.
Cincinnati OH 45219

Cleveland Memorial Society
216-751-5515
21600 Shaker Blvd.
Shaker Heights, OH 44122

Memorial Society of the
  Columbus Area
614-436-8911
P.O. Box 14835
Columbus OH 43214-4835
http://www.funerals.org/famsa/
msca1.htm

Memorial Society of Northwest
  Ohio
419-475-1429
2210 Collingwood Blvd.
Toledo OH 43620-1147

Oklahoma

All Oklahoma cities call:
800-371-2221

Oregon

Oregon Memorial Association
503-297-3513
888-475-5520
P.O. Box 25578
Portland OR 97298

Pennsylvania

Memorial Society of Erie
814-456-4433
Box 3495
Erie PA 16508-3495

Memorial Society of Greater
  Harrisburg
717-564-8507
1280 Clover Lane
Harrisburg PA 17113

Memorial Society of Greater
  Philadelphia
215-567-1065
2125 Chestnut St.
Philadelphia PA 19103

Pittsburgh Memorial Society
724-621-4740
605 Morewood Ave.
Pittsburgh PA 15213

Memorial Society of Central
  Pennnsylvania
780 Waupelani Dr. Ext.
State College PA 16801

Rhode Island

Memorial Society of Rhode Island
401-884-5933
119 Kenyon Ave.
East Greenwich RI 02818

South Carolina

*Funeral and Memorial Society of
  South Carolina*
803-772-7054
2701 Heyward St.
Columbia SC 29205

*Memorial Society of the Coastal
  Carolinas*
P.O. Box 4262
Wilmington NC 28406-4262

South Dakota

*Funeral Consumer Information
  Society of the Dakotas*
605-374-5336
HCR 66 Box 10
Lemmon SD 57638

Tennessee

Memorial Society of Chattanooga
3224 Navajo Dr.
Chattanooga TN 37411

East Tennessee Memorial Society
P.O. Box 10507
Knoxville TN 37939

*Memorial Society of Middle
  Tennessee*
615-661-7586
888-254-3872
1808 Woodmont Blvd.
Nashville TN 37215

Texas

*Austin Memorial & Burial
  Information Society*
512-480-0555
P.O. Box 4382
Austin TX 78765-4382
*http://www.funerals.org/famsa/
ambis.htm/*

Memorial Society of South Texas
800-371-2221
3125 Horne Rd.
Corpus Christi TX 78415

Memorial Society of North Texas
214-528-6006
(TX/OK) 800-371-2221
4015 Normandy
Dallas, TX 75205

Houston Area Memorial Society
713-526-4267
5200 Fannin St.
Houston TX 77004-5899

San Antonio Memorial Society
210-341-2213
7150 Interstate 10 West
San Antonio TX 78213

Memorial Society of Northern
  Texas, Central Texas Chapter
4209 N. 27th St.
Waco TX 76708-1509
(TX/OK) 800-371-2221

Vermont

Vermont Memorial Society
802-476-4300
802-875-3192 (SE Vermont)
802-482-3437 (NW Vermont)
800-805-0007
1630 Clark Rd.
East Montpelier VT 05651

Virginia

Memorial Society of Northern
  Virginia
703-271-9240
4444 Arlington Blvd.
Arlington VA 22204

Memorial Planning Society of
  Piedmont
804-293-8179
717 Rugby Rd.
Charlottesville VA 22903

Funeral Consumer Information
  Society of Virginia
804-745-3682
P.O. Box 3712
Glen Allen VA 23058-3712

Memorial Society of Tidewater
P.O. Box 4621
Virginia Beach VA 23454-4621

Washington

People's Memorial Association
206-325-0489
2366 Eastlake Ave. E.
Areis Bldg. #409
Seattle WA 98102
http://www.peoples-memorial.org/

Spokane Memorial Association
509-924-8400
P.O. Box 13613
Spokane WA 99213-3613
http://www.spokanememorial.org/

Funeral Association of Central
  Washington
509-248-4533
1916 N. 4th St.
Yakima WA 98901

West Virginia

NE area: See MD

Memorial Society of Greenbrier
  Valley
P.O. Box 1277
Lewisburg, WV 24901

Wisconsin

Memorial Societies of Wisconsin
414-868-3136
(WI) 800-374-1109
6900 Lost Lake Rd.
Egg Harbor WI 54209-9231

Funeral Consumer Information
  Society of Greater Milwaukee
414-238-0507
414-782-3535
13001 W. North Ave.
Brookfield WI 53005

Appendix F

ORGANIZATIONS

National Funeral Directors Association

13625 Bishops Drive
Brookfield, WI 53005
(414) 789-1880; (414) 789-6977 Fax
http://www.nfda.org

Largest educational and professional association of funeral directors. Established in 1882, with 14,000 members throughout the United States.

Cremation Association of North America

401 N. Michigan Ave.
Suite 2200
Chicago, IL 60611
(312) 644-6610; (312) 321-6869 Fax

Industry trade association of crematories, cemeteries and funeral homes that offer cremation. Provides brochures on cremation and on how to create memorials.

Funeral and Memorial Societies of America, Inc.

P.O. Box 10
Hinesburg, VT 05461
(802) 482-3437; (802) 482-5246 Fax
http://www.funerals.org/famsa

Nonprofit educational organization which serves as an umbrella to more than 120 nonprofit funeral consumer information societies.

American Association of Retired Persons

AARP Fulfillment
601 E. Street, NW
Washington, DC 20049
(202) 434-2277; (202) 434-6466 Fax
http://www.aarp.org/

Nonprofit organization helps elderly Americans have independent, dignified and purposeful lives. Free publications available are *Funeral Goods and Services* and *Pre-Paying for Your Funeral?*

Alzheimer's Association, Inc.

919 N. Michigan Ave.
Suite 1100
Chicago, IL 60611-1676
(312) 335-8700
http://www.alz.org/

Organization with 221 chapters and 1600 support groups. Research, education, support, public policy, family services. Provides information in newsletters and literature.

American Cancer Society

1599 Clifton Rd., NE
Atlanta, GA 30329-4251
(800) 227-2345 or (404) 320-3333; (404) 325-9341 Fax
http://www.cancer.org/

Sponsors self-help support groups and other services for cancer patients and their families. There are 58 divisions and over 3000 local groups. National programs of research and education.

Funeral Service Consumer Assistance Program

Carried on by: The National Research and Information Center
P.O. Box 486
Elm Grove, WI 53122-0486
(800) 662-7666 or (414) 789-6977

Run by a nonprofit organization, it receives about one complaint per week. It helps consumers and funeral directors resolve disagreements about funeral service contracts and provides consumer information on death, grief and funeral services.

National Hospice Organization

1901 N. Moore St.
Suite 901
Arlington, VA 22209
(703) 243-5900, or Hospice Help line: (800) 658-8898
(703) 525-5762 Fax

Sponsors national and regional meetings, develops standards of care, provides educational materials and newsletter, provides location of nearby hospice.

Hospice Education Institute

190 Westbrook Rd.
Essex, CT 06426
(860) 767-2746 or (800) 331-1620 Hospice Link, except:
(203) 767-1620 in Connecticut and Alaska

HEI refers callers immediately to the nearest hospice. Also coordinates regional, national, and international seminars and training for hospice professionals, health care providers and civic groups; presents community education programs; consultation to existing hospice programs and to groups seeking to begin hospice care.

The American Association of Tissue Banks

1350 Beverly Rd.
Suite 220-A
McLean, VA 22101
(703) 827-9582 or (800) 635-2282 for persons requesting tissue
http://www.aatb.org/

Group of physicians, nurses, lawyers, technicians and the general public not affiliated with the government. Develops standards for tissue banking with inspection and certification of tissue banks.

Eye Bank Association of America

1015 18th Street NW
Suite 1010
Washington DC 20036-5504
(202) 775-4999; (202) 434-6466 Fax
http://restoresight.org

Monitors government activity and the media while developing standards, professional training, and computer coordination.

International Order of the Golden Rule

13523 Lakefront Drive
Bridgeton, MO 63045
(314) 209-7142

International association of independent funeral homes; membership by invitation only. There are approximately 1500 funeral home members.

Jewish Funeral Directors of America, Inc.

Seaport Landing
150 Lynnway
Suite 506
Lynn, MA 01902
(781) 477-9300; (781) 477-9393 Fax

National trade association of funeral directors who serve the Jewish community with 200 members.

National Funeral Directors and Morticians Association

3544 Prospect
Kansas City, MO 64127
(816) 923-2121

National association primarily of black funeral providers with 1600 members in 27 states. One of the oldest African-American associations.

National Selected Morticians

5 Revere Drive
Suite 340
Northbrook, IL 60062
(847) 559-9569; (847) 449-9471 Fax
http://www.nsm.org/

National association of funeral firms, membership by invitation only and conditioned upon commitment of each firm to comply with the Association's Code of Good Funeral Practice.

Division of Transplantation, Health Resources and Services Administration, U.S. Dept. of Health and Human Services

5600 Fishers Lane
Park Lawn Bldg. 4-81
Rockville, MD 20857
(888) 90-SHARE or (301) 443-7577; (301) 594-6095 Fax
http://www.organdonor.gov

Provides information on organ donation and transplantation. Includes recorded information, brochures or direct phone contact with a specialist, encourages the notification of organ donors in obituaries.

International Conference of Funeral Service Examining Boards

P.O. Drawer E
Huntsville, AR 72740
(501) 738-1915; (501) 738-1922 Fax
http://www.cfseb.org/

Represents licensing boards in 47 states, providing information on laws in different states and fielding consumer inquiries or complaints about funeral providers.

Theos Foundation, Inc.

322 Blvd. of the Allies
Suite 105
Pittsburgh, PA 15222-1919
(412) 471-7779; (312) 471-7782 Fax

Dedicated to helping widowed people through the grieving process via psychological treatment, educational tools and support groups.

American Association of Suicidology

4201 Connecticut Ave. NW
Suite 408
Washington DC 20008
(202) 237-2280; (202) 237-2282 Fax
http://www.suicidology.org/

Provides information on coping with grief when faced with loss by suicide, also provides information on suicide prevention and can refer you to a local organization for support or information.

Emotions Anonymous

P.O. Box 4245
St. Paul, MN 55104
(651) 647-9712; (651) 647-1593 Fax
http://www.mtn.org/EA/

An international service providing services and referrals to counselors in your state, dealing with emotions, such as grief.

National Sudden Infant Death Syndrome Foundation (SIDS)

1314 Bedford Avenue
Suite 210
Baltimore, MD 21208
(800) 221-7437; (440) 653-8709 Fax
http://www.sidsalliance.org/
   Provides counseling and information on SIDS, and funds research.

The Compassionate Friends

P.O. Box 3696
Oak Brook, IL 60522-3696
(603) 990-0010; (630) 990-0246 Fax
http://www.compassionatefriends.org/
   National organization providing counseling and support groups for parents of children who have died.

Children's Grief Center

P.O. Box 6324
Kent, WA 98031
(253) 631-0158
   Provides support for children ages 3-18 who have recently lost a parent or loved one.

Cremation Society of the South

5754 Harrison Ave.
Suite B
Austell, GA 30106
(770) 941-5352; (770) 437-8181 Fax
http://www.cremation.org/georgia/georgia.html
   Membership with a one-time fee places your name on file. At the time of death, one call to them takes care of everything.

Center to Improve Care of the Dying

George Washington Univ.
2175 K St. NW
Washington DC 20037-1802
(202) 467-2222
   Committed to research and education to improve care of dying patients and for people suffering from a disabling disease.

Arlington National Cemetery

Superintendent Arlington Natl. Cemetery
Arlington, VA 22211
(703) 695-3250; (703) 614-6339 Fax
   Burial limited to specific categories of military personnel and veterans.

Choice in Dying

1035 30th St., NW
Washington DC 20007
(202) 338-9790; (202) 338-2042 Fax
http://www.choices.org/
   Non-profit organization providing advance directives, family and patient counseling, advocates for improved laws. Offers broad range of publications and services.

GLOSSARY

AARP: The American Association of Retired Persons.

Advance directive: A class of legal documents, such as living wills, that allow individuals to specify in advance what medical care they desire. They only go into effect if the person lacks the capacity to make valid decisions at the time they are necessary.

Anatomical gift: A donation of all or part of a human body to take effect upon or after death.

Anatomical Gift Act: Anatomical Gift Act, Part I, 1968 and Anatomical Gift Act, Part II, 1987 pertain to donating the body or organs to medical science or education.

Ark: Focal point of service in a synagogue or temple, the receptacle of the Torah (written law). It may be portable or an opening in a wall.

Aron: Hebrew meaning "container." A coffin or casket made entirely of wood and containing no metal parts.

Arterial embalming: The most common type of embalming. Chemicals are injected in a large artery while the blood is simultaneously removed from a large vein.

Arterial preservative: The chemicals injected into a body in the embalming process.

Autopsy: An examination of a dead body to determine the cause and manner of death.

Avelim: A mourner: (Abel, Avel, Ovel). The nearest of seven blood relatives; father, mother, husband, wife, son or daughter, brother and sister.

Batsudan: Small family altar in a Japanese home where daily prayers and meals are offered to honor the deceased.

Bet olan: To bury; (Bais, Olam, Bet Almin) everlasting home, graveyard or burialgrounds.

Bikkur Cholim: the mitzvah of visiting the sick in the Jewish religion.

Bimah: The portion of the Jewish synagogue or temple raised above the congregation seating.

Blood borne pathogens: Pathogenic microorganisms that are present in human blood and can cause disease in humans. These pathogens include, but are not limited to Hep B, HIV.

Burial certificate or permit: A legal paper issued by the local government authorizing burial. The permit may authorize earth burial or cremation.

CANA: The Cremation Association of North America.

Cannibalism: Eating all or a part of an individual from one's own species.

Casketing: Placing of the body in the casket upon completion of embalming, dressing and cosmetizing.

Catafalque: A stand upon which the casketed remains rest while in state and during the funeral service.

Cavity embalming: Instilling embalming chemicals into the chest or abdomen to preserve these areas. The method is usually accompanied by draining gas and fluid from the cavities and internal organs through a needle.

Cemetery services: Opening and closing graves, crypts or niches; setting grave liners or vaults; setting markers and long term maintenance of cemetery grounds and facilities.

Chevrah Kaddisha: In Judaism, the "Holy Brotherhood" Society whose members devote themselves to burial and rites connected with it.

Columbarium: The structure containing recessed memorial niches for cremated remains. In modern structures, the niches are faced with protective glass, bronze or marble. It may be outdoors or part of a mausoleum.

Committal service: Final portion of the funeral service at which time the deceased is interred and entombed. It may be held at the grave side immediately before burial or in a crematory chapel before cremation.

Consumer Preneed Bill of Rights: A document created by the NFDA specifying the rights of a consumer.

Cortege: The funeral procession.

Cremains: The ashes of a cremated body.

Cremation: The process of using heat and evaporation to reduce human remains to bone fragments/ irreversible process of reducing human remains to bone fragments through extreme heat and evaporation.

Cremation container: The container required to transport the human remains to the crematory. It could be the casket used at the funeral or a special rigid, leak resistant, combustible box designed for cremation.

Cryogenics: The science and technology which study the effects of extreme low temperatures on physical systems and materials.

Cryonic suspension: The freezing of a human at an extremely low temperature, in hopes that the body may be resuscitated after medical science improves.

Crypt: A space in a mausoleum or other building to hold cremated or whole human remains.

Decedent: A deceased person.

Dharma: The term for the actions of a Hindu during his or her lifetime resulting in a composite reward.

Direct burial: Burial of a body without prior viewing, embalming, or cosmetic restoration. Usually followed by a memorial service.

Document of gift: Card, statement attached to or imprinted on a motor vehicle operator's or chauffeur's license, a will or other writing used to make an anatomical gift.

Durable power of attorney for health care: A form of advance directive that empowers a person's agent to make health care decisions for him if he is unable to do so.

Embalming: The replacement of a corpse's fluids with disinfecting and preserving chemicals. A process of preserving a dead body by means of circulating preservative and antiseptic through the veins and arteries.

Entombment: Burial in a mausoleum.

Enucleator: An individual who is licensed/certified by the state board of medical examiners to remove or process eyes or parts of eyes.

Eternal light: Traditionally an oil lamp.

Flower car: A vehicle used for the transportation of flower pieces from the funeral home to the church and/or cemetery.

Funeral Rule: A rule issued by the Federal Trade Commission that requires funeral homes to disclose prices and follow other regulations.

Funeral service: Service with the body present. It is held soon after death occurs, in a religious setting or mortuary or even in a family home.

Funeral spray: A collective mass of cut flowers sent to the residence of the deceased or to the funeral home as a floral tribute to the deceased.

Grave liner: A term sometimes used interchangeably with vault. It is a concrete enclosure for the coffin. It is supposed to prevent collapse of the ground above.

Grave (or memorial) marker: A method of identifying the occupant of a particular grave. Permanent grave markers are usually of metal or stone which give such data as the name of the individual, date and place of birth, date and place of death.

Gusal: Washing ritual of a dead body by same gender person of a deceased Muslim.

Haaji: A Muslim priest.

House trust: A trust created to shield your house from taxes for its appreciation from the time you make your trust to the time you die.

Icon: Holy pictures, usually of Christ, the Mother of God and the Saints, found covering the walls.

Iconostasis: A solid screen, covered with icons, at the front of the church, dividing the sanctuary from the body of the building.

Ihai: In Japan, a tablet inscribed with the posthumous name given to the deceased, placed on an alter at the funeral home.

Immurement: The interment of a body in a mausoleum.

Infectious waste: Products from humans that can cause infection.

Inhumation: Burial in the ground.

In state: The custom of availing the deceased for viewing by relatives and friends prior to or after the funeral service.

Interment: Burial in the ground, inurement or entombment.

Inurement: (1) Placing the cremated remains (ashes) in an urn (2) placing the urn/container in its final resting place.

Kaddish: A prayer recited for the deceased by the direct mourners (parents, siblings, spouse, children) for the first time at the conclusion of the Interment service. It is recited by children for their parents at every service for eleven months, in Jewish religion.

Karma: Term for the deeds and actions during the life of a Hindu.

Keriah: Hebrew meaning rending or tearing; a symbol of grief, a tear in the upper corner of the garment or on a symbolic ribbon.

Kever: The grave, in Jewish religion.

Kevurah: Burial, in Jewish religion.

Kichu: In Japan, a notice of mourning written on a piece of white paper with a black frame, posted on the front door or gate of the house throughout the mourning period.

Koden: In Japan, incense or gift money brought by mourners to the house or to memorial services; in a white envelope tied with black or white or silver strings.

Koden gaeshi: A reply to koden, by the family members to people who have come to mourn for the dead; often token gifts.

Koran: Holy Book of Islamic religion.

Lifetime exemption: The amount of capital gains on the sale of a home that is exempted from taxes.

Living wills: A limited and inflexible form of advance directive.

Mausoleum: An above-ground structure, usually of stone, in which bodies are entombed, usually within areas called "crypts."

Memorial service: Service held without the body present and not requiring extensive services or the expense of a mortician.

Memorial society: A consumer movement to get an economical funeral.

Mikoto: Honorific title added after the name of the deceased in the Shinto funeral rite.

Mummy: A corpse whose skin has been preserved over a skeleton, either through natural or artificial processes.

Necrophagia: Scientific name for cannibalism.

Niche: A space in a columbarium, mausoleum or niche wall to hold an urn.

Oharai: Rinsing the mouth and washing with water performed by Japanese priest as a purification ceremony.

Osenko: Incense sticks used during Japanese memorial service.

OSHA: Occupational Safety and Health Administration. Under the U.S. Department of Labor, this organization establishes and enforces protective standards in the workplace.

Ossuary: Depository for the bones of the dead.

Pai Shou: In China, the party or banquet for a person who is elderly and near death literally meaning Honor Longevity.

Pallbearers: Individuals whose duty is to carry the casket when necessary during funeral service.

Perpetual care: The promise to maintain a cemetery forever.

Prearrangement: Arranging a funeral in advance of death. It is often formalized with an agreement to deliver specific goods and services .

Preneed: Purchase of funeral, burial or cremation services by a person before death.

Preparation room: A room in a funeral home designed and equipped for preparing the deceased for final disposition.

Probate court: A court where a judge legally transfers the ownership of the property of a deceased to his or her survivors.

Procurement organization: A person licensed, accredited or approved under the laws of any state for procurement, distribution or storage of human bodies or parts.

Pulverization process: The reduction of the cremated remains to an unidentifiable consistency to facilitate inurement and/or to make the cremated remains acceptable for scattering.

Rabbi: A teacher or ordained leader in the Jewish faith.

Sakaki: Branches of evergreen camellia used with shimenawa, a Shinto ceremony.

Shabbath: The Jewish Sabbath which begins at sundown on Friday and ends at sundown on Saturday.

Shalom: A word of many meanings: Good morning, Peace, Hello, Goodbye, Love, Until Tomorrow, Farewell.

Shaman: Leader in funeral ceremony who plays the reed horn at Hmong funerals.

Shimenawa: Bamboo poles and braided ropes decorating the funeral altar in Shinto ceremonies.

Shoko: Incense powder burned throughout the Japanese wake.

Shou Pao: Formal gown worn by the honored at the Pai Shou and to be kept for when the person dies to be part of the burial costume.

Solea: The open area before the altar in an Orthodox church.

Synagogue: Orthodox Jewish religious building.

Taper: A wax candle lit in the narthex of the Orthodox Church signifying prayers and petitions being offered up to God.

Temple: A religious building of the Reform and Conservative Jewish faith.

Thanatologist: An academic who is designed as an expert on death.

Tomb: A general term designating those places suitable for the reception of a dead body.

Torah: In Judaism, the book of law, instruction and learning.

Traditional funeral: Series of rituals and practices honoring the dead.

Trisagion: In an Orthodox Christian ceremony, three short services or blessings, conducted at the funeral home the evening before the funeral service, on the day of the funeral service before leaving the funeral home for the church and at the cemetery, following the funeral service.

Tsuya: The Japanese term for wake; observation of the body throughout the night to mourn for the dead and to pray for his soul.

Universal precautions: An approach to infection control. According to the concept of Universal Precautions, all human blood and certain human body fluids are treated as if known to be infectious for HIV, hepatitis B, hepatitis C or other blood borne pathogens.

Urn: A container to hold cremated human remains.

Vault: Burial structure or chamber usually made of stone to hold a casket and its contents.

Wake: Period between death and burial when the body is tended.

INDEX

A

AARP *see* American Association of Retired Persons

Advance directive (*see also* Living wills) 13, 14, 25, 26, 262, 328, 329

African 187

African-American

   funeral customs 244, 245

   funeral directors association 325

Agra, India 188, 281-283

AIDS 46, 175-177

Allah 215

American Association of Retired Persons (AARP) 4, 5, 9, 97, 99-101, 104, 322, 329

American Bar Association (ABA) 26, 27

American Indian *see* Native American

American Medical Association (AMA) 27

Amish funeral customs 240-244

Ammon, Jakob 240

Anabaptists 240

Anatomical gifts (*see also* Donation of body and organs) 27-35, 59, 257, 303, 329

   model forms 305-308

      Anatomical Gift by a Living Donor 305

      Anatomical Gift by a Relative 306

      Authorization for Permission to Use Eyes 308

      Uniform Donor Card 307

Apache 187

Archbishop of Canterbury 276

Ark 329

Arlington National Cemetery 133, 270-272, 328

Aron 329

Ashes (*see also* Cremains) xvi, 30, 67, 73, 74, 82, 109, 134, 194, 211, 225, 227, 240

At need xii, 39-44, 65, 100, 121, 165, 259, 264, 265

Attorney (*see also* Lawyer) 9, 22, 23, 26, 31, 147, 153, 258, 261, 264, 266

Australia 75, 186, 187

Autopsy 29, 35, 40, 44, 48, 59, 85-88, 91-94, 101-103, 151-153, 175, 179, 180, 257, 264, 270, 330

   without authorization 87, 151, 152

Avelim 330

B

Baby boomer xi, xvi

Barrie, J.M. 300

Batsudan 233, 330

Bedford, James H. 62

Benefits

   death 130, 135, 266

   insurance 6, 8, 110

   retiree 9, 127, 130, 131

   Social Security 9, 52, 110, 127, 135-139

   survivor 130, 131

   veterans 9, 52, 110, 127, 132-135

Bernhardt, Sarah 189

Bet olan 330

Bible, biblical readings 204, 209, 211, 240, 245, 275, 276

Biddle, P.H. 209

Bierce, Ambrose 147

Bikkur Cholim 201, 330

Bill of Rights (consumer) 4-7

Bimah 330

Blair, Robert 279

Blair, Tony 276

Blood borne pathogens 176-178, 330

Brochure, personal 9, 15, 16, 262, 263
Buckingham Palace 273, 274
Buddhism, Buddhist 229
    funeral customs 229-234
Burial 5, 40, 42, 43, 62, 63, 65-71, 73,
    93, 99-112, 115-117, 123, 129,
    132-135, 137, 138, 143-145,
    150-152, 160, 161, 165, 168-172,
    186-190, 194, 196, 198, 199, 202,
    206, 211-213, 216-218, 232, 240,
    243-248, 253, 256, 260, 265, 269,
    271, 272, 276, 303, 304, 334
  at sea 65-67, 134
  costs 67, 70, 71, 104-108, 112
  direct/immediate 14, 40, 43, 62, 65,
    66, 99, 103, 106, 108, 112, 115,
    116, 123, 332
  mistakes 151, 152
  monuments (see also Grave markers;
    Headstones) 99, 106-108, 112,
    188, 197, 279-286
  of cremains 65, 67, 109, 211
  overseas 101, 141-145

C

Campbell, Thomas 277
CANA see Cremation Association of
    North America
Canada xii, 115, 116, 170
Canary Islands 60
Cannibalism 186, 330
Cardinal John Cushing 271, 272
Care of deceased (see also Preparation
    of the body) 99-101, 103, 108, 109,
    127, 261
Carey, George 276
Carr, Wesley 275, 276
Carroll, David 282
Casket (see also Coffin) xii-xv, 4, 5, 7,
    9, 15-17, 40, 42, 43, 65-67, 70, 75,
    78, 79, 82, 98-105, 107-109, 111,
    112, 119-125, 135, 138, 150, 151,
    168, 170, 171, 197-199, 204-207,

    210, 212-214, 218, 219, 226,
    227,
Casket (continued) 231, 232, 234, 240,
    242, 244-246, 249, 255-257, 263,
    264, 270-272, 304
  for cremation 43, 99, 109, 123, 124
  defective 150
  rental 99, 104, 109, 112
Casketing 99, 101, 102, 127, 128, 217,
    242, 330
Catacombs 258
Catafalque 271, 330
Cathedral of Memories 69
Catholic/Protestant funeral customs
    189, 209-214, 249
Cemetery xii, xiii, xvii, 4, 5, 9, 15, 16,
    43, 65, 66, 70, 80, 100, 106-108,
    124, 128, 132-134, 150, 151,
    164-167, 169, 170, 198, 202, 203,
    205, 211-214, 229, 232, 234, 243,
    244, 246, 248, 260, 262-264,
    270-272, 303, 304, 331
  plot 3, 4, 7, 13-15, 66, 70, 82, 98, 99,
    105, 106, 112, 133, 134, 138, 154,
    196, 197, 243, 260, 262-264, 303
Charitable dead (see also Anatomical
    gifts; Donation of body and organs)
    27-35
Check list for funeral preparation
    261-266
Cheops (King) 280
Chevra Kaddisha 202, 203, 205, 206,
    331
Children 47, 48, 186, 188, 198, 202, 224,
    254, 264, 265, 296, 327
China, Chinese 61, 68, 186, 188-190,
    247, 248
  funeral customs 193-200, 335, 337
Choice in Dying 26, 154, 328
Christian funeral customs 110, 209-214,
    226
Church of Jesus Christ of Latter-Day
    Saints (see also Mormon) 245
Clodd, Edward 189
Code of Canon Law 211

Coffin (*see also* Casket) xv, 11, 91, 93, 189, 190, 205, 212, 218, 224, 227, 230, 232, 242, 243, 248, 249, 270, 271, 274, 276

Columbarium 67, 194, 303, 331

Computers xii-xiv,xvii

Conglomeration in the funeral industry xvi, xvii

Connolly, John 270

Consumer xi-xvii, 28, 30, 62, 159, 160
  Bill of Rights 4-7
  complaints 323, 326
  cremation information 76
  embalming tips 62
  guide 161, 261-263
  memorial societies and 115-117, 256
  overseas death and 141, 142, 144, 145
  Preneed Bill of Rights 4-7, 331
  protection 5, 161, 162, 175, 180
  rights 4-7, 164, 258, 331
  rip-offs 119-126
  tips to cut funeral costs 97-113

Consumer Guide 161

Consumer Preneed Bill of Rights 4-7, 331

Cortege 271, 274-276, 331

Cost of funerals xi, 4, 5, 8, 29, 41, 42, 44, 97-112, 115, 196, 256
  burial 70, 71
  casket 102, 103
  cemetery plot 70
  cremation 75
  funeral (average) 97-100, 116, 253
  Japanese funeral customs 229
  mausoleum 70, 71
  sea burial 67

Council of Bishops 213

Coward, Noel 300

Cremains (*see also* Ashes) 30, 65, 67, 145, 211, 225, 227, 266, 302, 331

Cremation xii, xiii, xv,40, 42, 43, 62, 63, 73-82, 99-105, 108-112, 115-117, 123-125, 133, 144, 145, 149, 153, 154, 161, 165, 168, 169, 193, 194,

Cremation *(continued)* 196, 206, 211, 214, 219, 224, 225, 227, 229, 230, 232, 240, 245, 246, 249, 253, 256-259, 265, 302, 304, 331, 332
  cost 109, 115, 123
  definition 73
  direct 62, 75, 99, 103, 109, 112, 115, 116, 123, 124, 168
  disposition after cremation 75, 77, 80-82, 227, 240
  incidence 73-75, 256
  liability 76, 81
  Model Cremation Authorization form 75, 77-82
  process 73, 78, 79

Cremation Association of North America (CANA) 73-76, 321, 330

Crematory xii, xvii, 73, 75-82, 99, 108, 109, 124, 149, 150, 164, 166, 169, 170, 262, 303

Cryogenics 331

Cryonics 61, 62, 332

D

De LaFontaine, Jean 3

Death benefits 130, 135, 266

Death certificates xiii, xiv, 31, 41, 43, 101, 107, 110-112, 130, 143, 164-166, 257, 260, 265, 266

Death tax 19

Death bell 191

"Death Hilton" 69

Death overseas 41, 101, 141-146, 203

Deaths, accidental 40, 46, 49, 88, 147, 264

Decedent 32, 34, 35, 76-78, 80-82, 129, 132, 142, 148, 150, 151, 164, 165, 170, 197, 332

Dharma 221, 332

Dickens, Charles 300

Dickinson, Emily 27

Directory of memorial societies 309-320

Disposition of dead 9, 27, 30, 42-44, 57, 65-71, 73-75, 77, 80-82, 99, 102, 103, 109, 110, 123, 125, 127, 128, 137, 141-143, 161, 164, 168-171, 175, 187, 193, 196, 211, 214, 218, 226, 229, 240, 253, 255, 257, 262, 301-304

Donation laws 31-35

Donation of body or organs 9, 28-35, 40, 44, 58, 116, 117, 153, 154, 175, 219, 224, 256, 257, 302, 303, 306, 325, 329

Donne, John 221

Dressing 99, 101-103, 204, 217, 229, 242, 247

Durable power of attorney for health care or health care proxy 24, 25, 154, 332

E

Eating of dead 186

Economics of funerals 44, 70, 97-113

Egypt, Egyptian 59-61, 68, 189, 279-281

Pyramids 67, 68, 279-281

Electronic death registration xiii, xiv

Embalming 31, 33-35, 40, 43, 44, 57-63, 65, 66, 86, 87, 98-101, 103, 112, 116, 123, 125, 138, 144, 151-153, 163, 164, 166, 168, 170-173, 175, 179, 180, 186, 193, 196, 203, 206, 210, 213, 216, 217, 224, 226, 229, 234, 238, 242, 248, 256, 258, 259, 264, 279, 281, 302, 303, 329, 330, 332

arterial 58, 59, 329

cavity 58, 59, 330, 331

costs 62

definition 57

donation of body parts and, 31, 33-35, 44, 58, 302

history 59-62, 279, 281

modern 61

tips 62

types 58

Enucleation, enucleator 31, 35, 308, 332

Environmental Protection Agency (EPA) 66, 153, 161, 175

Epicurus 300

Estate, estate planning (*see also* Will) 9, 12, 13, 19-24, 43, 110, 132, 141, 142, 147, 148, 154, 264

Ethical will 202

Etiquette, Japanese 230

Eulogy/eulogies xiii, 16, 198, 199, 214, 226, 231, 243, 246, 265

examples of 287, 288

F

Famous burial monuments 279-286

Famous funerals 269-277

FAMSA *see* Funeral and Memorial Societies of America

Federal help with funerals 127-139

Federal Trade Commission (FTC) 4, 5, 42, 119, 121, 122, 153, 161, 162, 175, 258, 333

Fellows, Lady Jane 274, 275

Forensic pathology 91

Forest Lawn 69, 71, 106

Formaldehyde 58, 176, 179, 180

Forms (samples) 301-308

France xv, xvi, 75, 186

FTC's Funeral Rule (*see also* Funeral Rule) 4, 5, 42, 119-126, 153, 161, 162, 333

Funeral

arrangements xiv, 3-18, 39-46, 50, 51, 65, 97-113, 116, 154, 162, 166, 167, 169, 229, 253, 256, 262-266

ceremonies 5, 45, 151, 194, 195, 197-199, 210, 213, 218, 224-226, 229, 230, 232-234, 238, 239, 243, 245-249, 269-277

costs *see* Costs, funeral

customs 185-192, 229, 233

African American 244, 245

Amish 240-244

Buddhist 229-234, 247

Funeral, customs *(continued)*

Chinese 61, 186, 188-190, 193-200, 247, 248, 335

Christian 209-214, 240, 245, 247

Egyptian 59-61, 189, 279-281

Hindu 190, 221-227

Hmong 247, 248

humanist 236-240

Japanese 229-234

Jewish 190, 201-207, 226

Mexican 249

Mormon 245, 246

Muslim 16, 17, 215-219, 221-227

Orthodox Christian 209, 213, 214

Roman 189

Shinto 229, 233, 234

Vietnamese 247-249

directors xii, 15, 16, 29-31, 34, 35, 40-44, 62, 65, 66, 70, 75, 76, 86-88, 92, 93, 97-105, 107-111, 116, 127, 128, 133, 134, 136, 141, 143, 144, 147, 149, 151-153, 159-173, 203, 206, 209, 210, 213, 216, 226, 227, 253, 257, 259, 261, 262, 264, 302, 308

association for 321, 323-325

feasting 187, 191

frauds 119-126, 161, 162

homes xii, xv, xvi, 40-43, 57, 66, 70, 76, 78, 79, 87, 99, 101-104, 106-109, 112, 115, 121, 122, 128, 130, 142, 149-152, 162, 163, 175-180, 193, 198, 199, 202, 203, 210, 213, 216, 218, 226, 229-232, 234, 238, 244-247, 249, 253, 256, 259, 260, 264, 304, 333

organizations for 321, 324

industry xii, 115, 119-122, 125, 160, 161, 175

laws 57, 62, 119-126, 141-145, 187, 189, 202, 203, 206, 221, 242, 326, 328

Funeral *(continued)*

of President Kennedy 269-273

of Princess Diana 273-277

planning xii, 3-10, 11-17, 65, 97-113, 149, 165, 196, 202, 206, 209, 210, 256, 261-266

at need 39-44, 65, 121, 259, 264-266

preneed 3-10, 11-17, 65, 100, 106, 112, 121, 137, 138, 149, 166, 172, 173, 195-197, 202, 206, 259, 262, 263

rip-offs 119-126

services xi, xii, xv, 3, 7, 15, 16, 33, 42, 43, 59, 86, 98, 102, 109, 110, 116, 127, 138, 164, 165, 168, 170, 173, 179, 193, 194, 197-199, 203, 204, 207, 209-211, 214, 218, 226, 230-232, 238, 243-247, 253, 256, 258, 263, 269-277, 330, 333

shops xi-xvii

Funeral and Memorial Societies of America (FAMSA) 116, 117, 321

Funeral Rule *(see also* FTC's Funeral Rule) 4, 5, 42, 119-126, 153, 333

Future of funeral care xi-xvii

G

Gammaliel, Rabbi 204

Ganga (Ganges) 67, 223, 225, 227

General price list 5, 42, 97-101, 122-124, 164, 166, 168, 171, 172

Ghost 187

Gift, gifting (estate) 20, 21, 24

Gift *(see also* Anatomical gifts; Donation of body and organs) 27-35, 305-307

Giza, Egypt 188, 280

Grave opening and closing 5, 15, 70, 99, 106, 108, 263, 331

Grave liner *(see also* Vault) 100, 106, 107, 112, 333

Grave marker (*see also* Headstone) xiii, 15, 17, 99, 107, 108, 112, 134, 263, 264, 304, 333

Grave site 7, 11, 17, 43, 70, 71, 100, 106, 108, 121, 125, 138, 187, 191, 197, 202, 203, 205-207, 218, 219, 249

Great Pyramid 188, 280

Grief, grieving (*see also* Mourning) 3, 39, 43-52, 87, 97, 110, 116, 119-121, 125, 147, 149, 159, 185, 191, 195, 197, 199, 201, 204, 209, 212, 215, 238, 239, 248, 254-256, 258, 261, 266, 272, 276, 282, 288, 291, 294-297

Theos Foundation 323, 326, 327

Grief, stages of 48-50

Gusal 217, 333

H

Haaji 16, 216, 333

Hallam, A. 91

Handbook of Forensic Pathology 91, 239

Hantsuya 230

Hardan, Richard 61

Hazardous substances 175, 176, 180

Headstone (*see also* Grave marker; Monument) 65, 70, 108, 134, 138, 244, 266

Healing 45, 50, 51, 185, 256

Henry I (King) 186

Hepatitis 175-180, 255, 337

Hepatitis B vaccine 177-179, 255

Hesse, Herman 4

Hindu, Hinduism 67, 190, 221

    funeral customs 67, 221-227

Hmong funeral customs 247-249, 336

Homa 224, 225

Hostetler, John 240

Hughes, Langston 237

House trust 20, 333

Housman, A.E. 300

Humanism, Humanist 236

    funeral customs 236-240

Hunter, William 61

I

Icon 213, 214, 333

Iconstasis 214, 333

Ihai 231, 333

Immurement 67, 333

India 67, 68, 74, 93, 148, 187, 188, 190, 219, 221, 223, 225, 226, 229, 281, 282

Infections 57, 333, 337

Ingersoll, Clark 293

Ingersoll, Robert Green 293

Inhumation 187, 334

Instructions, disposition 78, 80, 81, 99, 103, 110, 142, 154, 262, 301-308

Interment 7, 67, 99, 128, 132, 133, 150, 168, 169, 171, 202, 263, 334

Internal Revenue Service (IRS) 19

Internet xii-xvii, 104, 112

Inurement 334

Ireland 75, 91, 191

Islamic 12, 194, 215-219, 283, 284, 334

J

Jahan, Shah 188, 281-284

Japanese funeral customs 67, 229-234, 330, 333, 334, 336, 337

Jewish funeral customs 190, 201-207, 226, 329, 330, 334

    costume 190, 204, 206

    funeral directors association 324

JFK 269-277

John, Elton 276

Johnson, Lyndon B. 270-272

Johnson, Samuel 201

Joint Commission on Accreditation of Hospitals (JCAHO) 85

Judaism 201, 202, 206

K

Kaddish 334

Kahfre (Pharaoh) 188

Kapp 241

Karma 221, 222, 334

Kavod Hamet 201

Kennedy, Jacqueline 270-272
Kennedy, John F. 269-273
Kensington Palace 274
Keriah 204, 205, 207, 334
Kever 334
Kevurah 334
Khufu (Pharoah) 188, 280
Kichu 230, 233, 334
Koden, koden gaeshi 231, 232, 334
Koran 16, 215-217, 281, 283, 334
Kumbhas 224, 225

L

Laws 25, 27, 28, 31-34, 57, 62, 77, 81, 82, 88, 119-126, 137, 138, 141-145, 147-149, 151, 153, 161-173, 175, 187, 189, 202, 203, 206, 216, 217, 221, 242, 303, 305-307, 326, 328
   anatomical gift 27, 28, 31-34
   California 163, 171-173
   Florida 163-167
   New York 163, 167-171, 173
   tax 19, 21, 22, 24, 167
Lawyer (*see also* Attorney) 24, 147-149, 159, 302
Life Extension Foundation 62
Lifetime exemption 20, 21, 335
Lincoln, Abraham 270, 271
Lindbergh, Charles 11
Litigation 82, 86, 147
Living will (*see also* Advance directive) 13, 14, 16, 25, 26, 153, 154, 256, 258, 262, 329, 335
   definition 25, 256
Longevity robe 196
Loss (*see also* Grief, grieving) xi, xii, 45, 47-51, 159, 271, 277
   of child 48
   of parent 47
   of spouse 47

M

MacKinnon, John G. 298
Mankaure (Pharaoh) 188
Mantra 223
Mao Tse Tung 68, 188, 193
Mausoleum xii, 5, 43, 65, 67-71, 82, 99, 106, 108, 109, 138, 185, 206, 211, 214, 246, 258, 263, 264, 266, 281, 283, 303, 304, 332, 333, 335
McCorquodale, Lady Sarah 274, 275
McGinnis, Father Jack 50
McNamara, Robert 270
Mecca 14, 216, 218
Medical examiner 12, 28, 35, 40, 44, 85, 87, 88, 92, 93, 148, 164, 166, 260, 264
Melanesia 187
Memorial societies xii, 106, 107, 113, 115-117, 126, 256, 321, 335
   listing of 309-320
Memorials xii-xiv, 71, 263, 264, 266, 333
Mennonite 240
Methanol 176
Mexican funeral customs 249
Mikoto 233, 235
Military funeral policy (*see also* Veterans) 9, 127-129, 132, 133
Ming Dynasty 68, 186, 188, 193
Misrepresentations (*see also* Funeral fraud) 161
Mitford, Jessica 119
Model forms 35, 75-82, 301-307
Mogul 188, 281, 282, 284
Moksha 222, 227
Monk 231, 234
Mormon 245, 246
Mort bell 191
Moslem 215-219, 333
Mourning (*see also* Grief, grieving) 11, 45, 49-52, 60, 187, 191, 197-199, 201-206, 212, 215, 219, 225, 226, 230-233, 242-244, 247-249, 271, 274, 275, 276, 282, 288

Mummification, mummies 59-61, 186, 279, 280, 335
Mumtaz Mahal 188, 281-284
Muslim, Muslim funeral customs 16, 145, 194, 215-219

N

Napoleon 69, 280
National Funeral Directors Association (NFDA) 4-7, 31, 74, 97-101, 104, 111, 112, 127, 130, 160, 253, 321, 331
Native American 187
Navajo 187
Neptune Society 66
NFDA *see* National Funeral Directors Association
"Nightmares" of funeral directors 86, 149-153
Nirvana 222

O

Obon festival 233
Occupational Safety and Health Administration (OSHA) 87, 153, 161, 175-180, 255, 335
Oharai 233, 335
One-stop funeral shop xiv-xvi
Ordnung 241, 242
Organizations, funeral 321-328
Osenko 232, 335
OSHA *see* Occupational Safety and Health Administration
Ossuary 335

PQ

Pai Shou banquet 195, 196, 335
Pallbearer 11, 17, 111, 123, 205, 206, 213, 225, 232, 234, 243, 264, 265, 336
Panciera, Mark xv
Pandit 224
Parker, Dorothy 300
Parsees 187

Pathologist, pathology 12, 44, 59, 87, 91, 159, 180
Perpetual care xiii, 14, 99, 106, 107, 259, 336
Pharaohs 188, 279-281
Phenol 176
Polynesian 187
Power of attorney 24, 25, 154, 255
Prayer cards 110, 113, 265
Prayer(s) 11, 17, 51, 197, 202, 204, 209-214, 215, 216, 218, 219, 225, 226, 231, 233, 234, 241, 246, 265, 271, 272, 276
  examples of 287, 289-299
Preneed xii, xvi, 3-10, 12-14, 39, 65, 115, 121, 137, 138, 152, 166, 172, 173, 195-197, 259, 262, 263
Pre-paying 7-9, 262
Preparation of the body 57, 62, 65, 102, 103, 112, 127, 128, 144, 161, 168, 169, 171, 172, 189, 202, 210, 213, 216, 217, 224, 226, 336
Prepaying funeral 5, 8, 336
Preplanning a funeral xii, 3-10, 11-15, 19, 20, 97, 100, 106, 112, 149, 202, 206, 261-263, 336
Presidential Memorial Certificate 135
Preplanning a funeral xii, 3-10, 11-17, 19, 20, 149, 202, 206, 261-263, 336
Price disclosures xii, xiv, xv, 42, 100, 122-125, 162, 168, 171, 172
Prince Charles 273, 274
Prince Phillip 274
Princess Diana 273-277
Probate court 21, 22, 43, 52, 110, 266, 336
Protective claims 120, 125
Puckle, Bertram S. 93, 185, 186, 190
Purchasing a plot 3, 4, 7, 66, 105-107, 112, 196, 197, 202, 206, 262, 263
Pyramids 11, 67, 68, 188, 279-281
Qhuab Kev 247
Questions, common 253-260

R

Regale xv
Rental caskets 99, 104, 109, 112, 169, 170
Resurrection 188, 209-212, 246
Retiree benefits 9, 127, 130-133
Rice, Helen Steiner 45
Rigor mortis 259
Robbie, Joe 19
Roc Eclerc xiv, xv
Roman 68, 189, 239
Roman Catholic Church 210, 211, 249
Roosevelt, Franklin D. 271

S

Sabbath 202, 203
Sakaki 233, 236
Sanskrit 221
Santayana, George 11
Sati 190
Scotland 191, 210
Senreisai 233
Service Corporation International xvii
Shah Jahan 188, 281-284
Shakespeare, William 24, 25
Shaman 247, 336
Shaw, George Bernard 269
Shimenawa 233, 337
Shinto funeral customs 229, 233, 234, 335-337
Shiva 206, 221, 223
Shoko 231, 337
Shou pao 196, 337
Smith, Joseph 245
Social Security 9, 52, 110, 127, 135-139, 258, 262
Society for the Right to Die 25
Solomon Island 189
Soul 187, 191, 194, 202, 205, 216, 222, 225, 226, 230, 233, 247, 248, 275, 279, 281, 283
Soul bell 191
Southey, Robert 27
Spencer, Earl 274, 276

Spirit, spirit world 187-189, 193, 196, 210, 225, 230, 233, 245-248, 276
St. Matthew's Cathedral 271
State Department (U.S.) 141-145
Stone Age 186
Sutra 231-233

T

Tagore, Rabindranath 298, 299
Taj Mahal 68, 69, 188, 281-284
Tax, taxes 19-24, 147, 154, 167, 263, 335
Temple Ordinances 245, 246
Theos Foundation 52
Thomas, Dylan 294
Tibet 61, 194
Tilak 223
Tombs 60, 67-69, 71, 188, 193, 212, 270, 279-281, 283, 284, 337
Trisagion 213, 337
Trust account 7, 8, 20-24, 137, 138
Tsuya 230, 337
Tzdakah 204

U

United States (U.S.) Armed Forces 127, 128, 132, 139, 271
United States (U.S.) embassy 142, 143
United States (U.S.) Government 19, 127-139, 144, 147
Uniform Anatomical Gift Act 27, 28, 30-35
Uniform Donor Card 28, 30, 33, 35, 307
Urn xii, xv, 68, 79-82, 107, 109, 112, 138, 194, 198, 229, 232, 240, 302, 338

V

Vault xii, 4, 5, 7, 9, 15, 17, 43, 65-67, 70, 98, 99, 106, 107, 112, 119, 120, 125, 138, 169, 170, 199, 263, 264, 333, 338
Vedas, vedic verses 221, 223
Veterans Administration 132, 264

Veterans benefits 9, 52, 110, 127,
132-135
Vietnamese funeral customs 247-249
Visitation xiii, 71, 112, 164, 165, 213,
218, 225, 230, 234, 242, 243,
245-247, 249, 254, 255, 265

W-Z

Wake 191, 198, 199, 210, 229-231, 233,
245, 304, 338
Warhol, Andy 39
Westminster Abbey 274-276
Westwood Village Memorial Park 106
White House 270, 271
Will xi, 12, 13, 16, 22, 25, 26, 28, 30, 33,
34, 110, 153, 154, 256, 258, 262
Will, ethical 202
Will, living (*see also* Advance directive;
Living will) 13, 14, 16, 25, 26, 153,
254, 256, 258, 262
Wilson, Michael S. xiii
Woodlawn Mausoleum 69
Yin tribes 194
Zoser, King 280, 281

ABOUT THE AUTHORS

*A*bdullah Fatteh, M.D., PhD., LL.B., *former professor of pathology at* East Carolina University, has been a pathologist and medical examiner for over 39 years. After receiving his medical and law degrees and a Ph.D. in pathology, he taught in medical schools. Dr. Fatteh simultaneously worked as a Medical Examiner in several county, state and federal governments for 20 years. He has personally performed over 6,000 autopsies, and has supervised an additional 15,000. An attorney as well as a physician, he has had extensive training and practical experience in toxicology, medical jurisprudence, criminalization and firearms identification. Dr. Fatteh is the author of numerous papers and chapters, as well as of five other books: *Handbook of Forensic Pathology, How to Live with Heart Disease, Investigations of Skin Wounds, Medicolegal Investigations of Gunshot Wounds,* and *Prescriptions for Longevity* (due out in December, 1999). Dr. Fatteh has three grown children, all of whom are physicians, and lives with his wife in Plantation, Florida.

Naaz Fatteh, M.D. is certified in Infectious Diseases and Internal Medicine. She is currently the Director of Infectious Diseases for the Department of Obstetrics/Gynecology at Plantation General Hospital in Plantation, Florida.